DATE DUE

Demco, Inc. 38-293

HOW TO PLAY
CHESS ENDINGS

HOW TO PLAY
CHESS ENDINGS

By

EUGENE ZNOSKO-BOROVSKY

Translated by
J. DU MONT

DOVER PUBLICATIONS, INC.
NEW YORK

This Dover edition, first published in 1974, is an
unabridged and corrected republication of the work
first published in 1940 by the David McKay Com-
pany.

International Standard Book Number: 0-486-21170-3
Library of Congress Catalog Card Number: 74-82214

Manufactured in the United States of America
Dover Publications, Inc.
180 Varick Street
New York, N. Y. 10014

INDEX

TRANSLATOR'S PREFACE

The difference in playing strength between the master and the amateur is most marked, perhaps, in end game play.

The reason for this is twofold : games between amateurs do not reach the end game stage nearly so frequently as those of the masters, and then, chess literature has far fewer works to show on the end game than on the other stages, and the majority of these are not in English.

Several of the most famous of such books contain almost exclusively artificial, if artistic, studies and are of little practical and no pedagogical value.

Several modern works give greater prominence to positions from practical play and provide fine collections of examples of end game skill.

It was left to the pioneer spirit of Znosko-Borovsky to treat a notable subject in a notable manner. In "How to Play Chess Endings" we have a comprehensive text book in which the reader is taught the principles underlying end game play. Upon these principles an imposing edifice of logic is erected which covers the whole ground.

Memory plays little or no part in the development of end game skill if the precepts of this book are followed. It shows the way to logical but independent thinking.

Not the least achievement in the author's masterpiece, to my mind, is the fact that while showing that the end game is the most strictly logical and accountable part of a game of chess, he nevertheless discloses that it is capable of the utmost artistry, the most delightful and unexpected turns.

To have written such a thorough treatise on a difficult and reputedly arid subject in an entertaining and altogether fascinating manner is an achievement in chess literature.

J. DU MONT.

INTRODUCTION

The main difficulty in the study of the end game is the apparent impossibility of setting up general principles for this phase of the struggle. Here all seems to be a question of arithmetic; it is the kingdom of cold calculation. At no other stage is each single move of such importance : it either wins or loses. Neutral, non-committal moves are seldom available. Positions may appear similar, but each one, as a rule, has some special characteristic, which makes it an individual case : a pawn being advanced or not affects the result of the game ; often "the move" decides.

In these conditions how could relatively stable principles be established ? It is possible to tabulate types of positions leading automatically to some definite result and to learn them by heart. But would that really be chess, the game we love ?

In addition, it seems that a number of fundamental principles, applicable at any other time, have no bearing on the end game : in fact their very opposite frequently obtains. One single pawn can win, where two Knights remain helpless ; what can be said of the value of the centre, when a distant pawn on the wing wins against a centre pawn ? The result depends perhaps on but one *tempo*.

On entering upon the end game stage, we must forget all we have learned ; a new and different type of game begins. We pass from a game of chess, one is almost tempted to say, to a complicated species of draughts.

If we have failed in forethought, a very sudden change occurs at this precise moment, with, not seldom, a rude awakening.

With victory in sight, our fond dreams are shattered —there is a depreciation in values and the ending proves to be unfavourable, possibly lost.

Our opponent may have been more far-seeing, but,

at any rate, we have not taken the necessary precautions. An accident, perhaps, but we were not insured.

Once the end game is reached, it is too late to think out ways and means : there is nothing to be done but to deal with the situation as it is. But, if appropriate measures are taken in good time, there is nearly always some way of avoiding, or of delaying an end game, or at least of modifying its characteristics. If we realize that we shall be unfavourably placed in the forthcoming end game, we must try to eliminate weaknesses from our position. There are many ways of effecting this : we can conserve a piece which would make a win difficult for our opponent, or exchange a hostile piece which might become dangerous, and we must try to improve and consolidate our pawn formation.

To that end it is essential to have some knowledge of the main characteristics and requirements of end game play. We shall then realize that there are certain general principles applicable to this phase of the game. If we are conversant with them, they will guide us in our operations when we prepare for an ending before it actually occurs.

A good deal of theoretical learning thus becomes necessary and should be the object of concentrated study.

It is a pity when a well-contested game is utterly spoilt through the lack of knowledge of end game theory. And yet it is constantly happening. Instinct and inspiration can be trusted less in an end game than at any other stage of the game. Technique is all-important here, and is the deciding factor. Masters who give simultaneous performances know this very well. They frequently and deliberately bring about a perfectly even end game position, in the justified assumption that they will prevail, because their adversary is lacking in end game technique, even though he has conducted his game magnificently up to that point, and given free rein to his imagination. Imagination is of little value in an end game. There the artist must give way to the artisan, who is sure of his craft.

The student must therefore acquire this technique, see things as they are, without illusions. Once his mind can see clearly the why and wherefore of end game technique, he will be able to put his knowledge into practice. Then, if it is in him, he will be able to create exquisite works of art and to find surprising turns.

Those who are unable to play an end game can have no conception of the beauty which it contains, its subtlety, its *finesse*. It is the art of the jeweller, the art of the miniature. Middle game methods, at times, savour of the bludgeon, when compared with the filigree work of the ending. Often they seem coarse and disappointing by comparison.

I invite my readers, especially those who have studied my previous publications, to follow me on a fresh journey.

They must not expect to find here all there is to learn about the end game. Rather would I be their guide, telling them of essential facts, easy to comprehend and to retain, which will help them to find their way in a maze of complicated variations. They will learn to think correctly, to calculate rapidly without blundering, in short, to feel at home in the intriguing but delicious labyrinth, which is the end game.

After that it remains for the reader to take his chessboard and to become a practical end game player, and for the spectator to smile frequently and, at times, to admire.

The Elements

We shall now examine in what manner chess fundamentals affect the end game, how far-reaching is their influence there and to what extent their application varies as compared with the other phases of the game. It is assumed that, in a general way, the reader is familiar with the various elements. In any event, they are fully described in my book, "The Middle Game in Chess," and popularized in "How Not to Play Chess."†

The Chessboard

The chessboard represents a perfect geometrical figure, with 64 equal squares, and it would be easy to assume that any manœuvres on such a board would submit to the laws of geometry. Far from it ! It is interesting to note—and in practice of considerable importance—that here the straight line is not the shortest way between two points. There are a number of ways all equally short. For instance, in order to reach K R 7 from K R 1, the King requires 6 moves going up the R file. He can, however, move on a diagonal from K R 1 to K 4, and from there, again diagonally, to K R 7. By this lengthy route also he will take but six moves.

In point of geometrical distance, the diagonal Q R 1—K R 8 is longer than the file K R 1—K R 8. But the King can cover either of them in seven moves.

It is the number of squares that matters, and not the distance.

The facts are of the greatest importance in an end game, and to ignore them may cost you the game.

---

†Reprinted by Dover Publications, Inc.

The linear relations between ranks and files on the one hand and diagonals on the other, in other words between the oblique line and the straight, must not be overlooked in end game play. They perform a paramount *rôle* in most end game combinations.

But an approximative appreciation would be insufficient. It would not do, for instance, simply to count moves and squares : the intended *route* might suddenly become obstructed, the itinerary adopted by the adversary, which seemed innocuous, may be changed suddenly and without loss of time, thanks to his knowledge of linear relations.

No. 1. White to play.

Dr. Lasker *v.* Dr. Tarrasch
St. Petersburg, 1914

If we examine Diag. 1, Black appears to have a won game : he threatens to queen in seven moves by 1 ... P—B 5 ; 2 P × P, P × P ; 3 any, P—B 6 ; 4 P × P, followed by ... P—R 5—R 6—R 7—R 8 (Q).

As it is White's move, he might stop the pawn from queening after : 1 P—R 4, K—Kt 5 ; and the white King taking the diagonal from K Kt 7 to Q Kt 2, would reach the critical square Q Kt 2 on the 6th move, just

in time to hold up Black's Q R P, but for one fact :
after 3 ... P—B 6 ; 4 P × P, there is a white pawn at
Q B 3, which now obstructs the white King's progress
and stops him from arriving in time. The long diagonal
clearly is not the right one to select. White must use
another if he can do so without loss of time. But how
is it to be done ?

The great master who conducted the white pieces
may not have reasoned in this precise manner : but this
type of reasoning would help even a moderate player to
find the correct idea of what is to be done : and in that
case he also would find ways and means.

After 1 P—R 4, K—Kt 5 ; White, instead of playing
2 K—B 6, as one would expect, played 2 K—Kt 6,
threatening to queen his pawn by 3 P—R 5, etc. Thus
Black is compelled to lose a *tempo* by 2 ... K × P ; and
White has achieved his object : he has changed the
diagonal without losing time, and now, via the diagonal
K Kt 6—Q B 2, he reaches Q Kt 2 in the same number
of moves, which is not difficult to ascertain.

If he perseveres with his original plan, Black runs the
risk of losing the game, e.g. : 1 P—R 4, K—Kt 5 ;
2 K—Kt 6, K × P ; 3 K—B 5, P—B 5 ; 4 P × P, P × P ;
5 K—K 4, P—B 6 ; 6 P × P, P—R 5 ; 7 K—Q 3,
P—R 6 ; 8 K—B 2, P—R 7 ; 9 K—Kt 2, and the
white King is in time to stop the pawn. The whole
combination has failed because of a judicious change of
diagonal by White, and it is Black who must now play
for a draw. With three united pawns against a doubled
pawn, he has a precarious game, for his King, after capturing the R P, is further away from his pawns than is
the opposing King. Luckily for him the draw is not
difficult to obtain, e.g. : 3 K—B 5, K—Kt 6 ; 4 K—K 4,
K—B 7 ; 5 K—Q 5, K—K 6 ; 6 K × P, K—Q 6 ;
7 K × P, K—B 7 ; 8 K × P, K × P (Kt 6) ; etc.

This example is very instructive. Besides the change
of diagonal, we see a sacrifice to divert the opposing

King, another to obstruct his progress, and a third to obtain a passed pawn and this in various parts of the board.

The importance of the correct choice of a line is clearly demonstrated here ; for the object and direction of the alternative diagonals were the same. But we shall see that in choosing the right itinerary for the King, we can sometimes serve the needs of two or more alternative plans.

No. 2. White to play and draw.

Study by Réti

We perceive this clearly in Diag. 2, which, however, I shall not treat at length, as I have already given it in another book. After 1 P—R 4, Black seems lost, for the hostile pawn is two moves ahead, and, whatever line is chosen for the King, he cannot overtake the pawn. Therefore, if we take this pawn only into account, the game is lost. But if Black remembers that he also has a pawn, things may be different. For Black it is a case of combining two objects : he must approach his own pawn without giving up the pursuit of his opponent's. In this case again, the diagonal will serve him well.

After 1 P—R 4, instead of thoughtlessly playing

1 ... K—R 7 ; Black must play 1 ... K—Kt 7 ; 2 P—R 5, K—B 6. If then 3 P—R 6, then Black, after 3 ... K—Q 7 ; also queens his pawn in two. Therefore White must first stop the pawn with 3 K—Kt 3, and after 3... K—Q 5; White is faced with the same problem, 4 P—R 6, K—K 6 ; and queens in two, and so he must first capture the pawn 4 K × P, after which Black can overtake the pawn by 4 ... K—B 4 ; 5 P—R 6, K—Kt 3 ; and draws.

How has this reversal of chances been effected ? Black has forced his adversary to lose two moves in effecting the capture of the pawn, the two *tempi* which he lacked. The diagonal was the *deus ex machina* and, without increasing the distance to the passed pawn, enabled the black King to aim at both wings at the same time.

This example also shows the importance of the centre, which we might have been tempted to underestimate. Such a double mission can be best accomplished from a central position : from the centre we can observe and control both flanks. Thus we re-establish the relative value of the squares, and we revert to the fundamentals which are the basis of the game of chess as a whole. Thus also the unity of the game is established and the study of the end game becomes possible. We find there the same laws and principles which govern the other phases of the game. An essential difference is that in the end game, some at least of the basic ideas find no application, because it is more limited in scope ; there are fewer pieces and the ultimate object is now clearly defined.

In common with combinations, end game play achieves its aims by force in a greater degree than ordinary manoeuvres and often dispenses with considerations of a purely general nature. But the essentials are the same, as, for instance, the geometrical idea. Thus the position in Diag. 3 is akin to the preceding one and is derived from it.

No. 3. White to play and win.

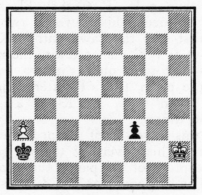

Study by Rinck

What is the difference ? The black King is at Q R 7 instead of Q R 8, the white King at K R 2 instead of K R 3, which does not appear to affect the position at all, and yet everything is changed, even the result.

The play is : 1 P—R 4, K—Kt 6 ; 2 P—R 5, K—B 5. But whereas in Diag. 2 as soon as the black King reaches the Q B file the white King has to move to stop the hostile pawn, in the present case there is no need for him to do so, for after 3 P—R 6, K—Q 6 ; 4 P—R 7, P—B 7 ; 5 P—R 8 (Q), P—B 8 (Q) ; 6 Q—R 6 *ch*, followed by 7 Q × Q, and Black is lost. Clearly the position of his King at Q B 5 is fatal : he must leave the unlucky diagonal and find a different route. Therefore : 2 ... K—B 6 ; and if now 3 P—R 6, K—Q 7 ; and if 3 K—Kt 3, K—Q 5 ; and in either case a draw results as in Diag. 2. But White takes advantage of his King's position at R 2 and first plays 3 K—Kt 1, stopping the B P whilst the black King cannot overtake the R P. For this time his King has only made one extra move, instead of two as in the preceding example.

By drawing a parallel between these two positions, we clearly see on which subtleties endings are based ;

they are made up of nice distinctions and *nuances*. That is why it is hardly possible to set up hard and fast rules, of a general character, to suit all cases. Although such rules do exist and find their application at all times, it is essential to take into consideration the peculiarities of a position and to recognize when any particular rule might apply.

The choice of the correct file or diagonal decides the issue in countless cases. Take, for instance, a simple example: White: K at Q 5, P at K R 6; Black: K at his K B 5 and P at Q R 6. The play is as follows : 1 P—R 7, P—R 7 ; 2 P—R 8 (Q), and Black's pawn is stopped. Imagine the same position with the respective pawns at their K Kt 6 and Q Kt 7. Now we have: 1 P—Kt 7, P—Kt 8 (Q) ; 2 P—Kt 8 (Q), Q—R 7 *ch* ; followed by 3 ... Q × Q; drastic examples of the importance of the correct choice of lines in an ending. That which happens but seldom in the middle game is here of constant occurrence.

It is fatal to disregard this characteristic of end game play. Here is another and more complicated example (Diag. 4).

No. 4. White to play.

Znosko-Borovsky *v.* Salve
Ostend, 1907

The continuation is : 1 R—R 8, P—B 7 ; 2 P—R 7, K—B 6 ; and the game appears irremediably lost for White, who is threatened with mate by 3 ... R—R 8. But there follows 3 R—R 8, R × R ; 4 P—R 8 (Q), R × Q stalemate !

From K R 8 the Queen commands Q R 1 where mate was threatened, as did the white Rook from Q R 8 on the preceding move. It would have been sufficient for Black to play his Rook to Q Kt 7 instead of Q R 7, and the whole combination would have failed. He pays the penalty for having neglected the geometrical idea and selected the wrong file.

As we proceed with our study of the end game, we shall notice that other general principles which occur in the middle game find their application in the end game also, e.g., the question of space, and many others.

In thus greeting old acquaintances, we must not shut our eyes to the fact that, in the end game, there are subtle variations in the application of these principles.

MOVES

In an end game time is of greater importance than space. The management of time is the very essence of end game play. After all, the question is who will be the first to make a new Queen, whose pawn will be at least a move ahead in reaching the queening square. Nowhere else does time play such an important part, and outside the end game, positions are rare in which one *tempo* can so completely alter the state of affairs. In endings, on the contrary, the result quite commonly depends on one *tempo*. The question as to who has the move is all-important in judging an end game position, whereas, in the middle game, where numerous pieces are in play, it often makes but little difference. Thus end games require to be handled with the utmost precision ; in that they are akin to combinations. There is nothing to equal end game play for developing powers of analysis and intricate calculation.

A curious and at times baffling circumstance is that frequently, in an end game, to have the move means to lose the game. This can upset all one's calculations, for from the very beginning of the game, the "move" is looked upon as a definite advantage, which we must try to increase, whilst to have few moves available is a sign of a deteriorating position. No doubt such cases also occur in the middle game, but they are extremely rare and are in the nature of exceptions : also the loser's game is usually compromised so that the onus of the move only precipitates the impending catastrophe.

In end games the compulsion to move often turns an even position into a loss, or a win into a draw, nor are such cases exceptions ; on the contrary they illustrate an essential element of end game technique.

Let us closely examine this anomaly, try to understand its nature and to identify any signs which might warn us of this transformation in values.

STALEMATE

Take one of the most usual cases : White : K at Q 6, P at K 7 ; Black : K at his K 1. Black has succeeded in stopping the pawn, but if he has the move, he must willy nilly play ... K—B 2 ; and after K—Q 7, the pawn queens. If it is White's move, the game is drawn, for after K—K 6, Black has no move—stalemate. Space is limited on the chessboard, whereas time is not. Thanks to the convention that a stalemate means a draw, stalemate becomes an important weapon in end game play. There are positions which are theoretically drawn on account of stalemate : in others it occurs through the opponent's inaccurate play. Even here it is a perfectly legitimate weapon. Frequently pawns are blockaded and therefore immovable, and it happens that there is but one piece left to the defender, the only

unit able to move : here is the germ of the idea of a
sacrifice, which is to eliminate this troublesome piece,
of which the drawback is what at other times we appraise
the most : mobility.   Subtle and pretty combinations
are based on this, as are also, at times, crude traps,
which rely on the possibility of a blunder, due to the
carelessness of an adversary who feels certain of victory.

We have already seen a stalemate combination in
Diag. 4 : here is another (Diag. *5*), a typical trap devoid
of all charm.

No. 5. Black to play.

Schlechter *v.* H. Wolf
Nuremberg, 1906

After 1 ... R—K 6 ; White could have played
2 K—B 1, or even 2 R—B 1 *ch*, winning easily.   Instead
of which he rushed on blindly 2 P—Kt 6, and the game
was drawn after 2 ... R—K 8 *ch* ; 3 R × R, stalemate.

On entering upon the end game stage, we must bear
in mind that it is the domain not only of the mate, but
of the stalemate as well, and its shadow hovers over all
our calculations, over all our plans.

ZUGZWANG

Often a stalemate is the result of a *Zugzwang*, a

compulsory move, which affects the result. In the first example it occurred on the edge of the board ; but it can well happen in the centre of the board and in extremely varied circumstances, depending in no way on the conflict between two essential elements, time and space.

Examine another position : White : K at K Kt 1, Ps at K B 6 and K R 6. Black: K—K Kt 1, Ps at K B 6 and K R 6.

Whoever has the move loses, e.g., 1 K—B 2, P—R 7 ; or 1 K—R 2, P—B 7 ; queening in either case. As the positions are symmetrical, the same applies to Black if he has the move.

Both adversaries have obtained the best possible arrangement of their forces, and in either case the position must of necessity get worse, if it has to be altered at all. This is far less likely to occur in the middle game, where many pieces are available which can threaten other points or create diversions. The end game, however, is inexorable ; the problem in hand must be faced at once, for better or for worse.

If we add a few pawns in the last position, say at Q R 2 and Q Kt 2 on both sides, will the result be affected ? In other words is the first player still lost ? As the position on the K side has not altered, the question will be whether, as the moves on the Q side become exhausted, one side or the other can gain a *tempo*. (This is an indication, to which we shall revert at a later stage, that the analysis of an end game position is dealt with in sections, at least, as here, in two.)

If 1 P—Q R 4, P—Q R 4 ; 2 P—Kt 3, P—Kt 3 ; and White's moves are exhausted. If 1 P—Q R 3, P—Q R 3 ; 2 P—Kt 3, P—Kt 3 ; 3 P—Kt 4, P—Kt 4 ; and again White has no move left. He must play the King, which loses as we have seen.

This shows clearly that, when the pawns are arranged symmetrically, the first player has no means of altering the order of the moves, nor is it difficult to gauge the situation when the pawns are not in symmetry. But the second player is in a different position. After 1 P—Q R 4, Black has only to play P—R 3 ; to alter the situation, or after 1 P—R 3, P—Q R 4 ; and in either case the first player has the move, which in this case, as it happens, is to Black's detriment, but which, in similar cases, might be desirable. Note also how important it is to have a pawn on the second rank, where it has the option of a double step, according to circumstances.

In an end game, where a *tempo* often means everything, this option is invaluable.

The first player must show his hand and reveal his intentions, and his adversary derives the benefit and plays accordingly.

This also happens in asymmetric positions in which there is no pawn on the second rank.

Imagine White's pawns to be at Q R 3 and Q 3, and Black's at his Q Kt 3 and K 3, if White plays 1 P—R 4, Black replies ... P—K 4 ; and White loses a pawn. If 1 P—Q 4, P—Kt 4 ; with the same result.

It is obviously essential to foresee clearly whether the "move" is going to be an advantage or whether it will be in the nature of a *Zugzwang* with its attendant fatal consequences. In addition it is necessary to ascertain whether one or the other of the players will be able to gain a *tempo* and which of the two will be the first to have exhausted all available moves. The result of a game frequently depends on that. To have a move in reserve is of inestimable advantage when all other moves are exhausted and a *Zugzwang* or a stalemate is threatened. With two white pawns at K Kt 4 and K R 3 and two black pawns at their K Kt 4 and K R 2, Black has an extra move in reserve, ... P—K R 3. Instinctively the average player will at once make this move, thinking that he is strengthening his position : he does

not realize that, in so doing, he throws away his strongest
weapon and, more often than not, causes his own
downfall.

In judging a position, it is always necessary to ascertain
how many available moves the contestants have at their
disposal, and which of the two has moves in reserve.
These represent additional chances of a win, or at least
of a draw. The science of end game play is based on
such details. The player who pays attention to them,
who will not neglect them at the crucial moment but
will assess them at their true value, that player is a
likely winner.

We have stated that *Zugzwang* positions can occur
in the middle of the board.

No. 6.

The Trebuchet and the Quasi-trebuchet

In these positions the first player loses the game or,
at the very least, the pawn. The difference between the
two positions shown in Diag. 6 is that in the first instance
the King is in front of his pawn and in the second he is
behind it, but the essential point is the same in both
cases, namely : that the King has only one square available from which to defend his pawn. Thus, if he is

compelled to leave that square, the pawn is lost. Such
a situation arises mostly from faulty play, from a player's
undue haste in attacking the hostile pawn and defending
his own, instead of compelling the adversary to be the
first to take up this unfavourable position. Judicious
manœuvring by the King is required to this end. For
the sake of practice place both Kings at the extreme
ends of the board and try to force one or the other into
this fatal position. The mechanism of these manœuvres
will be explained later, but we may say here that there
is nearly always a way of avoiding the worst by giving
up the pawn at the proper time.

Thus a *Zugzwang* is frequently the final point of a
lengthy manœuvre or a complicated combination. If it
can be foreseen and played for, it can also be avoided.
But how disappointing it is when, after having forced
your opponent into a position such as shown in Diag. 6,
you discover that he has a move in reserve. He makes
that move now and you are in trouble !

We have, so far, only considered *Zugzwang* positions
with pawns. A *Zugzwang* can also occur with pieces
and can be extremely complicated.

At the moment, we are dealing only with essentials,
and cannot deal with more elaborate matters. Let it
suffice to say that, usually, when a *Zugzwang* position
arises, it is the weaker party who has to submit.

One of the most frequent cases of *Zugzwang* is the
"opposition," and it can be safely stated that the opposition is the most important element in end game play.

THE OPPOSITION

If we place the white King at K 6 and the black
King at his K 1, whoever has moved *last* has the opposition. This is a matter of the utmost importance,
because the onus of moving implies that the King in
question cannot reach his objective, but must, on the
contrary, give a free passage to the adverse King. For

instance, in this case, if 1 ... K—Q 1 ; 2 K—B 7. As in the case of the *Zugzwang*, to have "the move" means to lose the game.

As, generally speaking, an advance on a file is the most effective, vertical opposition is the most telling ; the next best is horizontal opposition, as it often is essential to be able to reach one or the other wing, e.g., the white King at his K 6, the black King at his Q B 3. Finally, there is the diagonal opposition (the Kings at their Q B 3 and K 4 respectively). As can easily be seen, the Kings, when in opposition, are on squares of the same colour. This characteristic, which stands out clearly when the Kings are in *direct opposition*, that is with but one square between them, also obtains when they are in *distant opposition*. For such an opposition exists, although it is not quite so valuable or effective.

But if the Kings are at a distance of three or five squares and on the same line, they are in opposition ; e.g., the Kings at K 8 and K 2, at Q R 5 and K 5, at Q Kt 1 and at K R 7. This *distant opposition* must be taken into account as soon as the Kings start active operations. Moving the King without forethought brings about an early and disagreeable surprise ; there will be no good moves left, for the adversary will have obtained the *direct opposition*. Only a timely assumption of the distant opposition can prevent this.

Where the Kings are not in opposition, he who has the move can always obtain it. This sheds a new and strange light on the nature of the opposition, in which we have seen that "the move" loses. The direct opposition is but the culmination of lengthy manœuvres, in which "the move" wins. Having the move, we force the adverse King to the edge of the board, or to the limit of the field of action, where he in turn, having the move, must leave a free passage to our King.

In positions indicated without a diagram, the squares are named from the point of view of *White* unless stated otherwise.

Imagine your King to be at K R 1, and his rival at his Q Kt 1. Having the move, White obtains the opposition by 1 K—R 2, as would Black, with the move, by 1 ... K—Kt 2.

A more complicated example : the white King at Q B 1, the black King at his K B 1. After the first move, 1 K—Q 2, the black King cannot occupy the K file without allowing the adversary to take the opposition. Nor can he, for the same reason, occupy K Kt 2. He has only two good squares at his disposal : K B 2 and K Kt 1. If 1 ... K—B 2 ; 2 K—Q 3 (examine : he cannot occupy the K file, for the adverse King would gain the opposition). It is always essential to ascertain whether the opposing King can gain the opposition if we occupy certain squares and to avoid the squares which expose us to this danger. It is easy to see that Black has now available the squares K B 1 and K Kt 1. If 3 ... K—B 1 ; 4 K—Q 4, and wherever the black King moves, he has to abandon the opposition to his opponent.

This demonstrates the truth of our contention, namely : that, wherever the opposition is not yet established, the player who has the move will be able to obtain it. It might well be asked whether it would not be as well to allow the opposing King to assume the *distant opposition* at once instead of putting up a useless fight after which the opponent still gains the *direct opposition*. The result would be no better as can easily be ascertained by reverting to the last example : after 1 K—Q 2, let us say that Black plays 1 ... K—K 1 ; allowing his adversary at once to take the distant opposition by 2 K—K 2. We have stated that the opposition affords the King the opportunity of advancing, and so, after 2... K—Q 1 ; White is not compelled to maintain the same opposition by 3 K—Q 2, but he fearlessly approaches by 3 K—B 3, for again there is no opposition, and the player who has the move will obtain it.

It is essential, however, to keep in mind the real object of the journey and not to stray too far from it. It must also be remembered that it is always possible to turn the opponent's flank and to transform, when necessary, a vertical into a horizontal opposition.

In complicated positions, when we could easily miss our way in manœuvring to obtain the opposition, it is important to know what may be called *virtual opposition*. This occurs when the contending Kings occupy different lines at a distance. In such cases it is sufficient to count the squares on the files and ranks occupied by the two Kings up to the square where these lines cross : the number of squares on each line must be *odd*. For instance, in the last example, after 1 K—Q 2, the black King is at his K B 1, and the focal point between the two lines is at K B 2 (or Q 8). We count the squares, including those occupied by the Kings : 3 for the white King (Q 2, K 2, K B 2), 7 for the black King (his K B 1, K B 2, K B 3, K B 4, K B 5, K B 6, K B 7). This means that the Kings are in *virtual opposition*, which irrevocably leads to the *actual opposition*. In order to avoid error, it is always best to rely on this method of counting the squares in preference to observing the colours of the squares occupied by the Kings.

In cases of *virtual opposition*, the colour of the respective squares is by no means decisive. For instance, the white King at K 4 and the black King at his Q Kt 4 are on squares of the same colour, but they are not in *virtual opposition*.

All these notions about the opposition have no value at all on an empty board with a King on either side. Let there be but one pawn, and they become of paramount importance. Such endings can often be won only with the help of the opposition. No rule is of such general application, and it can be relied upon in all circumstances.

But it is only right to add at this stage, such is the complexity of end game play, that it happens sometimes, as a rare exception, that to have the opposition actually loses the game. It might be more correct perhaps to say that, even with the opposition, a lost position cannot always be retrieved. We shall learn later on when and in which circumstances the notion of the opposition does not answer the requirements of a position, and must be enlarged. But for the time being let us look upon our knowledge of the opposition as an acquirement of the utmost importance.

Let us repeat once again, that it is essential to think of these things in good time and before they happen, and not after we have missed our way, when a mistake is beyond repair.

From K Kt 1 to Q B 4 the way seems indicated: K B 2, K 3, Q 4. It is possible, however, for this route to be barren of results, and that the way leading from K Kt 1 to Q B 4 and victory, must pass through K R 1.

THE RULE OF THE TRIANGLE

There is, however, one condition which is essential for the success of such manœuvres by the King : he must have sufficient space at his disposal.

In order to obtain the opposition, the King must occupy a certain square : let us suppose that there is one of his own pawns on that square: his own pawn loses the game for him ! In such cases the rule of the triangle applies and is an indispensable complement of the rule of the opposition.

This rule is the first step to a wider understanding of the principle of the opposition both *distant* and *direct*. It is desirable to have the opposition, but it is equally important to be able to maintain it or to recover it, once lost, by skilful manœuvres. To that end it is essential to have, behind the opposition square, free space for manœuvring, and at least two squares from which we can reach the all-important opposition square.

No. 7. Black to play and draw.

Study by Neustadl

Let us examine Diag. 7. The important squares here are Black's Q Kt 2 and Q Kt 3, and White's Q 7 and Q 6. From these the black pawn can be defended and attacked. Black's King commands as much space as White's, as the white King cannot enter the K B file without the risk of losing his Kt P, nor can he gain the necessary time as the black King preserves sufficient space for his evolutions. Therefore, with "the move" Black draws the game, as he immediately takes the opposition and is able to maintain it, e.g., 1... K—R 1 ; 2 K—K 7 (2 P—Kt 5, K—Kt 2), K—R 2 ; 3 K—K 6, K—R 3 ; 4 K—Q 7, K—Kt 2 ; 5 K—Q 6, K—Kt 3 ; 6 K—K 5, K—Kt 4 ; 7 K—Q 6, K—Kt 3, etc. Thus the black King always maintains the opposition ; he leaves his pawn for the purpose, watches the opposing King's manœuvres and moves accordingly. He must always be able to occupy Kt 3, whenever his rival moves to Q 6, or Kt 2 when he moves to Q 7. As there is space enough behind these squares, he succeeds.

No. 8. White to play and win.

Study by Chéron

Now compare Diag. 8; the position is very similar to the preceding one, except that the black King is one file short and, for that reason, Black is lost. 1 K—Q 6 (threatening 2 K—B 6), K—Kt 2 ; (had Black another file, he would occupy it as in the preceding example) ; 2 K—Q 7, K—R 3 ; 3 K—B 6, K—R 2 ; 4 K—B 7, K—R 3 ; 5 K—Kt 8, K—R 4 ; 6 K—R 7, etc. Black must give up the struggle for the opposition and, as is always the case, the opposing King moves up and wins the pawn.

Diag. 9 is another example of the same kind. Here Black has the opposition but is unable to maintain it, for after 1 K—K 5 he cannot play 1 ... K—K 2 ; because of 2 P—B 6. He must play 1 ... K—B 3 ; as otherwise there follows 3 K—Q 6, and the classic evolution of the triangle would gain for White the necessary time to deprive his opponent of the opposition. 2 K—Q 4, K—Q 2 ; 3 K—Q 5, and now Black has the move, and he must give up the opposition. White's King penetrates to Q 6 and the game is won for him, 3 ... K—Q 1 ; 4 K—Q 6, K—B 1 ; 5 K—K 7, K—Kt 1 ;

No. 9. White to play and win.

O. Sander

6 K—Q 7, K—R 1 ; 7 P—B 6, P×P ; 8 K—B 7, P—B 4 ; 9 P—Kt 7 *ch*, etc.

It must be remembered that this manœuvre K (Q 5)—K 5—Q 4—Q 5 can be carried out by either side, the essential point being that the necessary space must be available ; on this *Hinterland* the fate of the game often depends in the same measure as on a reserve move. The object of this type of manœuvre is to obtain the identical position, but passing on "the move" to the other side.

We will now pass on to the study of related squares, one of the most interesting chapters in the science of end game play.*

RELATED SQUARES

The principle of "related squares" finds its application especially in blocked positions, in which there are but narrow lanes between pawns, or in which there are only definite and predetermined objects in view, which must, however, be attained at one particular moment.

---

*A short, but how precious, pamphlet is : "Die Oppositionslehre," by Otto Sander. (Curt Ronniger, Leipzig.)

The King's moves become more and more restricted as he advances down one of these lanes towards the crucial square. He must reach it at the precise moment when his rival will find it impossible to occupy an equivalent square. Something of the kind was shown in Diag. 7, but there it was a question of direct opposition ; when, however, the Kings are on different lines and at a distance from each other, matters become complicated and this opposition is no longer sufficient, if not actually unfavourable.

Let us examine one of the simplest instances (Diag. 10) which is, in that respect, similar to those which we have already studied.

No. 10.   White to play and win.

Study by Sackmann

The object here is indicated ; it is to attack the black pawns at Q B 5 and Q B 6. They can be attacked by the white King, without the black King being able to retaliate by attacking the white pawns. The proper plan is obvious : the attacker must attack the adverse pawns in such a way that they cannot be defended. For his part, Black must strive to have his King at all times in such a position that he can come to the rescue of his pawns whenever they are attacked. He must move with the utmost precision : when White plays K—Q 6, Black must be able to play ... K—Kt 3. If K—Q 7, Black must play ... K—Kt 2 ; a first instance of interdependence of related squares. We can go further still by analysing the position retrospectively, that is : starting from the intended final position. The corresponding squares to Q 6, Q 7, Q 8 are Q Kt 6, Q Kt 7, Q Kt 8. White can reach Q 6 from three squares, K 5, K 6 or K 7. These corresponding squares are Q R 5, Q R 6, Q R 7, all of them in direct, horizontal opposition. If White simply keeps manœuvring on the Q and K files, he will achieve nothing because the black King disposes of the same amount of space on the Q R and Q Kt files. But the white King has three more files at his disposal on the K side, and by making use of them he makes an end to the opposition and the effect of corresponding squares. If 1 K—B 6, Black can play K—Kt 3 ; maintaining the opposition. White therefore plays 1 K—B 5, and as Black cannot play ... K—Kt 4 ; he must upset the balance with ruinous consequences. We see that in order to attack the black pawns on the Q B file, White must first play K—B 5 ! An object lesson to the wise, that it is foolish to make straight for the obvious goal, without giving a thought to the subtleties of end game play. 1 K—Q 6 achieves nothing but a draw, whereas 1 K—B 5 wins easily : 1 K—B 5, K—Kt 3 ; 2 K—B 6 (assuming the opposition), K—Kt 2 ; 3 K—B 7, K—Kt 1 ; 4 K—K 6, K—R 2 ; 5 K—K 7, K—R 3 ; 6 K—Q 8, K—Kt 2 ; 7 K—Q 7, K—Kt 3 ; 8 K—B 8, and wins.

Although the idea of corresponding squares can clearly be seen here, the win is brought about by means of real and direct opposition. Allow the defending King an additional file, and the whole of White's manœuvre fails, as Black will be able to maintain the opposition.

In more complicated cases, which are perhaps more

characteristic of our subject matter, the "real" opposition fails to solve the problem, because the Kings are not on the same line. Another type of opposition arises here, which some authors propose to name the *heterodox opposition* in contradistinction to the ordinary *orthodox opposition*.

No. 11. White to play and win.

Study by Locock

Let us look at Diag. 11, which illustrates a case in point. First of all we must seek to establish what threats are available. In doing so we shall find that the white King will not be able to attack the doubled pawns from the Q side, as the black King will prevent him from getting in by taking the opposition. Even should the white King get through, there would be no danger, because Black's King can guard the pawns from his K 1 and K 2 and he has sufficient squares available on the adjacent files to maintain the opposition : we have seen a similar case in the preceding diagram. But White has two real threats : firstly, he can play his King to K B 4 in order to win the Kt P, and secondly he can play the King to Q 4, threatening to play P—K 5, and to force his way into the hostile camp. In order to parry these threats, Black must manœuvre his King in such a way that he can occupy his K Kt 4 as soon as the white King reaches K 3, or his K B 3 when White has played to Q 4. In this position it is essential to be the last to reach the all-important square, just as is the case in Diag. 6. The two related squares are therefore K 3 and K Kt 5, or, alternatively, Q 4 and K B 6. We see that the principle of the related squares is the saving clause for the weaker side, which will have recourse to these squares in order to maintain the balance. The stronger party, however, has no need to conform to the rules dictated by this principle ; he must rather break them so that his adversary cannot derive any benefit from their existence. We have seen a similar state of affairs, when discussing the real distant opposition : we give up the opposition in order to get closer to the field of battle, and do not try to preserve it, when it would clearly be of no advantage to us. As in all cases of this kind the manœuvres of our King have the object of gaining a move, so that we can transfer "the move" in the final and desired position or, conversely,

No. 12.

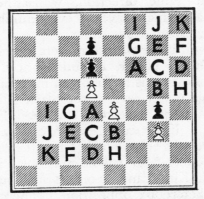

Related squares in the study by Locock (No. 11)

prevent the adverse King from being the last to reach the last and most important *related square*. Even a player having the advantage needs to be familiar with the idea of *related squares*, for only thus can he at all times judge which particular square his opponent will occupy in reply to any move he may make. Proceeding by the retrograde analysis already employed, we can easily see that Q 3 corresponds to K Kt 6, Q B 3 to K Kt 7, Q 2 to K R 6, etc. The arrangement of these squares is perfectly symmetrical, so that, if the diagram were folded along the diagonal K R 2—Q Kt 8, the related squares would cover each other.

In examining the related squares, however, we find that on the long black diagonal the related squares are in opposition, the number of squares between them being odd. The same applies to all the black diagonals going in the same direction, whereas on the parallel white diagonals the related squares have an even number of squares between them. This anomaly does not, however, depend on the colour of the diagonals. The reverse is the case on the long white diagonal where related squares have an odd number of squares between them. The same applies again to all the white diagonals going in the same direction, whilst here it is the black diagonals which have an even number of squares separating the related squares.

This rule will be helpful to players who like automatic methods. Others prefer, I think rightly, clear reasoning. Its application is as follows : in the initial position of the example under review, the black King, unlike his rival, is already on a related square. This simplifies White's task. If he could at once play his King to Q Kt 3 (the related square to K Kt 8) the problem would be solved at once. As it is he must play in such a way that the black King cannot, on his next move, take the orthodox or heterodox opposition. Therefore : 1 K— Kt 1, K—B 2 (1 ... K—B 1 ; 2 K—B 2) ; 2 K—Q 2,

K—B 3 ; 3 K—K 2, K—Kt 3 (3 ... K—Kt 4 ; 4 K—
K 3) ; 4 K—Q 3, and wins.

As in similar cases, lack of space has caused the black
King's downfall : if an additional file had been at his
disposal, White could not have succeeded.   But in all
positions, it is essential to realize whether it is possible
to attack a weak pawn, or to penetrate into the hostile
position : in other words, who has the attack and who
must assume the defensive ?   The whole method of
play becomes different according to the answer.

Here is a very well-known example :

In Diag. 13, as can easily be seen, White has the
advantage, because his King can break through via
Q Kt 5 or K Kt 5, which can be called the two poles.
We can at once establish the fact that, when the white
King reaches Q B 4, his adversary must be at his Q R 3
or Q Kt 3 ; when the white King is at K R 4, the black
King must be at his K Kt 3 or K R 3.   It is clear that
White's task is here much more difficult than in

No. 13. White to play and win.

Study by Dr. Lasker and Reichhelm

Diag. 12, because the black King enjoys greater freedom
of movement.   White must therefore play upon the two

threats, which in this instance are widely apart, whereas in No. 11 they were close together at Q 4 and K B 4.

The question is now whether the black King, after having obstructed the white King's ingress via Q B 4, will have time to reach the other wing and oppose his adversary's advance via K Kt 5. Let us establish the shortest route between these poles : White needs five moves, Q B 4—Q 3—K 3 (or K 2)—K B 3 (or K B 2)— K Kt 3—K R 4. Black's King cannot cover the necessary distance in the same number of moves. He would only move from his Q Kt 3 to K Kt 3 in the time and not from Q R 3—K R 3 (e.g., Q Kt 3—B 2—Q 2 (or Q 1)—K 2 (or K 1)—B 3 (or B 2)—Kt 3). Thus Q R 3 and K R 3 must be left out of our calculations, and the only related squares available are Q B 4 and Q Kt 6 or K R 4 and K Kt 6. Working backwards, we find that further related squares are : Q B 3 and Q Kt 7, Q 3 and Q B 7, etc. (see Diag. 14), and the

No. 14.

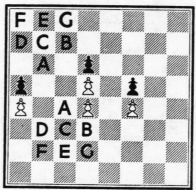

Related squares in the study by Dr. Lasker and Reichhelm (No. 13)

solution is therefore : 1 K—Kt 1, K—Kt 2 ; 2 K—B 1, K—B 2 ; 3 K—Q 1, K—Q 2 ; 4 K—B 2, K—Q 1 ;

5 K—B 3, K—B 2 ; 6 K—Q 3, and wins by making for K Kt 5. If the black King tries to prevent this, then 7 K—B 4, reaching Q Kt 5.

Again in this example White has an extra rank at his disposal, which the King relinquishes only when his adversary is forced to play to an unfavourable square, thus losing the opposition. Thanks to this extra rank, White is able to watch his opponent's manœuvres and to act accordingly. Therefore Black cannot enforce a draw, which he could do if he were able to occupy a related square *after* his adversary. In the additional territory which White controls—the additional rank—the rules of the *heterodox opposition* still apply to the same extent, and the King cannot be played haphazard on to any square. For instance, if White were to play K—R 2 on the first move, he cannot succeed in breaking the opposition after 1 K—R 2, K—Kt 1 ; 2 K—R 3, K—Kt 2 ; 3 K—Kt 2, K—R 1 ; 4 K—B 2, K—Kt 1 ; 5 K—Q 2, K—B 1 ; 6 K—K 2, K—Q 1 ; and the black King is able to follow up White's manœuvres and to act accordingly.

If we examine the related squares in this example, we see that here also they form identical groups on either side. But if the diagram is to be folded in two, so that the related squares cover one another, it must be on a horizontal axis, and not, as in a previous example, diagonally. Here the opposition is regular in character except that the group of related squares for Black is moved one rank to the left.

The whole of this analysis points to the fact that already the first move decides the fate of the game : no amount of skilful manœuvring will repair the damage

In this section we follow fairly closely the subject matter and even the technical terms of a wonderful volume : "L'Opposition et les Cases Conjuguées sont réconciliées, par M. Duchamp and V. Halberstadt." Edicions de l'Echiquier. Its presentment, unique in the annals of chess literature, is due to the artistic research and the unerring taste of the famous painter, M. Duchamp.

caused by a faulty first move. Nor is it surprising, for we have learnt that, where there is no opposition, the player, whose turn it is to move, will obtain it. And if this first move is incorrect there is no further hope. In order to find the *coup juste* it is essential to see clearly what the ultimate object is and, by a retrograde analysis, establish which are the related squares—the acme of co-ordination of time and space on the chessboard.

EXERCISES AND QUESTIONNAIRE

In Diag. 15, where Black has practically a certain win, he made a faulty combination : 1... Q × R ; 2 P × Q,

No. 15.

Yates *v.* Dr. Tartakower
Bad Homburg, 1927

P × P ; in the belief that the pawn ending was easily won. How does White succeed in drawing the game ?

In Diag. 16 White plays and wins. Indicate the method of winning, also the related squares, the two poles and the shortest route between them.

The replies to the questionnaire are given on pp. 253-262.

No. 16.

Study by Bianchetti

THE MEN

The third essential element in chess, namely *force*, is also affected by end game considerations; for many reasons, the relative value of the men undergoes very considerable changes.

In the first place, the object to be pursued alters everything. Whereas, in the middle game, the question of a mating attack arises fairly frequently, in endings the opportunity of a mate, barring exceptional cases, arises only after the creation of a new Queen. The King, in consequence, becomes an active and powerful force. There is no fear of a mate, and he can undertake what, in the middle game, would be inadmissible. He is, however, exposed to two dangers which he rarely encounters in the middle game : perpetual check and stalemate. This, in itself, illustrates the wide divergence which separates the principles governing the ending and the other phases of the game.

The King's increased power is accompanied by further changes : the pieces lose much of their importance. In the middle game, pawns are frequently sacrificed in order to clear a passage for the pieces, but in the end

game, where the queening of a pawn is usually the ultimate aim, pieces play a secondary *rôle* ; they are important
only in assisting the pawns, and are readily sacrificed
to facilitate the pawn's march forward.   Even in their
struggle against adverse pawns, the pieces often fall by
the way, when they can neither stop a pawn nor bring
about a mate.

In the middle game, pieces can, at times, lose their
value without, however, forfeiting their latent force :
conditions may change, the position may take another
aspect, when those same pieces again recover their
normal strength.   But in the end game everything is, so
to speak, definite : if a piece is ineffective, it will as a
rule remain useless and inoffensive to the bitter end.

Another point to remember is that, in the middle
game, pieces are numerous and can combine their efforts
on the vital points in a position : it is not their number,
but their joint effect which counts.

In the end game a strong piece effects but one threat
which, although perhaps dangerous, may be parried by
the King alone.   But a combined threat by two minor
pieces may prove too much for the defence by the King
and a major piece.

What a triumph when, in the middle game, the Queen
has been captured in exchange for two minor pieces :
but there comes the ending, and the two minor pieces
may well prove superior to the Queen.

We often lose an ending not because of bad play, but
because it is intrinsically lost.   The mistake occurred
at an earlier stage : we should have thought of it before
entering the end game stage.   It is essential, on approaching that stage, to proceed to a revaluation of forces from
yet another point of view.   In a difficult position we
may often be tempted to seek salvation in the end game,
but the middle game actually provides more resources,
for its possibilities are less limited. It certainly is possible
to turn a favourable middle game into an ending.   But

what a disappointment when the prognostication of its
value proves to be wrong, and our best chances are
thrown overboard !

A most telling example of the reversal of values is
given in Diag. 17.

Granted, this is an exceptional case, but how convincing as well as attractive !

The forces are equal.   At first sight, one might think
that White has the best of the fight, because his Knight
is more active than the adverse Bishop, which is entirely
passive, and moreover Black has doubled, isolated
pawns.   But Black succeeds in obtaining a passed pawn,

No. 17. Black to play.

Ortueta *v.* Sanz
Madrid, 1933

and with it a winning advantage.   He plays 1 ... R × P ;
thus sacrificing to this end his most powerful and active
unit.   2 Kt × R, P—B 6 ; White is already in a quandary : if 3 Kt—Q 3, in order to stop the pawn, then
3 ... P—B 5 *dis ch* ; 4 K—B 1, (4 R × B, P × Kt ;)
P × Kt ; 5 K—K 1, P—B 7 ; 6 K—Q 2, B—K 6 *ch* ;
and wins.   White therefore replies with a returned
sacrifice 3 R × B, counting on 3 ... P × R ; 4 Kt—Q 3,

but, amazingly, Black plays 3 ... P—B 5 ; depriving
the Knight of access to its Q 3. Then 4 R—Kt 4,
threatening R × P, stopping the passed pawn. But again
there is a surprise move : 4 ... P—R 4 ; and Black has
only two pawns against two pieces, but these pawns
win the game, for if 5 R × P, P × Kt ; and the pawn
queens.

Is this not charming ? It illustrates clearly the very
essence of end game play and shows, incidentally, the
upheaval in values which takes place in the last phase
of the game.

Another, and no less admirable example, comes from
the "Avro" Tournament, 1938 (Diag. 18). It begins
practically in the middle game by a sacrifice of the
exchange, continues by a sequence of Knight combinations and terminates with an advance by pawns : 1 ...
P—Q 4 ; 2 B × Kt, R × B ; 3 Kt—B 6, P × B ; 4 Kt × R,

No. 18. Black to play.

Fine *v.* Keres
"Avro" Tournament, 1938

P × P ; 5 Kt—Q 5, Kt—Q 6 ; (with the threat 6 Kt × B,
Kt—B 5 *ch* ; or 6 R × B, P—Kt 7;) 6 R—Q 2, P—Kt 7 ;
7 R—Q 1, P—B 4 ; (nicely calculated—although far

behind, this pawn arrives in time to support the far advanced Kt P) 8 R—Q Kt 1, P—Q B 5 ; 9 K—B 1, B—B 4 ; 10 K—K 2, B×P ; 11 Kt—K 3, P—B 6 ; 12 Kt—B 2, (12 K×Kt, B×Kt ; 13 K×P, B—B 8 ;) 12 ... Kt—K 8 ; 13 Kt—R 3, (13 Kt×Kt, B×Kt ; 14 K—Q 3, B—Q 7 ;) 13 ... B—B 4 ; 14 K×Kt, B×Kt ; 15 K—Q 1, B—Q 3 ; and wins. Note the speed with which the rearward pawn came up to the rescue of its bold and impulsive comrade.

It is of extreme importance to give the pieces their full mobility, even at the cost of sacrifices. A mobile piece, able to attack, is an irresistible force as long as the adverse force is reduced to the defensive.

In the middle game, a passive piece retains its latent powers : in an ending such piece is of little value. Although the end game is the pawn's especial *domaine*, it is there, nevertheless, that the individual piece can develop its full powers. But general notions must be looked upon with distrust, the end game is a special case in which values undergo a change. In order to comprehend well the peculiarities of the end game, it is necessary to know the part each piece and the pawns have to play and what scope they have in their manœuvres.

That is what we shall now learn.

THE KING

Of all the pieces, the King changes most in value in the end game and this circumstance imparts to it its particular character. There are no longer any threats of mate, there is no need for him to keep under cover, and he becomes an active piece. He requires no protection which fetters his own pieces : on the contrary, he rushes into the thick of the fray and often decides the issue. Acting in eight different directions, he becomes, instead of the weakest piece, one of the most formidable units. He is best able to stop a hostile passed pawn or to support his own. It is clear that the position of the King is of the greatest importance in the end game, which must be avoided if the King is far away and the hostile King is nearer to the field of battle. As soon as an ending is in sight, the first thing to do, in most cases, is to bring the King near, to facilitate his co-operation, and to throw him, without much concern for his safety, wherever the fight is hottest.

As we have said before, the germ of victory or defeat is found in the preceding phase : amongst the outward signs which enable a player to assess the prospects of an impending end game, the King's position is one of the most important and withal the most easily recognisable.

In some cases the King can take an active part in the middle game, but they are exceptional, and even then his *rôle* is rather passive. He defends a weak point, taking the place of a piece, which is needed for the attack. Thus in Diag. 19, White intends to play

No. 19. White to play.

Capablanca *v.* Chajes
New York, 1918

P—K R 5, but he perceives that after ... P × P ; P × P, Black would play ... Q—R 6 ; and create a difficult position. He therefore decides to bring his King to K Kt 3, in order to guard the squares on the K side which will become weak after the advance of the pawns : 1 K—K 2, K—Kt 1 ; 2 K—B 1, K—B 1 ; 3 K—Kt 2, K—Kt 1 ; 4 K—Kt 3, K—B 1 ; 5 P—K R 5, P × P ; 6 P × P, Q—K 2 ; 7 Q—B 5, K—Kt 1 ; 8 R—Q 7, B × P *ch* ; 9 K—Kt 4, Q—B 3 ; 10 Kt × B, Q—Kt 2 *ch* ; 11 K—B 4, and wins.

This can hardly be called an end game position, but, thanks to the unfavourable disposition of the black pieces, which are restricted and passive, the white King is in no danger of being mated, and this enables him to embark on his journey. Had Black not made a mistake on his eighth move, an end game might have resulted, and the white King would have been in the right place, where there is a majority of white pawns. In the present case, the game was decided before the end game stage ; the King undertook the defence of some weak points in the position and there was no call for him to exert any active force, as would have happened if an ending had been reached. In Diag. 20 we see a

No. 20. Black to play.

Schlechter *v.* Dr. Lasker
Match, 1910

similar manœuvre by the King in preparation for the end game.   As Black has a pawn majority on the Q side, he can obtain the initiative there.   Therefore his King rushes to this, the main field of battle, which is the reverse of what is done in the middle game, where we place the King where there is no play and when, normally, he would not be expected to support an attack.

The game went : 1 ... K—K 1 ; 2 Q—K 2, K—Q 1 ; 3 Q—Q 2, K B 2 ; and Black obtains chances of a strong flank attack.

Although the King plays a most important part in an end game and gains in power and activity as the number of pieces diminishes and he is exposed to few dangers, this change in most cases occurs very slowly and methodically.   It leads to disappointment to continue in the spirit of the middle game, with all the pieces ready to make a dead set at the opposing King, when everything points to the near approach of the end game stage.

Here is a curious illustration : the game finds an abrupt termination just before the end game is reached.

No. 21.

Czaya *v.* Michel
Berlin, 1938

The black King develops an extraordinary and almost excessive activity: 1 P—K 4, P—K 4 ; 2 Kt—K B 3, Kt—Q B 3 ; 3 B—Kt 5, P—Q R 3 ; 4 B—R 4, P—Q 3 ; 5 P—B 4, P—B 4 ; 6 P—Q 4, B P × P ; 7 Kt × P, P × Kt ; 8 Q—R 5 *ch*, K—K 2 ; 9 B × Kt, Kt—B 3 ; 10 B—K Kt 5, Q × P ; 11 Q—K 8 *ch*, K—Q 3 ; 12 B × Kt, B—Kt 5 ; 13 B × P *ch*, Q × B ; 14 Q × Q *ch*, K × Q; 15 B × KP, B—Kt 5 *ch*; 16 Kt—B 3, B × Kt *ch*; 17 P × B, K × B; 18 P—B 3 *ch*, K—Q 6; 19 Castles *ch*, K × P (B 6) ; 20 P × B, Q R—Q 1 ; 21 R × R, R × R ; White resigns.

Compare this victorious advance by the King to the compulsory outings of which I have given numerous examples in "The Art of Chess Combination."* There the King is driven from pillar to post and finds no rest until he succumbs to some brilliant mating combination. There is a striking difference between the position, the play and the King's *rôle* in these cases. One might be playing with entirely different pieces. The greater the prudence necessary for the King in the middle game, the greater the permissible temerity of his manœuvres once the chessboard shows a decreasing number of pieces.

These, however, are preliminaries. We must discuss the part to be played by the King in actual end game play: the following examples will show how important it is.

Here is an end game with Rooks and pawns (Diag. 22). The difference between the respective positions of the Kings is obvious : whilst the black King is confined to an outside rank, his rival enjoys full freedom of move-ment, and this circumstance tips the scales in White's favour. With the help of the Rook and of a passed pawn, the only one that matters, the white King will penetrate into the enemy position with decisive *élan*. Black's Rook appears to be well placed, attacking as it does the Q side pawns ; but the King is deprived of

---

*Chatto & Windus (7/6).

No. 22. White to play.

Capablanca *v.* Dr. Tartakower
New York, 1924

its assistance. Thus the duel between the two Kings
decides the game. White is quite willing to give up a
good number of pawns, keeping only one. But, assisted
by the King, whilst the Rook occupies a dominating
position, this pawn will be sufficient to win. Combined with a threat of mate, this is an ample return for
the pawns sacrificed.

This is how the game continued : 1 K—Kt 3, R × P *ch* ;
2 K—R 4, R—B 6 ; 3 P—Kt 6, R × P *ch* ; 4 K—Kt 5,
R—K 5 ; 5 K—B 6, K—Kt 1 ; 6 R—Kt 7 *ch*, K—R 1 ;
7 R × P, R—K 1 ; 8 K × P, R—K 5 ; 9 K—B 6,
R—B 5 *ch* ; 10 K—K 5, R—Kt 5 ; 11 P—Kt 7 *ch*,
K—Kt 1 ; 12 R × P, R—Kt 8 ; 13 K × P, R—Q B 8 ;
14 K—Q 6, R—B 7 ; 15 P—Q 5, R—B 8 ; 16 R—
Q B 7, R—Q R 8 ; 17 K—B 6, R × P ; 18 P—Q 6,
resigns.

Compare the white King's decisive action with the
passive attitude of his opponent and you will recognize
to what White's predominance is due : he plays with
one piece more and what a piece !

Sometimes the King shows his prowess in an even

No. 23. Black to play.

Dr. Tarrasch *v.* Schlechter
Match, 1911

more spectacular manner (Diag. 23). In this difficult
ending, the white King, at the beginning of his travels,
appears to be passive : all he does is to escape from the
checks by the Queen, who tries to obtain a perpetual
check. But in so doing, he has another and more
active mission : that of guarding the pawn at Q Kt 6.
After he has manœuvred in such a way that his opponent
is practically in a stalemate position, because his only
active piece, the Queen, is tied up by the necessity of
stopping the advanced passed pawn, White moves his
King across the chessboard a second time, with a
view to a decisive attack on the opposing King—again
a duel between the two Kings of which one is active,
the other passive. 1 ... Q—Q 5 *ch* ; 2 K—B 1,
Q—Q 8 *ch* ; 3 K—B 2, Q—B 7 *ch* ; 4 K—Kt 3,
P—B 5 *ch* ; 5 K—B 3, Q—B 6 *ch* ; 6 K × P, Q—Q 7 *ch* ;
7 K—B 3, Q—Q 8 *ch* ; 8 K—K 3, Q—K 8 *ch* ; 9
K—B 3, Q—Q 8 *ch* ; 10 K—K 4, Q—K 8 *ch* ; 11
K—Q 5, Q—Q 7 *ch* ; 12 K—K 6, Q × P ; 13 P—Kt 7,
Q—Kt 3 *ch* ; 14 K—Q 5, Q—B 4 *ch* ; 15 K—B 6,
Q—K 3 *ch* ; 16 K—B 7, Q—K 2 *ch* ; 17 K—Kt 6,

Q—Q 1 *ch* ; 18 K—R 7, Q—Q 5 *ch*; 19 K—R 8,
Q—K 5 ; 20 Q—Q R 5, Q—B 6 ; 21 Q—Kt 4,
Q—Q 4 ; 22 Q—Kt 1 *ch*, P—Kt 3 ; 23 Q—B 2,
P—R 4 ; 24 P—R 4, K—R 3 ; 25 Q—B 7, Q—K 5 ;
26 Q—Q 7, Q—B 6 ; 27 Q—K 7, Q—Q B 3 ; 28 K—
R 7, Q—R 5 *ch* ; 29 K—Kt 6, Q—Kt 6 *ch* ; 30 K—B 7,
Q—B 5 *ch* ; 31 K—Q 7, Q—Kt 4 *ch* ; 32 K—Q 8,
Q—Kt 7 ; 33 K—K 8, Q—K R 7 ; 34 K—B 8,
Q—Kt 1 *ch* ; 35 K—B 7, Q—B 5 *ch* ; 36 K—Kt 8,
resigns.

It would lead too far to analyse this ending of which
Lasker has extolled the rare beauty : it is haunted by
the spectre of most end games—the fear of the perpetual
check.   Let it suffice to emphasize the importance of
the King in end game play : and this holds good in end
games with Kings and Queens in which the respective
Kings are constantly exposed to various attacks.   It is
shown very clearly here that the King, in an ending, is
an active piece and must take an active part in the
struggle.   If he fails in this and is content with mere
passivity, he is heading for disaster more surely than
when facing the worst disappointments of an active policy.

In an inferior position the King can still, at times,
save the day.   But, as always, it is necessary to have a
definite conception of what is wanted.   Haphazard,
planless manœuvring is entirely valueless.

In Diag. 24, White's endeavour is to play his King
to Q R 1.   We shall see later on that a R P, helped
by a Bishop, can win only if the queening square is
controlled by the Bishop.   This is not the case here,
and therefore a draw is possible, although Black has
two extra pawns.

It is even necessary to get rid of as many pawns as
possible so as to leave the adversary as little scope as
possible to thwart our plans.   This explains White's
initial sacrifice of a pawn : 1 P—K 6, P × P ; 2 P × P,
B × P ; 3 K—K 5, B—Kt 6 ; 4 K—Q 6, P—B 5 ;

No. 24. White to play.

Maróczy *v.* Pillsbury
Munich, 1900

5 K—B 5, K—B 5 ; 6 K—Kt 4, P—R 7 ; 7 K—R 3, K—K 5 ; 8 K—Kt 2, K—Q 6 ; 9 K—R 1, and the game is drawn. The Bishop cannot be captured because of stalemate, and if 9 … K—B 7 ; 10 B—R 8, P—B 6 ; 11 B × P, and his King can no longer be dislodged from the corner. The King reaches his objective by a roundabout route, but how fascinating it all is ! Instead of 7 moves, K 4—K 5—Q 6—B 5—Kt 4—R 3—Kt 2—R 1, he could have tried to reach the desired square in 4 : K 4—Q 3—B 2—Kt 2—R 1. Why did he select the longer way? Because he would not have reached his objective by this seeming natural route, e.g., if 3 K—Q 3, (instead of 3 K—K 5,) then 3 … B—Kt 6 ; 4 K—Q 2, P—R 7 ; 5 K—B 1, P—R 6 ; and the King cannot reach Q Kt 2. If 5 B—Kt 2 (instead of 5 K—B 1), then nevertheless 5 … P—R 6 ; as the pawn cannot be captured. The obviously shorter route would have led to nothing, whilst the longer route reached the objective, because the King in following it, did so with incidental threats, and thus without

losing time.   Another and a most telling illustration of
the necessity of correct judgment in the choice of lines.

All these examples are very picturesque and the
King's manœuvres transparent.

Other and more difficult ones display far more subtle
manœuvres : they show us that such things as for the
King to gain or lose a *tempo* or to reach a certain square
at a certain time—to say nothing of the opposition—
the *Zugzwang*, the triangle, related squares, are by no
means strangers to practical play.

In "King and pawns" endings, the question to be
decided is whether, in the combined manœuvres of K
and pawns, the King or the pawns are to bear the greater
share of responsibility.

In Diag. 25 Black has a passed pawn on the K R
file which could be stopped by the adverse King, even
if he were posted at K 5.   Against this, White has two
united passed pawns at Q 6 and K 4.   But he cannot
simply play 1 P—K 5, for then the black King would
restrain the two pawns by repeating the moves K—Q 2
—K 3—Q 2, etc., and the white King is helpless, as

No. 25. Black to play.

Dr. Dührssen *v.* Demetriescu
Correspondence game, 1938

his Q 5 and K B 5 are inaccessible. He must therefore strive to bring his King to K 5, in front of his pawn. Only, if after Black's 1 ... K—B 2 ; White simply plays 2 K—B 4, there follows 2 ... K—K 3 ; and the white King cannot reach his K 5. White must invoke the aid of the magic triangle and play 2 K—B 3, K—K 3 ; 3 K—B 4, and he has reached his object. On the next move he penetrates into the game by 3 ... K—B 2 ; 4 K—K 5, K—K 1 ; 5 K—K 6, P—R 5 ; 6 P—Q 7 *ch*, K—Q 1 ; 7 K—Q 6, P—R 6 ; 8 P—K 5, P—R 7; 9 P—K 6, P—R 8 (Q); 10 P—K 7 mate.

White forces the win, not thanks to the triangle, but owing to his adversary's guileless play. For if Black had bethought himself of the theory of the *related squares* he could have drawn the game. As he cannot prevent the white King from reaching K 5, he should have hindered his further progress from there : in other words, he must place his King at his K B 2 as soon as the white King has reached his K 5, the first pair of related squares.

The King can reach K B 2 either from K 1 or K B 1 (K Kt 1 or K Kt 2 are out of the question, as then White's Q P queens straight away). But with the black King at his K B 1, there is no need for White to play his King to K 5, for he can win simply by P—K 5, and if ... K—B 2 ; then P—Q 7, K—K 2 ; P—K 6, and the pawns break through. If the black King leaves his post at K 2, White plays K—Q 6, and if, instead, Black advances the K R P, the white King captures it first and returns to K 5. It follows that Black cannot safely reach his K B 2 except from K 1 (second pair of related squares, K B 4 and K 8) ; and thus his first move already was a mistake, a decisive one : he probably had forgotten the "triangle." He should have played 1 ... K—Q 2 ; 2 K—B 3, K—Q 1 ; 3 K—B 4, K—K 1 ; 4 K—K 5, K—B 2 ; and White cannot force a passage.

End game play abounds in such subtle turns in which

the King is frequently the prime mover. It is a mistake to think that they are beyond the powers of the average player. But they need to be known in theory before they can be put into practice.

THE PAWNS

Next to the King the pawns experience the most complete reversal in values as soon as the end game stage is reached. From being mere drudges, they become protagonists, a striking change indeed. Whereas in the middle game we give, generally speaking, but half-hearted attention to the humble pawns, and are only ready to sacrifice one or the other for more important ends, we must watch over them with the utmost vigilance and pay special attention to their position. The object of the pawns' activities changes suddenly, as does the meaning of their relative positions : a very advanced pawn is judged differently in the end and the middle game.

No doubt there are certain values which remain the same, to within slight *nuances*, during the whole of the game : a supported passed pawn, a well-guarded pawn chain, etc. The same applies to certain types of weaknesses : doubled pawns, an isolated pawn. But even in these cases, about which there can be no argument, it is well not to lose sight of the fact that their application is entirely different in an end game. If, for instance, the isolated pawn is a passed pawn, it can become a tower of strength. For a passed pawn is nearly always an asset in an ending, as the main object there is, speaking generally, to obtain such a pawn. The possibility of obtaining a passed pawn is the first consideration when assessing the value of a position. It is therefore of importance to become familiar with ways and means of exploiting such possibilities.

There are simple and obvious ways, which need no special discussion, such as exchanges or the gain of a pawn which bars the forward march of a passed pawn,

or the sacrifice of a piece for a pawn which prevents
our pawn from queening, e.g., white pawns at Q R 5
and Q Kt 6, black pawns at their Q R 3 and Q Kt 2.
White would not hesitate to give up a Bishop by capturing the hostile Q R P, for after ... P × B ; the Kt P
queens unhindered. That is why a pawn on the sixth,
especially if protected, nearly always constitutes a crush-
ing advantage in an end game : there are opportunities
for the most varied combinations. Such a pawn is also
an ideal support for a Rook on the seventh. The
backward pawn which is opposed to it on its second
rank becomes a target for our forces and an obvious
object for our attack. To lose a pawn in the middle
of the board is bad enough, although it need not be
a catastrophe, as would be the loss of a pawn on the
second rank, when it blocks a hostile pawn on its sixth.

The most characteristic, and also fairly frequent
method of obtaining a passed pawn when there is an
equal number of pawns on either side, is as follows :
White pawns at Q R 5, Q Kt 5, Q B 5, Black pawns
at their Q R 2, Q Kt 2, Q B 2—the play is : 1 P—Kt 6,
R P × P ; (1 ... B P × P ; 2 P—R 6, P × R P ; 3 P—
B 6, etc.) ; 2 P—B 6, P × B P ; 3 P—R 6, and wins.
With a greater number of pawns, the same procedure is
available. Add two pawns, a White one at Q 5 and
a Black at its Q 2, and the continuation is : 1 P—B 6,
Q P × P ; (1 ... Kt P × P ; 2 P—Q 6, P × Q P ; 3 P—
Kt 6, P × P ; 4 P—R 6, or P × P,) 2 P—Kt 6, (another
line would be 2 P—Q 6, P × Q P ; 3 P—R 6, but not
3 P—Kt 6, P—R 3 ;) 2 ... R P × P ; 3 R P × P,
P × Kt P ; 4 P—Q 6, and wins.

In these examples, the loser could have employed the
same method of obtaining a passed pawn, which, in his
case, would have led to a loss, because his pawns were
insufficiently advanced, and his adversary would have
been the first to promote a pawn. Thus we have an
additional and fairly general rule, which also affects

isolated pawns : advanced pawns are a serious menace.

At R 6 a pawn is superlatively dangerous : two more moves and it becomes a queen.   At R 2 even a passed pawn requires five moves to queen ; therefore there is ample time to overtake and perhaps capture it.

With two pawns only, this procedure is not available, but it happens in practice and against weak play, that with but two pawns a passed pawn is forced through and wins because it is well advanced.   In Diag. 26, White should have played simply 1 P × R P, P × B P ; 2 K—K 1.   But he played 1 B × P, hoping that after 1 ... P × Kt P ; 2 P—Q 4, the black pawns would be stopped with advantage to himself.   But Black played 1 ... P—Kt 6 ; and he can no longer be prevented from making a Queen : 2 P × R P, P × P ; or 2 P × Kt P, P—R 7 ; in either case avoiding Q Kt 8 which could be defended by the Bishop.

No. 26.   White to play.

Van Nüss *v.* Schmidt
1926

When there still are pieces on the board, we frequently see charming combinations of which the sole object is to create a passed pawn.   It is sometimes possible to

sacrifice the whole of the remaining pieces for that
purpose, a tribute to the importance of the passed pawn
in end game play.

Examine, for instance, the position in Diag. 27.

No. 27. Black to play.

Lund *v.* Nimzowitsch
Oslo, 1921

Here Black accomplishes his task in an admirable
manner : 1 ... P—Kt 5 ; 2 P × P, R × Kt ; 3 P × R,
P—Kt 6 ; 4 P × P, P—B 6 *ch* ; 5 P × P, P—R 6 ;
and White resigns, for if he stops the R P with his
K, Black captures the Bishop and queens his Q P.
He has sacrificed everything, remaining with but the
material necessary to make a Queen.

An advanced passed pawn can also be exploited in
another manner. It can be used and sacrificed to decoy
the adverse King from the centre or from the real battlefield. For this reason, distant passed pawns are the
most dangerous. Whilst the adverse King has to travel
a long way, his rival has full leisure before his return
to play havoc with the remaining pawns. This explains
also why a majority of pawns on the Q side is valued
so highly. In normal positions, both Kings having

castled on the K side, whoever has a pawn majority on
the Q side will easily obtain a passed pawn there, and
with it a winning advantage.   The reverse holds good
where both Kings have castled on the Q side.

From this it follows that even the opening can lead
to a more or less favourable ending.   The player who
has an advantage which can be exploited only in the
end game will try to reach that stage as quickly as
possible : there is no need for him to look for brilliant
combinations in the middle game, which, for him, will
merely be a stage which he must traverse without
losing his advantage.   His adversary, on the contrary,
will do his utmost to avoid the end game.

A good many openings present peculiarities which
indicate from the first the proper line to follow.   Take
the exchange variation of the Ruy Lopez : 1 P—K 4,
P—K 4 ; 2 Kt—K B 3, Kt—Q B 3 ; 3 B—Kt 5,
P—Q R 3 ; 4 B × Kt, Q P × B ; 5 P—Q 4, P × P ;
6 Q × P, Q × Q; 7 Kt × Q.   Black now has doubled
pawns on the Q side and will obtain a passed pawn only
with the greatest difficulty, whereas White already has
an extra pawn on the K side.   White therefore will not
be afraid of the end game, which Black will try to avoid
by exploiting the advantage of the two Bishops in the
middle game.   These simple considerations are all too
often neglected in planning for the future.

Thus we see that even in the opening, one should
allow for the possibilities of the end game : without this
it is at times impossible to formulate a strategic plan,
which conforms to the requirements of the position.

It is an obvious advantage to be able to obtain a
passed pawn, but the kind of passed pawn secured is
not a matter of indifference.   A supported passed pawn
is manifestly stronger than an isolated one.   Take, for
instance, a position with white pawns at K 4 and K B 5,
and black pawns at their K 4 and Q R 4 : Black is lost,
as his King will be unable to defend his R P, which

must fall, as otherwise the white K B P will queen. The distant position of the Q R P is fatal. With the isolated pawn nearer the centre, the defending King might achieve the double task of keeping the adverse pawn under observation and of guarding his own. Place the white pawns at Q 4 and K 5 and the black pawns at their Q 4 and Q R 4 ; in this case the black King, from his Q Kt 3, could accomplish this double mission. White will probably succeed in winning a pawn by letting his own passed pawn be taken, but in that case the black King should be able to maintain the opposition and to stop White's remaining Q P. For instance, with the white King at Q R 4 and the black King at his Q Kt 3, the continuation is : 1 P—K 6, K—B 3; 2 K×P, K—Q 3; 3 K—Kt 5, K×P; 4 K—B 5, K—K 2 ; 5 K×P, K—Q 2 ; and the game is drawn.

However, it would be a mistake to think that united pawns are invulnerable : it may usually be so in the case of an extended pawn chain, but two pawns can easily be undermined provided one of them, for preference the defending one, can be challenged by an adverse pawn. Suppose the white pawns to be at K B 5 and K Kt 4, with the black King at his K B 3 or K Kt 4, with a pawn at K R 2. It is sufficient to play ... P—R 4 ; to wipe out the two white pawns. This stratagem is worth remembering, for this one pawn becomes the equal of two, which is of even greater importance than to secure a passed pawn. Conversely, we shall avoid placing our pawns in such a position that they are controlled by a smaller number of opposing pawns, which would be the equivalent of being a pawn down.

Imagine two white pawns at Q R 4 and Q Kt 3, and a single black pawn at its Q R 4 will hold them both. It would be a different matter if they were far advanced, in which case, by sacrificing the Kt P the R P could queen ; here, too, the strength of an advanced pawn finds an illustration.

Sometimes a pawn can prove to be the equal of three.

With white pawns at Q R 2, Q Kt 3, Q B 2, a single black pawn at its Q Kt 5 reduces them to impotence, and somewhere on the K side Black is sure to have a winning advantage of two pawns. It is unpardonable to allow such a position to arise ; beware of backward pawns. A useful rule is : advance the pawn which has no opposite number.

In order to specify the conditions under which two isolated pawns can be expected to win even without the support of their King, a rule has been suggested which might be called the "rule of seven."

The more distant two pawns are from each other and the more advanced, the more certain they are to win through. The minimum distance which can ensure the win appears to be seven, which number represents the number of squares separating the pawns from each other and from the eighth rank. Thus pawns at Q 4 and K R 4 are at a distance of four squares from each other and of three squares from the eighth rank and will win without the support of their King. This useful rule must not be regarded as infallible and allowance must be made for exceptional cases.

The following are a few always recurring cases which it is well to remember :

Pawns at K 5 and Q 6 (united pawns) : the black King cannot capture the supporting K P as the Q P would queen.

Pawns at Q R 5 and Q B 5 : the King can capture one of these and yet overtake the other.

Pawns at Q R 5 and K 5 : the King can capture neither pawn as the other one would queen.

Pawns at Q R 5 and Q 5 : if it is White's move and the black King is at his Q Kt 4, White plays P—Q 5 and wins; if he is at his Q B 4, White plays P—R 5.

Pawns at K B 6 and K R 6, black King at his K Kt 1 : Black, with the move, loses. If he plays to the B file P—R 7, if to the R file P—B 7.

Pawns at Q 6 and K 7. These pawns cannot win without the help of their King. The black King remains on his K 1 and Q 2 and the "move" matters little.

Thus we gain an insight into the value of united pawns, isolated pawns distant from one another or otherwise, doubled pawns, backward pawns, distant passed pawns, pawns scattered, unconnected, across the chessboard, pawns blockaded by a lesser number—we must note all this if we are to assess our chances in the end game correctly, without losing sight of what we have learnt concerning the King's *rôle*, the influence of time and space, the spare move, etc. We are already able to judge the scope of a complete analysis of a position with Kings and pawns only : to effect it, we only want to learn the peculiarities of the race for promotion. In the meantime, we can already draw up a balance between profit and loss in any position.

THE SINGLE PAWN

As has already been stated, the pawns are the most important force in an end game which they can win, where a piece or even two pieces, often would fail, and they at times win against pieces. With the disappearance of the pieces, their power increases still further, for an extra pawn does not ensure victory when there is a piece on the board, but normally it does so when there are only pawns left.

It is therefore a mistake to change off pieces when in a minority of pawns : it may be thought that an extra pawn supported by a piece is stronger than the pawn by itself. The contrary, however, is the case, although a particular piece may increase the value of a pawn. It is therefore important for the weaker side to preserve such pieces which afford the best drawing chances. These are the Queen, the Rooks, or Bishops of opposite colours.

Logically, an ending leads in the end to play with a single pawn, the question then arising being whether the remaining pawn can be queened.

The first thing to ascertain is in which circumstances a single pawn can be stopped by a King.

Place a pawn at Q B 4. In order to stop this pawn the hostile King can be posted as far off as his K R 6, and, with the move, he will be in time : 1 ... K—Kt 5 ; 2 P—B 5, K—B 4 ; 3 P—B 6, K—K 3 ; 4 P—B 7, K—Q 2. This is the rule of the "square," which always applies in such cases. There are four squares in front of the pawn at Q B 4. Now imagine a square of which the sides are equal to these squares, including the square on which it stands. If the adverse King is in, or can enter, this square, he can overtake the pawn and stop it from queening.

In the case of the pawn at Q B 4, the "square" is Q B 4—Q B 8—K Kt 8—K Kt 4. The King, in order to succeed, must be on any square within these lines. It may appear more straightforward in practice to count the respective moves of the King and the pawn. But the *rule of the square* is of theoretical value, being a formula which covers all cases.

A point to be remembered is that, on its first move, the pawn can take a double step. In this case it is necessary to count the third rank, and not the second, as the base of the "square." With a pawn at K Kt 2, the opposing King is within the "square" at his K R 7. But after 1 P—Kt 4, he is left out in the cold and cannot re-enter the "square."

Yet another important point arises only when there are other pieces or pawns on the board. When referring to the *rule of the square*, it is implied that the King takes the shortest route : he would, therefore, march straight along a diagonal.

In the first illustration, with White's pawn at Q B 4 and the black King at his K R 6, place a black pawn at its K 3. The King's direct route becomes obstructed and he can no longer arrive in time to stop the pawn.

It can well be imagined that combinations can arise on this theme. In the said illustration add a white pawn at K 5 and a black pawn at its K B 2. After 1 ... K—Kt 5 ; White plays first 2 P—K 6, P × P ; and then only 3 P—B 5, and the pawn can no longer be overtaken.

The defending King has no opportunity to change the lines in time. Care and foresight must therefore be used, when applying the rule of the square ; there are traps for the unwary.

In these examples the pawn has been holding its own, by itself, against the King, an unequal contest except in certain well-defined cases. When it has the support of its own King, matters are very different. In order to prevent the pawn from queening in these circumstances, there is only one way. The defending King must be placed in front of the pawn : even then the draw is by no means assured, but it is the defender's only chance ; he must make use of the opposition and try to secure a stalemate, the only real resource in such cases.

When a R P is in question, the matter is very easy. Once the defending King is at R 7 or R 8, the pawn can never get through. There is another way of securing a draw against the R P : if the King of the stronger side is already at R 7 or R 8, in front of his own pawn, all the defence has to do is to play the King alternately to B 8 or B 7 ; his adversary is shut in, and if he advances the pawn there is a stalemate.

The case of the Kt P is less straightforward, and only careful play will win against the best defence, e.g. : White : K at Q B 7, P at Q Kt 5. Black : K at his Q R 2. If after 1 ... K—R 1 ; White plays impulsively

2 P—Kt 6, Black is stalemated.   He lacks another file
by which to escape.

White can avoid this disaster in the following manner :
1 ... K—R 1 ; 2 K—Kt 6, K—Kt 1 ; 3 K—R 6,
K—R 1 (... K—B 2 ; 4 K—R 7,) ; 4 P—Kt 6, K—Kt 1 ;
5 P—Kt 7, K—B 2 ; 6 K—R 7, and wins.

These two types of stalemate occur only with the
R P and Kt P.   There is yet another which applies to
all pawns.

If, for example, White's King is at K B 6, with a
white pawn at K 6, the black King being at his K B 1,
and White has the move, the continuation is 1 P—K 7 *ch*,
K—K 1 ; 2 K—K 6, stalemate.   This position represents both the object which the defender must seek to
attain, and the snag which the stronger side must try
to circumvent.   Remember that if the pawn reaches the
7th rank with check, there is a stalemate and the game
is drawn.   In order to win, the pawn must reach the
7th without giving check.   If, in the last example,
Black has the move, there follows 1 ... K—K 1 ; 2 P—
K 7 (without check), K—Q 2 ; 3 K—B 7, and queens
next move.

Both sides, in such cases, will have recourse to the
opposition, e.g., White : K at K B 5, P at K 6, Black :
K at his K 2.   Black must play 1 ... K—K 1 ; 2 K—
B 6, K—B 1 ; resuming the opposition.   But if Black
were to play 1 ... K—B 1 ; then White gains the opposition by 2 K—B 6, and after 2 K—B 6, K—K 1 ;
3 P—K 7, wins.   Another instance : White : K at
K 6, P at K 5, Black : K at his K 1.   After 1 ...
K—Q 1 ; 2 K—B 7, and Black can no longer get in
front of the pawn.

This manœuvre is available on any rank as long as
the King is *in front* of his pawn.   But in this case, if
White has the move he must lose the opposition by
1 K—Q 6, and yet he wins the game as follows : 1 ...
K—Q 1 (taking the opposition) ; 2 P—K 6, K—K 1 ;

3 P—K 7, and wins. Thus there are cases where the opposition is of no avail to the weaker side, namely : when the *King is in front of his pawn*.

Let us now examine how a pawn queens and which are the guiding principles of this manœuvre.

We have seen that it matters very much whether the King is in front of his own pawn or by the side. In the latter case, he can win only with the opposition. If he is in front, he wins in either event. It is not even essential for the King to be on the same file as his pawn. Imagine the King to be at K B 6, his pawn at K 5, the opposing King at his K B 1. The play is : 1 P—K 6, K—K 1 ; 2 P—K 7, and wins. With Black to move, the result is the same : 1 ... K—K 1 ; 2 K—K 6, (take note of 2 P—K 6, K—B 1 ; 3 P—K 7 *ch*, draw) 2 ... K—B 1 ; 3 K—Q 7, and wins.

But all this applies only when the King has reached the sixth rank ; when he is further back the win is far more difficult. If the King is next to the pawn, it is actually impossible to force a win : White : King at K B 4, pawn at K 4, Black : K at his K 3. 1 P—K 5, K—K 2 ; 2 K—B 5, K—B 2 ; 3 P—K 6 *ch*, K—K 2 ; 4 K—K 5, K—K 1 ; 5 K—B 6, K—B 1 ; 6 P—K 7 *ch*, draw. Or 1 ... K—B 3 ; 2 P—K 5 *ch*, K—K 3 ; 3 K—K 4, K—K 2 ; 4 K—B 5, K—B 2; etc. The defending King never allows his rival to get in front of the pawn and always succeeds in obtaining the opposition on the last rank.

Let us now examine what happens when the King is in front of his pawn, e.g., White : King at K 5, pawn at K 4, Black : King at his K 2. If White has the move the game is drawn : 1 K—B 5, K—B 2 ; 2 P—K 5, K—K 2 ; 3 P—K 6, K—K 1 ; 4 K—B 6, K—B 1 ; 5 P—K 7 *ch*. But White wins if it is Black's move, for the latter then loses the opposition : 1 ... K—B 2 ; 2 K—Q 6, K—K 1 ; 3 K—K 6, K—Q 1 ; 4 K—B 7, and the pawn gets through.

To sum up, being in front of the pawn but not yet on the 6th rank, the King wins if he has the opposition, or if the pawn is a square further back affording a reserve move which can be played in order to maintain the opposition. Thus White can always win when his King is two squares ahead of his pawn. It is clear that a doubled pawn will always win, as there is then always a reserve move available.

The King, in all cases, should advance as far as possible in front of his pawn, which should be advanced only when necessary. The defending King also will always try to advance as far as possible, to prevent his antagonist from getting in front of his pawn.

This, the simplest explanation of the advance of a single pawn, can also be expressed in a different manner from the point of view of the pawn. It is then a question of the selection of squares for the King. Some of these are fully effective with or without the opposition, and some only conditionally so, which means that the King must have the opposition. If the pawn is on the second, third or fourth rank the squares conditionally effective are the three squares immediately in front of it; all other squares in front, three on each rank, are fully effective. With the pawn on the fifth rank the nine squares in front are fully effective. Finally, with the pawn on the 6th rank, the two adjacent squares are conditionally, the six squares in front fully, effective.

The foregoing should make the principle of pawn promotion easy to understand.

In the case of the doubled pawns it should be remembered that the second pawn should be moved only when absolutely necessary, the best time being after the first pawn has reached the seventh, and it is necessary to wrest the opposition from the opponent. By wasting the second pawn's moves, a certain win can easily be missed as can be seen in the following example.

White : K at K B 6, pawns at K Kt 5 and K Kt 6,

Black : K at his K B 1. On his last move, White played P—Kt 5, wasting a valuable reserve move, and he can no longer win : 1 P—Kt 7 *ch*, K—Kt 1 ; 2 K—Kt 6, or P—Kt 6, stalemate. Even if Black has the move, White can win only by an astute stratagem : 1 ... K—Kt 1 ; 2 P—Kt 7, K—R 2 ; and if now 3 K—B 7, Black is stalemated, and if 3 P—Kt 6 *ch*, K—Kt 1 ; draw. But White regains the opposition by giving up his pawn : 3 P—Kt 8 (Q) *ch*, K × Q ; 4 K—Kt 6, K—R 1 (... K—B 1 ; 5 K—R 7,) ; 5 K—B 7, and wins.

It is remarkable how a simple ending can become complicated by a careless move. It cannot be over-emphasized that the greatest care is needed in the initial stages of an ending ; all chances of a win are often and definitely compromised by following the wrong trail. It is even possible to miss an obvious and easy win with two extra pawns, not doubled, through such a premature advance. Generally speaking, the win with two extra pawns is so easy and devoid of complications that it does not seem necessary even to refer to it ; we have seen that the isolated pawns can often win without the help of their King. We shall therefore give but one example in which the win cannot be enforced in spite of two extra pawns.

Here is a study by Fahrni : White : K at Q 5, pawns at Q R 5 and Q B 7, Black : K at his Q R 2. Black plays 1 ... K—Kt 2 ; 2 K—Q 6, K—B 1 ; and now either 3 K—B 6, or 3 P—R 6, stalemates, whilst any other move loses the B P and draws, as the R P cannot win. The bold counsel "Advance first and see what happens" is never applicable to the end game. Rather should it be "See what happens first and then advance."

EXERCISES

The first exercise, No. 28, consists in marching a pawn from his initial square, obstructed by the hostile King and supported by his own, the whole length of

No. 28.

From a 17th-century manuscript

the board, and thus to apply all the suggestions made in the course of our study of this particular ending.

The object of No. 29 is to illustrate the contest between a lone King and three united passed pawns. This needs no special study, being at all events of infrequent occurrence. But it is useful practice, as endings often produce

No. 29.

Préti *v.* Carrera

unusual positions which are not to be found in books. It is essential to be able to cope with such cases without any outside help.

What is the result in these two examples with either White or Black to move ?

Pawn Against Pawn

If there is one pawn on either side, the ending presents no difficulty, nor is it hard to foretell the issue. It is only a question of finding out which of the pawns will be the first to queen, which of them can be stopped by the opposing King, whether the geometrical idea can find its application, etc. Yet, these endings also have their finer points, and it is easy to miss a win if their possibility is not taken into account.

In these cases, the King nearly always plays the principal part and his manœuvres demand judicious handling : although the procedure is already familiar to us, its application requires thought and a certain amount of elasticity.

In order to ensure success, the ultimate object must first be clearly defined, and the peculiarities of the position be thoroughly grasped. Then all its possibilities must be exploited, be it by making use of the opposition or else of the related squares, the geometrical idea, the *Zugzwang*, etc. Only after realizing the difficulty of the position and how it could turn to our disadvantage, will it become easy to decide which particular means to apply.

In Diag. 30 we have pawns on the Q R file. We know that against a R P the weaker side can draw the game by occupying the queening square with the King, or else by confining the adverse King to his Q R 7 and Q R 8. The question for the attacking party is therefore : how can the hostile King be prevented from reaching Q B 2 or Q B 1 ? In this example it is White's move. He will reach the pawns first and

No. 30. White to play.

Schlage *v.* Ahues
Berlin, 1921

capture Black's R P and he must prevent the black King from reaching his Q B 1 or Q B 2 at that precise moment.

Therefore White must execute the manœuvre illustrated in Diag. 1 : in getting his King nearer to this Q side he must force away his rival from the position he desires to reach : 1 K—K 6, K—B 6 ; 2 K—Q 5 (2 K—Q 6, K—Q 5 ; draw), K—Kt 5 (... K—Q 6 ; 3 K—B 6,) ; 3 K—B 6, K—R 4 ; 4 K—Kt 7, K—Kt 4 ; 5 K × P, K—B 3 ; 6 K—Kt 8, and wins. Instead of moving horizontally in a straightforward manner and merely drawing the game (1 K—K 7, K—B 6 ; 2 K—Q 7, K—Q 5 ; 3 K—B 7, K—Q 4 ; 4 K—Kt 7, K—Q 3 ; 5 K × P, K—B 2 ;) White's King took the diagonal *route*, in order to keep his rival from forbidden territory. We have seen a similar manœuvre by the King in Example No. 1.

The King's manœuvre, in this instance, was not complicated ; they often have to be much more elaborate and also more subtle. The main thing, however, is, in all cases, to grasp the essential point which forms the basis of these manœuvres.

In Diag. 31, for instance, it is easy enough to see that

No. 31. White to play and win.

Study by Dedrle

White's King can capture the R P and occupy a favourable position in front of his own pawn, e.g., 1 K—B 3, K—K 3 ; 2 K—Kt 4, K—Q 3 ; 3 K × P, K—B 3 ; 4 K—R 5, K—Kt 2 ; 5 K—Kt 5, and wins. The drawback is that Black threatens to sacrifice his own pawn by ... P—R 6. If White captures it, he will have a R P and Black will reach the corner without difficulty and draw the game. If White refrains from taking the pawn, it is obvious that he will lose a great deal of time, which will allow the hostile King to occupy a favourable position and to maintain the opposition. These are the threats which must be taken into account, and White must find another way of winning the R P : 1 K—Kt 1, P—R 6 ; (if, instead, the King approaches, his rival will be able to win the R P and to occupy the desired position two ranks in front of his passed pawn) ; 2 P—Kt 3, (very subtle play ! The King must be placed *in front* of the pawn. The reader will easily see for himself that this could not be achieved after 2 P—Kt 4,) K—K 4 ; 3 K—R 2, K—Q 4 ; 4 K × P,

K—B 4 ; 5 K—R 4, K—Kt 3 ; 6 K—Kt 4, K—B 3 ;
7 K—R 5, and wins.

This example is both beautiful and subtle, and yet
it contains nothing new to us.   It is merely a case of
putting into practice principles which we have learnt
already.   In addition a little ingenuity is needed, which
cannot be learnt.

When we have two pawns against the adversary's
one, there is usually no difficulty in winning the game,
the most common method being to force the exchange
of one of the pawns and to queen the other.   It is,
however, necessary to make sure that the remaining
pawn shall be able to queen.

Take the following position : White : K at K Kt 5,
pawns at Q R 5 and K R 6, Black : K at his K R 2,
pawn at Q R 3.   If we play simply 1 K—B 5, K × P ;
2 K—K 5, K—Kt 3 ; it is easy to perceive that the
black King will reach his Q B 2 at the precise moment,
when his R P has been taken, with a drawn conclusion.

It is therefore necessary to gain a *tempo*.   We already
know the method, which is not difficult : 1 K—R 5,
K—R 1 ; 2 K—Kt 6, K—Kt 1 ; 3 K—B 6, K—R 2 ;
4 K—K 6, K × P ; 5 K—Q 6, K—Kt 3 ; and two ranks
separate the Kings with White to move.   When the
R P falls the black King will be at his K 2 and unable
to restrict the opposing King.

In all endings of this type the more time you gain,
the more you force the adverse King away from your
second pawn, the easier the win.   This does not, however, absolve you of the necessity of counting the necessary moves with the utmost precision.   Often a *tempo*
or even "the move" makes all the difference between a
win and a draw.

Even in these simple endings, subtle *finessing* is often
imperative.   In Diag. 32, for instance, if it were Black's
move, he would lose at once, for after a King's move
by Black, White plays 2 K—Kt 6, winning the R P.

No. 32. White to play.

Fahrni *v.* Alapin

White must therefore *lose the move*, in other words bring about the identical position with Black to move. Therefore : 1 K—Q 5, K—B 1 ; 2 K—Q 4, and Black is already in a quandary. If he plays 2 ... K—B 2 ; then 3 K—B 5, and White has attained his object. Therefore 2 ... K—Q 1 ; 3 K—B 4 (3 K—B 5, K—B 2;), K—B 1 ; 4 K—Q 5, K—B 2 (... K—Q 1 ; 5 K—Q 6, K—B 1 ; 6 P—B 7,) ; 5 K—B 5, *consummatum est.*

Note that White had two squares, Q B 5 and Q 5, from which to reach Q Kt 6 or Q 6, whereas Black had only one, his Q B 2, to parry both threats.

When our two pawns are united and under mutual protection, they are impregnable and so only cases in which they are obstructed by the single pawn afford any interesting features. There are two methods of winning : capture of the single pawn by means of the related squares, the opposition, the triangle, etc., or sacrifice or exchange of one of the pawns in order to queen the other.

Let us examine the position : White : K at Q 4, pawns at Q B 5 and Q 6, Black : K at his Q 2, P at Q B 3. A simple advance would win, but it would

take a long time, e.g. : 1 K—K 5, K—Q 1 ; 2 K—K 6,
K—K 1 ; 3 P—Q 7 *ch*, K—Q 1 ; 4 K—B 6, K × P;
5 K—B 7, K—Q 1 ; 6 K—K 6, K—B 2 ; 7 K—K 7,
K—B 1 ; 8 K—Q 6, K—Kt 2 ; 9 K—Q 7, K—Kt 1 ;
10 K × P, K—B 1 ; 11 K—Q 6, and wins.   But a far
quicker way is : 1 K—B 4, K—B 1 ; 2 K—Kt 4,
K—Kt 1 ; 3 K—R 5, K—Kt 2 ; 4 P—Q 7, K—B 2 ;
5 K—R 6, K × P ; 6 K—Kt 7, and wins.

A position with two united passed pawns is so strong
that it can be won even if the opponent has a passed
pawn somewhere on the board.   The King would set
out to win it and come back at leisure to execute the
manœuvre indicated above.   A supported passed pawn
nearly always wins.

If one of the united pawns is backward, and, although
not a passed pawn, is susceptible of becoming one,
some special care is needed ; this pawn might be
taken by the opponent with impunity and then the
sacrifice is not so simple, e.g. : White : K at K B 3,
pawns at Q 5 and Q B 4, Black : K at his K B 3, P at
Q 3.   After 1 K—B 4, K—Kt 3 ; 2 P—B 5, would
not do because of 2 ... P × P ; 3 K—K 5, K—B 2 ;
4 K—Q 6, P—B 5 ; but 2 K—K 4, K—B 3 ; 3 K—Q 4,
K—K 2 ; 4 K—B 3, the manœuvre applied in the preceding example is also effective here : 4 ... K—Q 2
(not 4 ... K—B 3 ; 5 K—Kt 4, K—K 4 ; 6 K—Kt 5,
K—Q 5 ; 7 K—B 6, K × P ; 8 K × P) ; 5 K—Kt 4,
K—B 2 ; 6 K—R 5, K—Kt 2 ; 7 K—Kt 5, K—B 2 ;
8 K—R 6, K—B 1 ; 9 K—Kt 6, K—Q 2 ; 10 K—Kt 7,
K—Q 1 ; 11 K—B 6, K—K 2 ; 12 K—B 7, and wins
the pawn.   If, foreseeing and trying to prevent this
manœuvre Black were to move his King as quickly as
possible to the Q side, the white King would carry out
a similar plan on the K side : 1 K—B 4, K—K 2 ;
2 K—Kt 5, K—B 2 ; 3 K—B 5, K—K 2 ; 4 K—Kt 6,
K—K 1 ; 5 K—B 6, K—Q 2 ; 6 K—B 7, etc.

If, however, the white King lacks the space necessary

for this manœuvre, the game is drawn, as for instance here, if the white position were moved one rank to the left.

If we bear in mind, however, the special feature of a position, simple and natural play is normally sufficient to win.

In Diag. 33 it is obvious that Black cannot hope to win the R P. He will therefore have to push forward his Kt P and to exchange it for the R P. The essential condition for a win is that the pawn must reach its Kt 7 without check. In other words, ... P—Kt 6 ; must be played with the white King at his K R 1. But it is not enough simply to advance the pawn, for then White's King will move to K B 2 and K Kt 2 preventing his rival from getting in front of the pawns. White must be forced to place his King at K Kt 1 or K R 1 for the defence of his pawn. After that, a calculation of the moves necessary for the intended manœuvre will

No. 33. Black to play.

Marshall *v.* Schlechter
San Sebastian, 1911

indicate the way to follow.

1 ... K—Kt 5 (1 ... K—K 5 ; would not win : 2 K—B 2, K—Q 6 ; 3 K—B 3, P—Kt 4; 4 K—B 2, K—K 5 ; 5 K—Kt 2, K—B 5 ; 6 K—B 2, K—Kt 5 ; 7 K—Kt 2, P—R 5 ; 8 P—R 3 *ch*, etc.) ; 2 K—B 2,

K—R 6 ; 3 K—Kt 1, P—R 5 ; 4 K—R 1, P—Kt 4 ;
5 K—Kt 1, P—Kt 5 ; 6 K—R 1, P—Kt 6 ; 7 P × P,
P × P ; 8 K—Kt 1, P—Kt 7 ; and wins.

In order to complete this section, I give here an
example in which the weaker side is able to draw.

We have already noted by what surprising means
such a feat can be achieved.   The resource of the stalemate in the corner often helps the weaker side to that
end, e.g. : White : K at Q B 4, pawns at Q R 5 and
Q Kt 6, Black : K at his Q Kt 2 and pawn at Q R 3.
White cannot win, with or without the *move*.   He can
never win the R P without stalemating his adversary,
e.g. : 1 K—Q 5, K—B 1 ; 2 K—B 6, K—Kt 1 ;
3 P—Kt 7, K—R 2 ; or 1 ... K—B 3 ; 2 K—Q 4,
K—Q 3 ; 3 K—K 4, K—B 3 ; 4 K—K 5, K—Q 2 ;
5 K—Q 5, K—B 1 ; etc.

We have given a considerable amount of space to these
simple end games, because they form the basis of all pawn
endings and we shall find there very similar manœuvres.

EXERCISES

In Diag. 34 White plays and wins.   Find the subtle
manœuvre which forces the win.

No. 34.

Study by Duras

In Diag. 35 the contest is between two united pawns and two isolated ones.

No. 35.

Study by Horwitz and Kling

The white King must be handled with much elasticity, for the two isolated pawns, at a distance of three ranks, can win even without outside help, and yet, with the move, White wins.

PAWNS

Endings with several pawns are in the nature of things more difficult than those with but one pawn or two, for the number of variations which must be fathomed increases considerably. But these endings contain also numerous resources both in attack and defence, and so ingenuity comes into its own, unexpected turns can be discovered, whereas an end game with one pawn only leaves no room for "play," everything being regulated beforehand and all the possibility exhausted by the theory. It may be said that endings with numerous pawns present far greater interest and are of greater importance in practical play. Consequently, their study also differs greatly from the analysis of the positions treated hitherto : there we have drawn largely on artistic studies, whereas now we shall have recourse, in the main, to end games from master practice.

Although these endings present an infinite variety, and each one contains something individual and frequently some original twist, we shall constantly meet the same ways and means which are employed in the more simple and typical end games.

As always, the difficulty lies in their application and in particular to the choice of procedure to be applied in each case and on what grounds a particular method is selected.

That is why it is essential to analyse a position very minutely before developing any sort of plan, the basis of such an analysis being the principles which we have established in the course of our study up to this point.

First of all we must pay attention to the respective positions of the Kings, and to establish which of the two is the better placed. Then, passing on to the pawns, if necessary we bisect their position in order the better to gauge the weaknesses, peculiarities as well as advantages on either flank : passed pawns, guarded, isolated, doubled pawns, spare moves, chances of creating a passed pawn, backward pawns, a minority of pawns holding a larger number, etc.

After thus bisecting a position, we cannot fail to realize its essential points and then we must revert to the position of the Kings to confirm the relative values of their positions in the light of the essential characteristics of the pawn formation. Then our plan of action will take shape, then we shall know what means to employ in order to surmount the difficulties and the obstacles which we shall find in our way. And then only shall we be able to play the end game with a complete grasp of the situation and with full confidence in our resources.

In studying the examples given here, we shall frequently make analyses of this type, and this will lead

us naturally to the very elaborate analysis which will
have to be made when we come to study, not only the
pawns, but also the pieces. The evolutions of the
pieces will be made on the background of the pawn
formation, which fact invests the study of pawn play
with singular importance.

When one side is a pawn up, the matter becomes
comparatively easy, not only because an extra pawn,
in the majority of cases, leads to a win without much
difficulty, not only because such an ending can easily
lead to one of the typical positions with which we are
already familiar, but also, in the first place, because we
immediately perceive an object to follow ; we rarely
have to seek far for a plan of campaign. It becomes
mostly a case of exploiting the material advantage
acquired, of creating a passed pawn and queening it.

Of course it happens that matters do not run smoothly
and that even in a simple end game there are subtle
points which must be noted and which, if overlooked
or misinterpreted wrongly, could compromise the whole
position.

Examine, for instance, the position in Diag. 36 :

No. 36. White to play and win.

L. Rödl

White has an extra pawn, a passed pawn in the centre with the King in front of it. In addition he has a spare move on the K side. With so many advantages, the win should be easy ; one might think that White must win whatever he does. And yet, even in this instance, it is possible to miss the win altogether if some details are neglected or the peculiarities of the position and the proper procedure are not thought out with sufficient care.

In order to force the win, the white King must break into the hostile position, but there is only one passage in front of him : via K 5. But this square is easily guarded by Black, and White's spare move is of no value and the black King has two appropriate squares available, his Q 3 and K 3. If another path could be found, say via Q B 5, the win could be secured at once, and thus the proper method becomes clear : 1 P—R 5, and if 1 ... P—Kt 4 ; 2 P—R 3 (the point : the spare move now is effective), P—R 4 ; 3 P—R 4, and, as Black's pawn moves are exhausted, he must allow free passage for his opponent's King. Similarly after 1 ... P × P ; 2 P × P, P—R 4 ; 3 P—R 4, Black's King cannot guard the two squares at his Q B 4 and K 4.

As this is our first example of an ending with a number of pawns, let us find out, by means of a brief analysis, whether White really has a win after this, although any average player should be able to analyse the position by himself and a cursory glance should show how the win is to be secured. Let us imagine that, after 1 P—R 5, P × P ; 2 P × P, P—R 4 ; 3 P—R 4, Black plays 3 ... K—B 3 ; then 4 K—K 5, (here White can also win by 4 K—B 4, K—Q 3 ; 5 P—Q 4, K—B 3 ; 6 P—Q 5 *ch*, K—Q 3 ; 7 K—Q 4, P—R 4 ; 8 P—R 4) K—Kt 4 ; 5 P—Q 4, K × P ; 6 P—Q 5, and wins.

Clearly an easy win ! Yet, had White thoughtlessly played 1 P—Kt 5, there is no more than a draw after the reply 1 ... P—Q R 4. If, misjudging the position, he had played 1 K—B 4, he could have won only with great difficulty and the win would have required lengthy and precise calculation, e.g. : 1 ... K—B 3 ; 2 P— Kt 5 *ch*, P × P *ch* ; 3 P × P *ch*, K—Q 3 ; 4 P—Q 4, (the author of this study quotes 4 P—R 4, giving up the spare move and leading to a draw) P—R 4 ; (trying to force White to use up his spare move, as he sees that if he employed the stratagem of the "triangle," by play- ing 4 ... K—K 3 ; 5 P—Q 5 *ch*, K—K 2 ; 6 K—Q 4, K—Q 3 ; White would put in his spare move 7 P—R 3, forcing Black to give up the opposition) 5 P—Q 5, (the only move, as 5 P—R 4 would use up his spare move, and if 5 P—R 3, P—R 5 ; and it is Black who gains a *tempo*), P—R 5 ; 6 K—Q 4, P—R 6 ; 7 K—B 4 (this is what Black overlooked ; the white King can manœuvre on Q B 4 and Q 4 without leaving his Q P unguarded), K—Q 2 ; (Black in turn utilizes the triangle, and proposes to move his King to his Q 3 as soon as White's King moves to Q 4) 8 K—Q 3, K—K 2 ; 9 K—K 3 (here is the unexpected opportunity, afforded by the advance of Black's K R P ; but it is the only way to win), K—Q 2 (K—Q 3 ; 10 K—Q 4) ; 10 K—B 3, K—Q 3 ; 11 K—Kt 3, K × P ; 12 K × P, and White's R P queens two moves ahead of Black's Q Kt P. Compare the two methods of winning. The first required five moves, the second about fifteen. And in the latter case White's K R P wins against Black's Q Kt P ; clearly that is not the right way. Thus chances are lost, and even though White wins by the second method also, he has nothing to spare.

If we reverse the situation and give the defending King a dominating position, the result immediately is altered (Diag. 37). Here White also has a passed pawn in the centre, but his King is behind it and it is blockaded by the adverse King. In addition Black has a spare move on the K side, even though he cannot

obtain a passed pawn there. In consequence, White is
virtually a pawn ahead, but to no avail, for the black King
is the more active of the two. It is the black King
who threatens to penetrate into the enemy camp via his
K 5 or Q B 5 : the first-named square is guarded only
by the white King, but the second can, in addition, be
protected by P—Q Kt 3. If Black could eliminate

No. 37. White to play.

Pirc *v.* Alatortzev
Moscow, 1935

this pawn by exchanging it, he would ensure a choice
of either route, as White did in the preceding example,
after which he would have chances of winning : the
advantage of the King's mobility would outweigh that
of the extra pawn. Therefore White must, at all cost,
avoid the exchange : he will, in fact, play a purely
defensive game and be only too happy to secure the
draw : 1 P—Q R 4, P—Q R 3 ; 2 P—Q Kt 3, (not
2 P—Q Kt 4, P—Q Kt 4 ; and Black would break
through) P—B 3 ; 3 P—R 4, P—R 3 ; 4 P—Kt 3,
P—K Kt 4 ; 5 K—K 3, P × R P ; 6 P × P, P—K R 4 ;
7 K—Q 3, P—Kt 4 ; 8 P × P, P × P ; 9 K—K 3,
K—Q 3 ; 10 K—Q 2 (the "triangle"), P—Kt 5 ; 11

K—K 3, etc., with the well-known manœuvre in which
Q 3 and Q 5 are related squares. Thus we see that
the pawn alone does not win ; the position is all-important.
It is necessary to look for or create minute advantages
and then only to seek to turn the advantage in material
to account. With a proper grasp of the situation, an
insignificant advantage can lead to a win ; without it, a
quite considerable advantage in material may be of no
avail.

In Diag. 38 Black is a pawn ahead, but this pawn is
doubled and cannot become a passed pawn. There is
practically no advantage in material for Black, but he
has a spare move, and a spare move, combined with
some positional asset, can easily mean a won game.
Again an analysis of the position is imperative.

No. 38. Black to play.

Teichmann v. Blackburne
Berlin, 1897

A glance is sufficient to recognize that the black King
has the superior position. There is another point in
Black's favour : he threatens to obtain a distant passed
pawn on the K R file. In that case, the position would
be won for him, for whilst the white King would stray

to the K R file looking after the hostile pawn, Black
would capture the K B pawn and set out to win the
Q side pawns as well.   This advance by the K R P also
threatens to render White's K B 4 unguarded and leave
the way open for the black King : if, however, 1 ...
P—R 5, 2 P—Kt 4, White remains with a backward
pawn at K B 3, against an advanced and protected pawn
at Black's K R 5.   Therefore, White will strive to
force his opponent to make the exchange at K Kt 3,
so that his King recaptures at K Kt 3 and stops the
black King from penetrating to his K B 5.   Now Black's
real difficulties begin, but it is already clear what kind
of manœuvres his King must undertake : he must arrive
on his K B 4 as soon as the adverse King will have
moved to his K Kt 3, and thus force him to leave a way
clear at his K B 5.   But Black must not follow the line
of least resistance by using up his spare move ; he must
leave this until later when the adverse King, retiring,
shall have the opposition : that is when the spare move
becomes useful by forcing the adversary to give up the
opposition.   If the first pair of *related squares* is K B 5
and K Kt 3, the second is K B 4 and K B 2.   The spare
move is the last trump in Black's hand and will decide
the fate of the battle.   And if a win cannot be forced
in this way, then there is nothing else to be done.

Thus the whole plan is established : 1 ... K—B 3 ;
2 K—Kt 2, K—Kt 3 ; 3 K—R 2, P—R 5 ; 4 K—R 3,
P × P ; 5 K × P, K—B 4 ; 6 K—Kt 2, K—B 5 ; 7
K—B 2, P—B 4 ; 8 K—K 2 (8 K—Kt 2, K—K 6),
K—Kt 6 ; 9 K—K 3, K—Kt 7 ; 10 K—K 2, K—R 6 ;
(taking advantage of the fact that White has no access
to his Q 6, by assuming the distant opposition) 11
K—B 2, K—R 7 ; 12 K—B 1, K—Kt 6 ; 13 K—K 2,
K—Kt 7 ; 14 K—K 3, K—B 8 ; and wins.   In this
most striking example we see the convincing application
in practical play of the laws of the opposition, the related
squares and the "triangle."   In the actual game,

however, the continuation was different. On the 6th move
White played the inferior 6 K—B 2, which shows that
he was unfamiliar with the correct procedure, and he
lost the game much quicker than necessary : 6 ...
K—B 5 ; 7 K—K 2, K—Kt 6 ; 8 K—K 3, P—B 4 ;
9 K—K 2, K—Kt 7 ; and wins.   This game was played
forty years ago when even a master could not really
grasp certain things which were little known, not properly
analysed, and certainly not yet proved.   To-day any
player should be conversant with them.   But the slightest
inaccuracy can alter the course of a game, change a win
into a draw, a draw into a loss.   For example, in Diag.
39 White's position is clearly superior : his King is
active, he has a passed pawn as well as a spare move.
These are appreciable advantages, especially in view of
the weaknesses in Black's camp, namely : the backward
Kt P and the weak K B P which will immobilize the King
for its protection.   But if we confine ourselves to this
cursory survey, an unpleasant surprise is in store for
us.   For it seems a simple matter to win the game by
1 K—B 4, K—K 3 ; 2 P—Kt 3, and the spare move

No. 39. White to play.

Iljin-Genevsky *v.* Botvinnik
Leningrad, 1938

enables us to win the B P. We should have investigated whether the adversary has a threat of his own, whether he has another method of guarding the pawn.

Once the question is raised, the answer is soon found : Black can guard his K B P by ... P—Kt 3 ; which also threatens ... P—Kt 4 ; by which he himself would obtain a supported passed pawn, or, in the case of an exchange, the contest is reduced to one of two isolated pawns on either side. This is White's problem. He must guard against this threat or, better still, he must be prepared to exploit the position resulting from the exchange of pawns. For if he plays as first suggested 1 K—B 4, then 1 ... P—Kt 3 ; 2 P × P *ch*, (2 P—Kt 3, K—Kt 2 ; 3 P—K 6, K—B 3,) K × P ; 3 P—Kt 3, P—R 4 ; 4 P—K 6, K—B 3 ; 5 P—K 7, K × P ; 6 K × P, and the game is drawn. And why ? Because the white King was already posted at B 4 when the black King moved to his Kt 3. And so White must, in this case also, first gain a *tempo* : he must move to B 4 only when the black King is already at his Kt 3 or K 3. Then Black's threat is inoperative. White plays 1 K—B 3. If Black wishes to mark time and plays 1 ... K—K 2 ; then he no longer threatens ... P—Kt 3 ; and we can play 2 K—B 4, K—K 3 ; 3 P—Kt 3, winning the B P. Therefore, in reply to 1 K—B 3, Black must at once play 1 ... P—Kt 3 ; but then 2 P × P *ch*, K × P ; 3 K—B 4, P—R 4 ; 4 P—Kt 3, and the King must leave his B P which is lost and, with it, the game. Nothing could be simpler. And yet, in actual play, 1 K—B 4, was played and the game was drawn.

It is clear that White failed to win the game because he did not anticipate his adversary's reply 1 ... P—Kt 3. This is a common failing which arises from inattention, lack of appreciation or faulty judgment of the opponent's counter-chances or of our own true object ; they are the most frequent causes of perverted results.

A cursory glance at Diag. 40 shows at once that

No. 40. White to play.

Eliskases *v.* Schmidt
Bad Oeynhausen, 1938

White's advantage consists in his ability to penetrate into the hostile position via Q R 5 and in his spare moves P—B 3 and P—R 4. If White's King reaches Q R 5 it will be impossible, on account of his spare moves, to prevent his playing to Q Kt 6. This is his principal threat and the question for Black now is the extent of the danger accruing from White's King being posted at Q Kt 6, and if it is serious, how to cope with it.

Supposing that Black undertakes nothing to prevent the arrival of the white King at his Q Kt 6, one of White's spare moves (P—R 4) will suffice to force away the black King from his Q B 2 to Q B 1. That is the position which both sides must visualize clearly. What would then be White's threat with his King at Q Kt 6 and his rival at his Q B 1? The solution is not difficult to find : 1 P—Kt 5, R P × P ; 2 P × P, P × P ; 3 K × P, K—B 2 ; 4 P—B 3 (the second spare move), K—Q 2 ; 5 K—Kt 6, K—B 1 ; 6 P—B 6, P × P ; 7 K × P, and White's King, in command of the sixth rank, will capture the K side pawns with impunity.

The threat is certainly serious and Black must do his

utmost to prevent the occurrence of this position. Is he powerless ? His King is much nearer to the Q side pawns and there should be some appropriate pawn advance to cut across White's intentions.

Once the problem is thus clearly stated, it is less difficult to find ways and means. Even without fore-seeing the exact manœuvres, opportunities often arise in the course of play. Black strategy may be described as an active defence, since a passive defence clearly loses. There are several ways of stopping the entry of the white King at his Q Kt 6, but their efficacy varies accord-ing to the changes in the position. The basic idea is to eliminate the backward Q Kt P. Let us see how this can be achieved. Firstly : 1 ... K—Q 2 ; 2 K—K 3, P—R 4 ; 3 K—Q 3, P×P ; 4 P—R 4 (4 P×P, K—B 2 ; 5 K—B 4, P—Kt 4 *ch* ; draw), P—Kt 3 ; 5 P×P, P—Q B 4 ; and the united passed pawns on either side secure the draw. Had he missed his oppor-tunity on the second move and instead of 2 ... P—R 4 ; played passively 2 ... K—B 2 ; 3 K—Q 3, K—Kt 1 ; 4 K—B 4, K—R 1 ; 5 K—Kt 3, K—R 2 ; 6 K—R 4, he could now still retrieve the situation by 6 ... P—Kt 4 *ch* ; 7 P×P *e.p. ch*, K×P ; 8 K—Kt 3, P—Q B 4 ; again drawing the game.

As in the preceding example, Black did not grasp the meaning of his adversary's threat, and allowed him to carry it out without let or hindrance ; the result was a lost game.

In nearly all the examples shown so far, the King only was responsible for ingenious manœuvres, the pawns advancing as and when required. This is not always the case : pawns must also be manœuvred with skill, and the co-ordination of their evolutions with those of the King is a difficult feature of end game play, but lends it extraordinary beauty.

The first example (Diag. 41) is very lucid in concep-tion, but its execution is extremely complicated. White

has an extra pawn, but it is backward and blockaded by
Black's Kt P, which, supported by its Q R P, stops
all three white pawns. White can win only if he can
obtain a passed pawn by P—B 4 ; but his difficulty is
that his King cannot leave the K side without great
risk, for his K Kt P would fall, leaving the adverse
K R P free to queen. This would take seven moves :
K—Kt 4 ; K×P ; P—R 4 ; P—R 5 ; P—R 6 ;
P—R 7 ; and P—R 8. White has therefore this
amount of time in which to carry out any scheme,
and, deducting the essential move K—K 3, to stop
Black's prospective passed pawn resulting from P—B 4,
P × P, *e.p.* ; etc. After that White can also obtain a
passed pawn by P—R 3, P—Kt 4, but this will also
require six moves and the black King at his K Kt 5
will be in the square of White's Q Kt P and will
therefore be able to stop it. It follows that White must

No. 41. White to play.

Berger *v.* Bauer
Correspondence game, 1889-91

queen the Q R P if he is to succeed, for not only will
this pawn be outside the square, but it will queen ahead
of Black's K R P and stop it from queening : White

must take recourse to the geometrical idea. Nor is it
necessary to play P—R 3, for P—R 4 at the proper
time will gain a move.   Thus he will queen on the
sixth move and Black on his seventh only, and White
will be two moves ahead.

And so the whole plan is laid out : 1 P—B 4,
P × P *e.p.* ; 2 K—K 3, K—Kt 4 ; 3 P—R 4, K × P ;
4 P—Kt 4, P × P.   But now White has to provide
against a serious contingency, for Black has now two
united passed pawns.   Can he use them to advantage ?
White can certainly stop them, but, in two moves,
Black's King will come to their assistance at his K 7.
And so, if White plays simply : 5 P—R 5, the continuation is 5 ... P—Kt 6 ; 6 K—Q 3, P—Kt 7 ; 7
K—B 2, K—B 6 ; 8 P—R 6, K—K 7 ; 9 P—R 7,
P—Kt 8 (Q) *ch* ; 10 K × Q, K—Q 7 ; 11 P—R 8 (Q),
P—B 7 *ch* ; 12 K—R 2, P—B 8 (Q) ; and Black
remains a pawn ahead, although the game will be drawn
by perpetual check.   It is clear that White must not
allow this diversion : he must stop the advance of the
two passed pawns and, to that end, lose another move :
5 K—Q 3, P—R 4 ; 6 P—R 5, and White queens
first just in time to prevent his adversary from doing so.

It is instructive to note the precision which was
required in this ending, and the finer points in which it
abounds.   Such skill is not acquired in a day, but one
object of this book is to teach the student to think on
right lines in the end game, and this presupposes a
grasp of its fundamentals, the ability to create a plan
based on these.   In addition it is essential to pay the
strictest attention to the subtleties and peculiarities that
are liable to occur, without losing sight of the fundamentals of end game play.

The student will now be able to tackle the next
position (Diag. 42) which is far more complicated
although the forces are reduced.   Here there is one
finesse after another and the play of Kings and pawns

is closely interconnected.   Almost constantly one side
or the other has to win or lose a *tempo*, and on nearly
every move there is a chance, even a likelihood, of a
mistake being made, which would reverse the legitimate
result.

Let us first examine the characteristics of the position.
Black can obtain by force a distant passed pawn on the

No. 42.   White to play.

Tchekhover *v.* Bondarevsky
Leningrad, 1938

K R file, but it would soon fall, and if he does so at once,
he will be unable to capture White's K B P in return.
Also the white King can advance to Q 5 and still remain
"in the square."   Black's threat is, all things considered, not very serious and can become dangerous
only in certain circumstances.   Black can also win the
Q R P which White's King cannot support, as he has
to watch the black K R P.   But it will take Black four
moves to effect this capture and the white K B P would
queen unhindered in the meantime.   Black's two threats
are thus seen to be fictitious and need occasion no great
anxiety.   White's threats are more substantial.   First
of all, the black K R P is under threat of capture by the

King ; and if it advances, the K Kt P is in jeopardy.
The white King is by far the more active of the two.
His every move contains a threat and, thanks to this
circumstance, he will reach K 5 without loss of time.
On the other hand, it will not be easy to effect the capture of the K Kt P, because, with the white King at
K 5, Black will play ... P—K R 4 ; and although this
pawn must fall, so must also White's K B P, and the
black King will return in time to the Q R file and force
a draw. White's problem is therefore : how to manœuvre his King, his K B P and Q R P, so that the black
King cannot get back to the Q side in time to save the
game. Black must be made to lose several *tempi* in
useless manœuvres.

Here is the continuation which occurred in the game,
with a few variations suggested by the winner : 1 K—
B 4, P—K R 3; (if, instead, 1 ... K—Q 3 ; 2 K—Kt 5,
K—K 4 ; 3 P—B 3—the first *finesse*—P—K R 4 ;
4 P—B 4 *ch*, K—K 3—here 4 ... K—K 5 will not do
because of 5 P × P, P × P ; 6 P—B 5, and the black
King is on the wrong diagonal, whereby the new black
Queen may be lost at her K R 8—5 P—B 5 *ch*, P × P ;
6 P × P, and White wins, thanks to the distant passed
pawn) 2 K—K 5, P—K R 4 ; 3 P × P, P × P ; 4
P—R 4, (a fresh subtlety: with 4 K—B 5, K—Q 3;
5 K—Kt 5, K—K 4 ; 6 P—B 3, P—R 3 ; 7 P—R 4,
P—R 4 ; 8 P—B 4 *ch*, K—K 3 ; the game is drawn.
White is in time to stop the adverse Q R P) 4 ...
P—R 4 (P—R 5 ; 5 K—B 4, K—Q 3 ; 6 K—Kt 4,
K—K 4 ; 7 P—R 5, K—K 5 ; 8 P—R 6, P—R 6 ;
9 K—Kt 3, P—R 7 ; 10 K × P, K—B 6 ; 11 K—Kt 1) ;
5 K—B 5, K—Q 3 ; 6 K—Kt 5, K—K 4 ; 7 P—B 3,
(again the same *finesse*) 7 ... K—K 3 (P—R 5 ; 8
K—Kt 4) ; 8 P—B 4, P—R 5 ; 9 K × P, K—B 3 ;
10 K—Kt 3, K—Kt 3 ; 11 K—B 3, K—B 3 ; 12
K—K 4, K—K 3 ; 13 K—Q 4, K—B 4; 14 K—B 5,
K × P ; 15 K—Kt 6, K—K 4 ; 16 K × P, K—Q 3 ;

17 K—Kt 6, K—Q 2 ; 18 K—Kt 7, and wins. By a
sequence of subtle manœuvres, White has managed to
capture the pawn with the Kings at an interval of two
files, after which his own pawn can get through, if
sufficiently advanced.

It would be a mistake to suppose that such precision
is not for the rank and file. With a clear understanding
of what is required and of what is possible, all the
necessary calculations will be made with surprising ease ;
the student will marvel at his own unsuspected powers.

In the last example we witnessed co-ordinated manœuvres by King and pawns. As we shall see in Diag. 43,
everything sometimes depends on a point in the handling
of the pawns. Here Black's position is very much
compromised, his pawns are isolated, one of them
doubled. In addition, White has two spare moves with

No. 43. Black to play.

Flohr *v.* Capablanca
Moscow, 1935

his R P, and if his King reaches K B 4, Black's pawn
at his K B 4 is lost. It seems impossible to prevent
White's King from getting there on account of his spare
moves. Nor can Black retaliate by capturing the white

K P (K—K 4; K—K 5 ; K—Q 6 ; in reply to K—Q 2,
K—K 2, K—B 2,) because White would capture all the
opposing pawns and queen his Kt P, which, as can easily
be ascertained, Black could not succeed in capturing.
Is there any salvation ? Remember the example in
Diag. 40 : there also it was essential to prevent the
intrusion of the opposing King, and this was achieved
by calling upon the active co-operation of the pawns.
There is no question of Black advancing his K B P.
White would simply capture it with a magnificent unifi-
cation of his disjointed pawns. But what about the
advance of the R P ? After P × P, Black can play
... P—B 5 ; and stop the R P with his King. Let us
analyse 1 ... K—K 4 ; 2 K—Q 2, K—K 5 ; 3 K—K 2,
P—R 5 ; 4 P × P, P—B 5 ; 5 P—R 5, and Black cannot
capture the K P because the R P would queen. It
follows that Black must advance the R P only at a time
when White cannot reply to the capture of his K P by
advancing his own R P, in other words the K P must
be captured with check, e.g.: 1 ... K—K 4 ; 2 K—K 2,
K—K 5 ; 3 K—B 2, P—R 5 ; 4 P × P, P—B 5 ;
5 P—R 5, P × P *ch* ; 6 K—K 2, K—B 4 ; and Black
stops the R P. Thus the way to a draw is found, and
now White must try to find a win. He must recognize
that Q 2 and K B 2 must not be occupied by his King
and that he must have recourse to his spare moves :
1 ... K—K 4 ; 2 K—K 2, K—K 5 ; 3 P—R 3. But
the problem no longer presents any difficulty for Black,
for he has sufficient space for "the triangle" by means
of which he can keep the hostile King at bay and cause
him to make use of his remaining spare move : 2 ...
K—Q 4 ; 3 K—B 3, K—K 4 ; 4 P—R 4, K—Q 4 ;
5 K—B 4, K—K 3 ; and the game is drawn. If White
had yet another move in reserve, he would now win.
But his astute opponent made him exhaust them all at
the proper time.

The foregoing examples are sufficient evidence that

there exists no universal *panacea* for the proper handling of an end game. Each one has its own peculiarities, which must be taken into account. But the same principles form the basis of all manœuvres, and the analysis of the position and the plan built upon it guides us in this selection. There constantly occur, however, *finesses* and subtle turns, which experience teaches us to discover, provided the object aimed at is properly understood.

This is the fundamental idea of end game play, which thus becomes an integral part of the game of chess, and calls upon intelligence and understanding in the same degree as upon simple calculation and mere technique.

EXERCISES

Try your skill on the next two examples (Diags. 44 and 45), find the proper continuation, single out the principles which should be applied and the appropriate

No. 44.   No. 45.

Colle *v.* Grünfeld
Carlsbad, 1929

Stoltz *v.* Nimzowitsch
Berlin, 1928

means to employ, the objects to pursue. In the first example, White has an extra pawn and he has the move : how does he force a win? In the second, the forces are equal and Black has the move. What is the result ?

THE PIECES

We have already ascertained that, in the end game, the pieces undergo remarkable changes in value, and we have seen in what these changes consist. The secondary *rôle* which is theirs in the end game, namely that of supporting the pawns on their march to the queening square, affects their relative degree of usefulness : it frequently happens that the same forces on either side vary in their effectiveness, and also that a normally weaker piece equals or even exceeds the stronger one in power. In entering upon, or preparing for the end game stage, it is essential to see clearly which piece will be the more appropriate.

On the other hand, the mere presence of a piece gives the ending a different turn. Many of the general principles, which we have discussed so far, no longer apply. The *Zugzwang*, for instance, is hardly applicable, for the piece is there, able to mark time ; to gain or lose a move with the King, a spare pawn move—what is their use, when the adverse piece can at will make a long or a short move, or reach a given point in one or more moves ? And so the manœuvres by King and pawns no longer have the vital importance, nor even the character, which they had in endings with Kings and pawns only. The pieces nearly always monopolise the dynamic aspect of the play and supply the combinations, thus maintaining their middle game character. It is surprising, however, that even in these circumstances, the ordinarily inert forces, the Kings and the pawns, can display a genius for speed and fantasy. When a piece initiates a combination it is not remarkable, but when a

King does so, there is both surprise and charm in an unlooked-for event. The measure of a King's powers in that direction is given in the next example (Diag. 46). On the last move Black's Rook has attacked the K P,

No. 46. White to play.

Dr. Alekhine *v.* Capablanca
Match, 1927

whilst his Bishop keeps the K R P under observation. As White cannot advance his K P because his K B P is unguarded, it is the King which comes to its aid by a most subtle and clever manœuvre : 1 K—Kt 2, and if 1 ... R × P ; 2 K—B 3, followed by 3 R—K 5 *ch*, winning the Bishop.

In judging the relative value of the pieces in an end game, notwithstanding the variety of their functions, there is one criterion which can be said to be of general application, in the same way as a King in the centre, or a supported passed pawn, and that is : their degree of mobility.

An active piece, able to roam freely over the chess-board, attacking pawns, forcing their advance and dis-locating their formations, creating weaknesses, is a fearful weapon, especially when opposed to a piece which is reduced to a passive defence. In such cases the attacker could rightly claim to be a piece ahead, and the defender's best course frequently is to put an end to this state of things by sacrificing a pawn. However important a pawn may be in the end game, its loss is preferable to being deprived of the use of a piece. The sacrifice, to be at all promising, must of course give back to the piece its full mobility and, as far as possible, reduce that of the opposing piece : if that piece remains as active as before, there is merely an ending with a minority of one pawn and a probable loss.

It would, however, be a mistake to generalize, and it can well be that even an active piece has no practical value, if it can neither attack nor stop the hostile pawns, e.g., a white-square Bishop having the freedom of the board, but quite useless against pawns on black squares. It is therefore not quite enough to ascertain the degree of mobility of a piece when entering upon the end game stage. This particularly refers to minor pieces. The analysis must therefore take into account the King's position, the characteristics of the pawn formation, and then the value of the pieces with reference to that formation.

Finally, we must not forget that certain pieces are of special value to the weaker side in increasing the chances of a draw : we have already quoted, in that respect, Queen, Rook, Bishops of opposite colours. According to the position, a decision must be taken as to which pieces to exchange and which to preserve, and the study of the different pieces, our familiarity with their advantages and shortcomings in various circumstances will teach us which will, at any time, answer our requirements.

End games with pieces fall quite naturally under five headings :

(1) King and piece *v.* King : mates by one or the other piece or by two pieces in concert.

(2) Piece *v.* passed pawn.

(3) Piece and pawn *v.* the same piece : the piece's part in supporting and defending the pawn.

(4) Piece and pawns *v.* the same piece and pawns— the true endings, of which the most important and frequent are the Rook endings.

(5) Various pieces : the most frequent combination is that of Knights and Bishops, which will claim most of our attention.

The immense variety of all these endings precludes a thorough study of all of them, and we must confine ourselves to a study of the most typical and representative cases.

THE QUEEN

The strongest piece on the chessboard, the Queen maintains her supremacy in the end game. But let it not be thought that the character of it remains unchanged : it is precisely her preponderance over all other pieces and her ability to act in eight directions which affect her adversely. If in the middle game the Queen requires more space in which to develop her strength, in an ending on an almost empty board, her wide radius, her ubiquity is of little use, for the Queen finds few objects of attack. She cannot mate without the help of her King and the adversary is not incommoded to any great extent ; on the other hand, the weaker side derives great benefit from the fact that his Queen can usually threaten a series of checks from which it is difficult to escape. The stronger party should preserve the Queen only if he has a positional advantage : as soon as this has been turned into one of material, he is well advised to exchange the troublesome Queen. It is a matter of pure arithmetic which is here confirmed : the advantage of a pawn, paramount when there are no pieces, considerable when there is a minor piece on either side, becomes insignificant where the tremendous force, which is represented by the Queen, is still on the board.

There is also a reversal of values in the end game in that, in the middle game, to gain the Queen for two pieces is usually a satisfactory transaction. In the end game the possibility of concentrating two threats on the same objective counterbalances the difference in power. Here a Rook and minor piece are nearly always a match for the Queen, whilst two Rooks are definitely superior : they can win a pawn defended by the Queen, they can enforce the queening of a pawn, which the Queen cannot achieve against them. The Queen is not at home in the end game, where all is *finesse* and subtlety : she is like the *Queen Mary* floating on the Avon. Besides, the Queen is essentially a piece for the middle game and rarely survives until the end. That is why Queen endings are of rare occurrence.

THE QUEEN ALONE

The Queen has one great advantage, which she shares only with the Rook. She can effect a mate with the sole help of the King. This mate is so easy that it is not necessary to illustrate it. A few observations will suffice.

This mate can only be effected on an outside rank or file and the assistance of the King is essential. In order not to waste time, we must force the King towards the square on which stands our King. If away from the centre, we must prevent him from getting there. If the adverse King is in the centre, as the four centre squares cannot be simultaneously attacked by the Queen, we must bring up our own King.

A mate can be administered in the corner (beware of stalemate in that case), but also equally well on an outside line. In this case the opposition is useful, although not always essential. There are in fact several aspects of the mate by the Queen, e.g., White : K at Q B 6, Q at Q Kt 7, Black : King at his Q R 1, or—White : K at K 6, Q at Q 7, Black : King at his Q 1, or—

White : K at Q B 7, Q at Q R 1, Black : K at his Q R 1,
or—White : K at Q B 6, Q at Q B 7, Black : K at his
Q B 1, or—K at Q B 6, Q at K R 8, Black : K at his
Q B 1.   Only in the last case is the opposition essential.

According to the advice given, the play in the following position, White : K at K R 8, Q at Q Kt 1, Black :
K at his Q 5, would be as follows : 1 K—Kt 7, K—K 4 ;
2 Q—Kt 4 (for the black King has entered enemy
territory), K—Q 4 ; 3 K—B 6, K—B 3 ; 4 K—K 6,
K—B 2 ; 5 Q—Kt 5, K—B 1 ; 6 K—Q 6, K—Q 1 ;
7 Q—Q 7 or Kt 8 mate.

QUEEN *v.* PAWN

It is no difficult task for a Queen to stop a pawn :
she only needs to place herself in front of it and she
cannot be dislodged.   The only cases, therefore, to be
discussed are those in which the pawn, supported by
the King, has reached the seventh rank without the
Queen being able to occupy the square in front.   Even
then the Queen can still prevent the pawn from queening.
The procedure is simple.   The Queen pins the pawn,
and by successive checks, the stronger King approaching
the pawn at every opportunity, the weaker King is forced
to defend the pawn and to occupy the queening square.

In the position White : K at K Kt 8, Q at K R 8,
Black : K at Q B 7, pawn at Q 7, the method is ; 1
Q—R 2 (1 Q—R 7 *ch*, is also playable), K—B 8 ;
2 Q—B 7 *ch*, K—Kt 7 ; 3 Q—Q 6 (or 3 Q—Kt 6 *ch*),
K—B 7 ; 4 Q—B 5 *ch*, K—Kt 7 ; 5 Q—Kt 4 *ch*
(approaching the pawn step by step), K—B 7 ; 6 Q—
B 4 *ch*, K—Kt 7 ; 7 Q—Q 3, K—B 8 ; 8 Q—B 3 *ch*,
K—Q 8 (the desired position is reached and the white
King approaches) ; 9 K—B 7, K—K 7 ; 10 Q—B 2,
K—K 8 ; 11 Q—K 4 *ch*, K—B 7 ; 12 Q—Q 3, K—K 8 ;
13 Q—K 3 *ch*, K—Q 8 ; and again the King gets
nearer and the same manœuvre is repeated until the King
is near enough to collaborate in the capture of the pawn.

Therefore such positions end in a draw, where the Queen is unable to check, e.g., White : K at Q 6, Q at K 8, Black : K at his Q 7, pawn at K 7. There are, however, positions in which the Queen can check, and yet the result is a draw : in these cases stalemate plays a part. One is the case of the R P which has reached its R 7 with the King at R 8. The adverse Queen has just driven the King into the corner by a check at her Kt 3, and now nothing can be done because of stalemate if the attacking King moves nearer.

The same thing occurs in the case of either B P (at B 7). After 1 Q—Kt 6 *ch*, the King moves to R 8, and not to B 8 as with other pawns, and the pawn cannot be captured because of stalemate.

Such positions can be won only if our King is sufficiently near : then there are two possibilities: either, we allow the pawn to queen if we can effect an immediate mate, e.g., White : K at K Kt 3, Q at K 3, Black : K at Q 8, pawn at Q B 7. The continuation is 1 K—B 2, P—B 8 (Q) ; 2 Q—K 2 mate, or, with the R P, it is even possible to play a waiting move as follows : White : K at Q R 5, Q at K 2, Black : K at Q Kt 8, pawn at Q R 7. The play is 1 K—Kt 4, P—R 8 (Q) ; 2 K—Kt 3, and whatever Black plays White mates in three moves. The same finish occurs also with other pawns if the stronger side succeeds in reaching a favourable position as, for instance : White : K at K 5, Q at Q Kt 2, Black : K at K 8, pawn at Q 7. Then 1 K—K 4, P—Q 8 (Q) ; 2 K—K 3, and Black has no check and is mated or loses the Queen. But such positions are of rare occurrence, as in most cases the win is easy by the simple procedure shown above.

It is clear that the Queen would normally win an ending against a pawn. Even against two pawns, if they are not too far advanced, the Queen will prevail by first winning one of them and then stopping the other. It is even possible for the second pawn to make the defender's task more awkward, for then there can be no stalemate, and all combinations based on stalemate are eliminated.

QUEEN AND PAWN *v.* QUEEN

We have already indicated that, with Queens on the board, the advantage of a pawn becomes almost insignificant and hardly ever sufficient to win. The defending Queen nearly always succeeds in giving endless checks with an occasional approach by the King in order to hold up the pawn. The pawn has a chance only when it has already reached the seventh rank, and even then a draw is by no means uncommon, e.g. : White : K at K R 8, Q at Q B 2, pawn at K Kt 7, Black : K at his Q Kt 5, Q at K Kt 6. Black plays : 1 ... Q—R 5 *ch* ; 2 Q—R 7, Q—Q 1 *ch* ; 3 P—Kt 8 (Q), Q—B 6 *ch* ; with perpetual check.

What means has White at his disposal in order to force a win ? He can exchange Queens, especially if he can interpose his own with check, or by making play with the "geometrical idea." For example, in this position : White : K at K 8, Q at K 6, pawn at Q 7, Black : K at his K R 2, Q at Q Kt 5. In order to stop the pawn, Black plays : 1 ... Q—Kt 4 ; 2 K—B 8, Q— Kt 1 *ch* (2 ... Q—Q B 4 *ch*; 3 Q—K 7 *ch,*); 3 Q—K 8, Q—B 4 *ch* (3 ... Q—Kt 4 *ch* ; 4 Q—K 7 *ch,*); 4 Q— B 7 *ch*, and wins.

These endings occur very seldom and do not require any special study. We shall now go on to end games with a number of pawns, which are far more interesting.

QUEENS AND PAWNS

As in other endings, we must, in order to assess the relative value of the positions, first examine separately the King's position, that of the pawns, and finally that of the piece. The Queen's characteristics give this valuation a new aspect, and we must take them into consideration if we wish to avoid errors of judgment.

For instance, we have stressed that a King's central position is of inestimable value for the final victory. But with the Queens on the board, the King in the centre is exposed to the dangers of a perpetual check and can compromise the chances of victory. A well-covered King, immune from checks by the Queen, is in itself an advantage and this immunity enables the stronger side to exploit any other advantage which may be obtained. There is one drawback, when the King has sought a safe refuge, his Queen has to carry on the battle by herself, and often the King has to come out at the proper time to support the advance of the pawn. Perpetual check of course has no terror for the weaker side, but a long sequence of checks is apt to result in the gain of another pawn or a further pawn advance. But when, hidden in the corner, the defending King requires in addition the protection of his Queen, then two pieces are out of action and the attacker has the field to himself.

In Diag. 47 both Queens are equally active and there

No. 47. White to play.

Maróczy *v.* Marshall
Carlsbad, 1907

appears to be little difference between the respective pawn formations. But the white King is entirely safe, whilst his rival is "in the air" and exposed to all kinds of attacks, and so the threats by White's Queen will be far more serious than Black's.

The ending is lengthy and laborious, which is why we shall be content to quote the moves only. 1 Q—B 8, P—K 4 ; 2 Q—Kt 8 *ch*, K—R 3 ; 3 P—K R 4, Q—B 7 ; 4 Q—B 8 *ch*, K—Kt 3 ; 5 P—R 5 *ch*, K × P ; 6 Q—Kt 7, Q—Q 7 ; 7 Q × P *ch*, Q—R 3 ; 8 P—Kt 4 *ch*, K—Kt 4 ; 9 Q × P, K—B 5 ; 10 Q × Kt P, Q—R 8 ; 11 Q—Kt 4 *ch*, K × P ; 12 Q × P, K × P ; 13 P—B 4, P—K 5 ; 14 P—B 5, P—B 4 ; 15 P—B 6, Q—R 1 *ch* ; 16 P—B 3, P—K 6 ; 17 Q—Kt 6 *ch*, K—B 5 ; 18 P—B 7, P—K 7 ; 19 Q—K 6, K—B 6 ; 20 Q × B P *ch*, K—Kt 7 ; 21 Q—Kt 4 *ch*, K—B 7 ; 22 Q—B 4 *ch*, K—Kt 7 ; 23 Q—K 3, K—B 8 ; 24 Q—B 3 *ch* (the well-known manœuvre in Q *v.* P endings), K—K 8 ; 25 Q—B 4, Q—Q B 1 ; 26 Q—Q 6, K—B 7 ; 27 Q—Q 8, P—K 8 (Q) ; 28 Q × Q, Q—Q 7 *ch* ; 29 K—R 3, Q—B 8 *ch* ; 30 K—R 4, Q—B 5 *ch* ; 31 P—B 4, and Black resigns.

Where, however, the King is in an exposed position, it is best to use him for the support of the pawn's advance, always trying to effect an exchange of Queens.

In Diag. 48, the black King occupies an exposed post in the centre ; in addition his Q Kt P is attacked : therefore, for the time being, he does not attend to his own safety, but defends the pawn indirectly by threatening the exchange of Queens : 1 ... K—K 3.

If now 2 Q × P, then 2 ... Q—Kt 7 *ch* ; 3 K—R 5, Q—B 6 *ch* ; followed by ... P—K 7. Therefore White decides to give up a pawn so that his Queen obtains increased mobility and is able to threaten a perpetual check. 2 P—B 5 *ch*, Q × P *ch* ; 3 K—Kt 3, P—K 7 ; 4 Q—B 3, Q—B 8 ; 5 Q—K 3 *ch*, K—B 2 ; 6 Q—R 7 *ch*, K—Kt 3 ; 7 P—R 5 *ch*, K × P ; 8 Q—R 7 *ch*, K—Kt 4.

No. 48. Black to play.

Sämisch *v.* Nimzowitsch
Carlsbad, 1923

Now begins a long journey across the board in order to support the passed pawn : 9 Q—Kt 7 *ch*, K—B 4 ; 10 Q—B 7 *ch*, K—K 4 ; 11 Q—K 7 *ch*, K—Q 4 ; 12 Q—Kt 7 *ch*, K—Q 5 ; 13 Q—Kt 6 *ch*, K—K 5 ; 14 Q—B 6 *ch*, P—Q 4 ; 15 Q—K 6 *ch*, K—Q 5 ; 16 Q—Kt 6 *ch*, K—Q 6 ; 17 Q × P *ch*, K—B 7.

White resigns, for after a further check at Q B 6 or Q B 5 the King escapes to Q Kt 7 or Q Kt 8, respectively, and the pawn queens.

In comparing the two Queens, the greater activity of one of them is a considerable advantage. The adverse Queen is restricted to the defensive, and the King at once obtains full liberty of action and embarks upon the fight with the same freedom as the pawns.

Thus in Diag. 49 the white Queen is reduced to defending her pawns and guarding against a mate.

Gradually her moves give out and White is soon compelled by the advance of the hostile pawns to give up one of his and to seek salvation in a possible perpetual check—the only saving clause for the weaker side in such positions.

No. 49. Black to play.

Marshall _v._ Maróczy
Ostend, 1905

1 ... Q—Q 8 *ch* ; 2 Q—K 1, Q—Q 6 *ch* ; 3 K—Kt 1, Q—B 7 ; 4 Q—R 1, P—Q R 4 ; 5 P—K Kt 3, P—R 5 ; 6 P—B 4, K—Kt 1 ; 7 P—R 3, P—R 4 ; 8 P—R 4, K—Kt 2 ; 9 K—R 1, Q—B 7 ; 10 Q—K Kt 1, Q × Q Kt P ; 11 Q—B 5, P—Kt 5 ; 12 P—B 5, K P × P ; 13 P—K 6, Kt P × P ; 14 P × P, K × P ; 15 Q—B 7 *ch*, K—K 3 ; 16 Q—B 6 *ch*, K—K 4 ; 17 Q × R P, P—R 7 ; 18 Q—K 8 *ch*, K—Q 4 ; 19 Q—Q 7 *ch*, K—K 5 ; 20 Q—B 6 *ch*, K—K 6 ; 21 Q—B 5 *ch*, Q—Q 5 ; 22 Q—R 3 *ch*, Q—Q 6 ; 23 Q—R 7 *ch*, K—B 6 ; 24 Q × P, Q—B 8 *ch* ; 25 K—R 2, Q—B 7 *ch* ; 26 Q × Q *ch*, K × Q ; and wins.

It is a considerable asset to have the Queen in a dominating position, and the addition of even a minute advantage elsewhere may well make it decisive. Not that it is altogether easy to take proper advantage of such a state of things : it may be required to reduce the activity of the adverse Queen, to exploit the insecure position of the King or a disjointed pawn formation. In Diag. 50, Black's Queen occupies the best possible post : not only is she in the centre, blockading an isolated pawn, but she is attacking three adverse pawns, which renders the position of the white Queen precarious. For she is, if not stalemated, then at least

No. 50. Black to play.

Lissitzin *v.* Capablanca
Moscow, 1935

under *Zugzwang* ; she guards all the pawns from her post at Q Kt 2 and is therefore unable to relinquish it. In the same manner as in the preceding example, Black takes advantage of the situation in reducing more and more his adversary's available moves : 1 ... K—K 3 ; 2 P—R 4, P—B 3 ; 3 K—K 3, Q—B 5 ; 4 P—Kt 3, P—Kt 4 ; 5 P × P, P × P ; 6 Q—K R 2 (White is in difficulties and has hardly a good move left), Q—Kt 6 *ch* ; 7 K—K 4, P—Kt 5 ; (threatening mate by ... Q—B 6 ;) 8 Q—K 2, Q × K Kt P; 9 Q—B 4 *ch*, K—K 2 ; 10 Q—B 8, Q—B 6 *ch* ; 11 K—K 5, Q—B 3 *ch* ; 12 K—Q 5, Q—Q 3 *ch* ; and White resigns on account of the threat ... Q—K 3 *ch*.

Reverting to the characteristics of a pawn formation, they should conform to the usual requirements. Isolated and widely-dispersed pawns cause the most trouble, for it is against such pawns that the Queen exercises her

powers the most successfully. A compact pawn position is far more desirable, for it gives the adverse Queen
no purchase, and the defending King can find an asylum
there. Such a formation can in itself provide chances
of a win.

An important part is played by a passed pawn. The
stronger and the more advanced it is, the brighter our
chances. But if blockaded, as in the last example, it
can become the source of much anxiety. But two
passed pawns, especially if guarded and united, lead
almost infallibly to victory ; it is even possible to sacrifice pawns elsewhere if it means the displacement of the
hostile Queen and, consequently, greater freedom for
our pawns. Generally speaking, the sacrifice of a pawn
in a Queen's ending presents less risk than in any other,
for the reason already adduced that next to the powerful
Queen the pawn cuts a poor figure. A positional
advantage, such as an advanced passed pawn, is often
of far greater value. In other types of endings it is
possible to give up the last piece for an advanced pawn
and then to make fight with the remaining pawns
against a piece : but what could even three pawns do
against a Queen ? A desperate enterprise except in
freak positions. If instead of one passed pawn there
are two and they are united, they have the additional
advantage of being able to guard the King against a
perpetual check. In return the King can the more
effectively support their advance.

In Diag. 51 Black is terribly handicapped by the
threatened advance of the two passed pawns, whereas
his own isolated pawn is held up in the middle of the
board, and so he decides to undertake to attack the pawns
on the opposite wing. White resolutely sacrifices these
and wins by steadily advancing one of his passed pawns :
1 ... Q—R 7 ; 2 P—Kt 5, Q×P *ch* ; 3 Q—K 2,
Q × R P ; 4 P—Kt 6, Q—Q 2 ; 5 Q—B 4, K—Kt 3 ;
6 Q—Q B 7, Q—K 3 ; 7 Q—B 2 *ch*, P—B 4 ; 8 Q—

No. 51. Black to play.

Maróczy *v.* Janowski
London, 1899

Kt 3, Q—K 4 ; 9 P—Kt 7, Q—Kt 1 ; 10 K—Q 3,
K—B 3 ; 11 Q—Kt 6 *ch*, K—K 2 ; 12 Q × R P,
Q—K 4 ; 13 Q—R 7 *ch*, K—K 3 ; 14 Q—Kt 8 *ch*,
K—K 2 ; 15 P—Kt 8 (Q), Q—K 6 *ch* ; 16 K—B 4,
Q—B 6 *ch* ; 17 K—Kt 5, and Black resigns.

In Diag. 52 we see another sacrifice with, however,

No. 52. White to play.

Maróczy *v.* Bogoljubow

a different object, namely that of obtaining a passed
pawn, the importance of which procedure we have
already extolled.   White has an extra pawn, but it is
backward and has no important part to play.   He cannot capture the Q B P because of the perpetual check
which is threatened.   He therefore decides to obtain a
passed pawn by sacrificing his backward pawn, but its
advance will require much prudence as the threat of a
perpetual check is still operative : 1 P—Kt 5, P × P ;
2 P—B 6, Q—B 7 ; 3 Q—Q 5, K—R 3 ; 4 Q—Q 6,
Q—B 5 ; 5 P—B 7, K—R 2 ; 6 Q—Q 7, (White now
submits to a number of checks, as he sees his way to
escape.   We have already seen several instances of
similar journeys across the board) 6 ... Q—B 5 *ch* ;
7 K—Kt 1, Q—B 8 *ch* ; 8 K—B 2, Q—B 4 *ch* ; 9
K—K 2, Q—Q B 7 *ch* ; 10 K—K 3, Q—B 4 *ch* ; 11
K—K 4, and Black resigns, for the King escapes to
Q Kt 7 or Q 8.

Our subject is far from exhausted.   But we have at
least given examples of the most representative types of
this end game, and the manner of their treatment, the
procedure to be followed by either side.   What these
endings require most is patience ; in an ending between
Keres and Alekhine no fewer than 45 moves were needed
to gain a decision.   In addition to patience, of course,
there must be no lack of ideas.

EXERCISES

In Diag. 53 White has the move : who has the advantage and why, and can this advantage, if any, be brought home (indicate general lines) ?

No. 53.

Dr. Vidmar *v.* Yates
Hastings, 1925

In Diag. 54 White has an extra pawn, but, by a

No. 54.

Dr. Alekhine *v.* Maróczy
New York, 1924

momentary lapse, he becomes a victim of a perpetual check which his adversary obtains by means of an astute pitfall.

The Rook

Of all the chess pieces, the Rook can rightly be considered as an end game piece *par excellence* and particularly adapted to this phase of the game. Here the qualities of the Rook stand out brilliantly, here it deploys its full power, often repressed in the opening and middle game, and its admirable qualities are right royally demonstrated.

It is easy to understand why the Rook is more powerful in the ending than in the middle game. Its action on the files is obstructed by pawns, and in order to exert the Rook's powers, the pawn formations must first be thinned out. But the Rook's action on the ranks, usually non-existent in the middle game, is its particular patrimony ; on a rank the Rook attains the zenith of its power. In such rare cases where the Rook has the freedom of a rank in the middle game, the truth of this assertion stands out clearly. It is clear that this is still more marked in the end game in which pawns are of paramount importance. Owing to the fact that pawns are posted on ranks and move on files and that the Rook is able to move in either direction, it becomes the most dangerous weapon in the end game and surpasses here all other pieces. We have already seen that the Queen's powers suffer a slight deterioration in the ending ; a Bishop ambling along diagonals of a certain colour often is entirely harmless to pawns, which in any case can always move to a diagonal of the opposite colour. As for the Knight, after being attacked by a pawn, it loses a great deal of time when returning to the attack. One move by the pawn may necessitate lengthy manœuvres by the Knight before its attack can be renewed. No pawn can escape from a Rook once it has got under fire.

Against the other principal end game piece, the King,
the Rook also exercises a terrible pressure : it can prevent the King from reaching any given point and
establish an impassable barrage, which is not the case
with a barrage set up by a single Bishop. Two Bishops
are required to this end.

It is, however, necessary, if the Rook is to exercise
these powers to the full, that it should enjoy freedom of
action and a wide space. When supporting a pawn,
for instance, it should do so not from the front, but
from the rear, so that, with every advance by the pawn,
its own radius of action should increase. For the same
reason, the Rook will stay behind an adverse passed
pawn, where it will enjoy entire freedom and restrict
the opposing Rook more and more, as, in the nature of
things, that Rook will be placed in front of its pawn.

A Rook placed *in front* of the hostile passed pawn
may in the end be confined to one square on its first
rank, and unable to make even a single move.

We shall see in the next examples that there may be
special reasons for selecting certain posts for the Rook,
but the main principle is always the preservation of the
greatest possible space and freedom. A free and active
Rook against a passive and restricted Rook is worth a
pawn and sometimes more.

In Diag. 55 Black, to escape from an imminent
attack on the K side, has induced the exchange of
Queens and minor pieces in order to obtain this end
game position with, it is true, a pawn less, but with a
Rook on an open file, able at once to occupy the 7th
rank. After 1 ... R—B 7 ; White replies with 2
K R—Q B 1, giving up the pawn, for after 2 ... R × P ;
there follows 3 K R—Q Kt 1, R × R ; 4 R × R, P—
Q Kt 3 ; 5 R—Q B 1, and it is White who has the open
file and threatens to occupy the 6th or 7th rank. That
is why Black plays 2 ... K R—B 1 ; 3 R × R, R × R ;
4 R—Q Kt 1, K—R 2 ; 5 K—Kt 3, K—Kt 3 ; 6 P—B 3,

No. 55. Black to play.

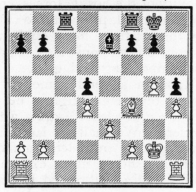

Dr. Alekhine *v.* Capablanca
Match, 1927

P—B 3 ; 7 P × P, B × P ; 8 P—R 4, K—B 4 ; 9 P—
R 5, R—K 7 ; and White again sacrifices a pawn in
order to free his Rook, 10 R—Q B 1, R × Kt P ; 11
R—B 5.   Although this last sacrifice, in the opinion of
Alekhine himself, was not necessary nor even good, it
illustrates, as does the preceding play, with the exchange
of a pawn against freedom of action for the Rook,
the importance which great players attach to the full
expansion of the Rook's powers.

When a Rook, leaving its own camp, invades an
empty centre, it attacks all the pawns one by one, forcing
their advance, creating weaknesses and reducing the
opposing forces to the defensive.   When it succeeds in
penetrating into the enemy formation on the seventh
rank, it attacks the pawns in their initial position and
not only reduces the adverse Rook to passivity, but also
prevents the King from leaving his prison and from
occupying the centre and taking part in the battle.

Thus a new significance is given to the Rook's manœuvres : it is not merely a case of obtaining for the Rook

complete and selfish freedom.   The object should be to
reduce the mobility of the hostile forces, create weakness
in the opposing camp and, primarily, to cut off the King.
Such general considerations must guide us when con-
ducting an ending, but we must also gauge in this light
the value of an impending end game.   The defensive
powers of a Rook in an end game are so great, its
resources so vast, that it can rightly be considered as
the most likely piece to secure a draw when practically
no chances are left.   We shall see later on what means
can be employed to that end ; let it suffice to say now
that the weaker side should never exchange the Rook.
But the active force of a well-placed Rook usually leads
to a win.

Rook endings are amongst the most interesting, because the action of the Rook is rich and inexhaustible
in its variety, more interesting than those of minor
pieces and Queens.

The King, the pawns, the Rooks, these are the real
heroes of the end game.

THE ROOK BY ITSELF

The Rook mates with almost the same ease as the
Queen, but it takes considerably longer, first of all
because the Rook cannot force the King to the edge of
the board as quickly as the Queen and then because the
Queen can mate in more varied ways.   The Rook can
mate in only one way, on an outside rank or file with
the Kings in direct opposition except when the defending
King stands on a corner square.   Unlike the Queen, which
can with advantage be placed at a Knight's distance from
the opposing King, the Rook must not be placed near
him, because it can be attacked and so lose time and
space.   The task of forcing the opposing King to the
last rank or file devolves in the main on the King.
He will always try to force his rival to take the direct

opposition, after which a check by the Rook will make him lose another rank or file.

Note also that in the case of the Queen the number of moves is of little importance, but with the Rook, although a mate can generally be forced in less than twenty moves, with careless play, it is quite possible to exceed the regulation fifty moves. The play here has to be far more exact. Two important hints : it is sometimes useful to lose a *tempo* with the Rook, when it forces the adverse King to assume the opposition so that a check on the next move forces him to leave the rank or file ; secondly, it is often possible and advisable to alter the direction in which the opposing King is being driven. Originally, out of four possible directions, one is chosen, but it may pay to make a change, in which case a vertical direction would be changed into a horizontal one or *vice versa*, a change to an adjacent field and not a complete reversal.

Examine the following example :

White : K at K R 1, R at Q R 8, Black : K at his Q 4. There are several ways of forcing a mate, of which the following, one of the shortest, is the most sensible. It conforms closely to the essential principles : 1 K—Kt 2, K—K 5 ; 2 R—Q 8, K—K 6 ; 3 K—Kt 3, K—K 5 ; 4 K—Kt 4, K—K 4 ; 5 K—B 3, K—K 3 ; 6 K—B 4, K—K 2 ; 7 R—Q 5, K—K 3 ; 8 K—K 4, K—B 3 ; 9 R—K 5, K—B 2 ; (K—Kt 3 ; 10 R— K B 5,) 10 K—B 5, K—Kt 2 ; 11 R—K 7 *ch*, K— B 1 (K—R 3 ; 12 R—K B 7,) ; 12 K—B 6, K—Kt 1 ; 13 K—Kt 6, K—B 1 ; 14 R—K 1, K—Kt 1 ; 15 R—K 8 mate.

It may be possible to reduce the number of moves by some subtle stratagem, but the method shown is simple and lucid. According to his experience, each player could no doubt find some astute turn, shortening the process, but it is not worth while making a study of it, as it may well happen that in a player's chess career the opportunity for such a mate never occurs.

ROOK AGAINST PAWN

Normally a Rook should win easily against a pawn. Any other result would be due to some exceptional characteristic of the position. It is however useful to show a few points of general application, which may affect the outcome.

First of all, the pawn requires the protection of its King, who has the double mission to chaperone it on its way and to prevent the rival King from approaching. It is an essential requirement for the weaker side to keep the hostile King away from the pawn so that the Rook has to contest the advance of the pawn by its own exertions. When the adverse King is in a specially bad position, the pawn might even win, provided only

No. 56. White to play and win.

Study by Rev. Saavedra

This position was known as the "Lasker position," because he has quoted it in some of his lectures, without, however, claiming to be its originator. Later on the real author was discovered. The Russian author Rabinovich indicates another source—a game, Potter-Fenton, 1881. But long before that a French book on the end game stated that this game was played in 1875 with the colours reversed and with the black King at K R 6 instead of Q R 8, an important difference. The manner of winning the game in this position was indicated by J. H. Zukertort in the *City of London Chess Magazine*, 1875, and is similar to an earlier study by Horwitz and Kling, 1853.

that it cannot be exchanged for the Rook as soon as it has queened. This extraordinary result occurs in Diag. 56. White wins as follows : 1 P—B 7, R—Q 3 *ch*; 2 K—Kt 5, R—Q 4 *ch*; 3 K—Kt 4, (the King cannot occupy the Q B file because of 3 ... R—Q 8 ; threatening ... R—B 8 *ch* ;) 3 ... R—Q 5 *ch* ; 4 K—Kt 3, R—Q 6 *ch* ; 5 K—B 2, this procedure is applicable in any position when the adverse King is far away ; his position here allows a *finesse* in two ways, which adds an unusually charming turn to the solution, 5 ... R—Q 5; (threatening, after 6 P—B 8 (Q), R—B 5 *ch* ; 7 Q × R, stalemate) ; 6 P—B 8 (R), (threatening 7 R—R 8 mate) ; 6 ... R—Q R 5 ; 7 K—Kt 3, and Black has no resource against the double threat of 8 K × R and 8 R—B 1 mate.

This final combination with the stalemate and the double threat of mate is possible only when the King is in a corner.

It sometimes happens that the pawn draws the game, even when the opposing King is fairly near. Generally speaking, the rule of the square finds its application in such cases, and the adverse King often has the task of

No. 57. Black to play.

Dr. Alekhine *v.* Bogoljubow
Match, 1929

preventing his rival from entering the "square." In Diag. 57 Black lost the game after : 1 ... K—Kt 5 ; 2 P—Kt 7, P—B 4 ; 3 P—Kt 8 (Q), R × Q ; 4 R × R, P—B 5 ; 5 K—Q 5, P—B 6 ; 6 K—K 4, P—B 7 ; 7 R—K B 8, K—Kt 6 ; 8 K—K 3, etc.   Had he played 1 ... K—K 5 ; at the outset, preventing the white King from occupying his Q 5, he would have drawn the game.   This manœuvre by the King, holding off his rival, is well known, and, as is seen here, finds its application in the most varied endings.

No. 58. White to play.

Mérenyi *v.* Znosko-Borovsky
Tata-Tovaros, 1935

Another and exceptional method of securing the draw is shown in Diag. 58.   It is most instructive : 1 K—Q 5, P—B 6 ; 2 K—Q 4, P—B 7 ; 3 R—Kt 2 *ch*, K—Q 8 ; 4 K—Q 3,—if now 4 ... P—B 8 (Q); 5 R—Kt 1 mate, but—4 ... P—B 8 (Kt) *ch* ; and the game is drawn.

It must be noted that the draw can be ensured only on condition that the Knight remains close to its King. In a game Neumann-Steinitz, Baden-Baden, 1870, a similar position was reached with the colours reversed :

White : K at K B 8, P at K Kt 7, Black : K at his K B 3, R at Q B 2.   Here White lost because he neglected to take this precaution.   The play was : 1 P—Kt 8 (Kt) *ch*, K—K 3 ; 2 Kt—R 6, R—K R 2 ; 3 Kt—Kt 4 (the mistake), R—R 5 ; 4 Kt—K 3, R—K 5 ; 5 Kt—Q 1, R—B 5 *ch* ; 6 K—Kt 7, R—B 6 ; 7 Kt—Kt 2, K—Q 4 ; 8 Kt—R 4, R—Kt 6 ; etc.

Another point to remember is that there is no salvation if it is a R P which has to be promoted to a Knight, for then the Knight is irremediably lost.   Thus, in a position by Stamma : White : K at Q 5, R at K 4, Black : K at his Q Kt 8, pawn at Q R 6.   White wins as follows : 1 K—B 4, P—R 7 ; 2 K—Kt 3, P—R 8 (Kt) *ch* ; 3 K—B 3, Kt—B 7 ; (3 ... K—R 7 ; 4 R—Q Kt 4, K—R 6 ; 5 R—Kt 8, K—R 7 ; 6 R—Kt 7,) 4 R—K 2, Kt—R 8 ; (... Kt—R 6 ; 5 K—Kt 3) 5 R—K R 2, and wins.

In passing on to endings in which the Rook has to contend against two pawns, we find matters radically changed.   Although a Rook wins in most cases, the pawns sometimes prevail, nor is it always necessary that they should be supported by the King.   It is only necessary for the pawns to be sufficiently advanced with the opposing King some distance away.   Often, however, the result depends on who has the move. Generally speaking, if the two pawns have reached the sixth rank, success is assured.   An extraordinary case of a drawn conclusion occurs in Diag. 59.   The game continued as follows : 1 P—R 7, R—Q R 7 ; 2 P—Kt 6, K—B 6 ; 3 K—Kt 1, R—R 3 ; 4 P—Kt 7, R—Kt 3 *ch* ; 5 K—B 1, R—K R 3 ; and was given up as drawn.   Why ?   The sequel could be : 6 K—Q 1, K—Q 6 ; 7 K—K 1, K—K 6 ; 8 K—B 1, K—B 6 ; 9 K—Kt 1, R—Kt 3 *ch* ; 10 K—R 2, R—R 3 *ch* ; and White cannot escape perpetual check. Even more curious would be the alternative line of play : 1 P—Kt 6, K—B 6 ; 2 K—Q 1, K—Q 6 ; 3 K—K 1,

K—K 6 ; 4 P—Kt 7, R—K R 7 ; 5 K—B 1, K—B 6 ;
6 K—Kt 1, R—R 1 ; 7 P—R 7, R—Kt 1 *ch* ; 8 K—
B 1, R—K R 1 ; 9 K—K 1, K—K 6 ; 10 K—Q 1,

No. 59. White to play.

Keres *v.* Eliskases
Noordwijk, 1938

K—Q 6 ; 11 K—B 1, K—B 6 ; 12 K—Kt 1, R—
R 8 *ch* ; 13 K—R 2, R—R 7 *ch* ; 14 K—R 3, R—R 8 ;
15 K—R 4, K—B 5 ; 16 K—R 5, K—B 4 ; (17 K—
R 6, R—R 8 mate) ; 17 K—R 4, K—B 5 ; repeating
the whole manœuvre over again and duplicating a study
by Moravec (1924), White : K at Q B 6, R at Q Kt 1,
Black : K at his Q R 2, pawns at K Kt 7 and K R 7,
drawn game.

Diag. 60 illustrates the normal procedure by which
two pawns win against a Rook provided the adverse
King is not in close attendance—and it is essential to
keep him away. That is why White's first move is
1 K—Q 4.

The game went on : 1 ... K—Kt 6 ; 2 K—K 5,
K—B 5 ; 3 P—Kt 6, R—K 8 *ch* ; 4 K—Q 6, R—
K Kt 8 (actually Black played the weaker 4 ... R—

No. 60. White to play.

Dr. Tarrasch *v.* Janowski
Ostend, 1907

Q 8 *ch* ; 5 K—K 7, R—K 8 *ch* ; 6 K—B 7,) ; 5 P—
Kt 7, K—Q 5 ; 6 K—B 6, K—B 5 ; 7 K—Q 7, (if,
on the preceding move, the King had entered the 7th
rank, the reply would have been ... K—K 4 ; attacking
the B P) 7 ... K—Q 4 ; 8 K—K 8, K—K 3 ; 9 P—
B 7, R—Q R 8 ; 10 P—B 8 (Kt) *ch*, followed by
11 P—Kt 8 (Q).

To conclude, let us repeat that pawns should be
pushed forward without their looking to the King too
much for their protection, provided they can safely
reach the sixth rank : otherwise the King must go to
their assistance, trying always to keep the rival, King
away.

EXERCISES

In Diag. 61 Black is to play and win : how ? In
Diag. 62 the two isolated pawns win their way to victory
against a Rook, taking advantage of the absence of the
opposing King. (White to play.)

No. 61.

Löwenthal *v.* Morphy
Match, 1858

No. 62.

Study by Berger

ROOK AND PAWN *v.* ROOK

Although pawn endings cover a wide field of end
game strategy, those with Rooks and pawns are perhaps
even more important. It is easy to understand why
Rook endings are in the majority. This piece is the
last to enter the fray, and naturally the most likely to

survive to the end. How often does it happen that several minor pieces have been exchanged before the Rooks have left the first rank ! In addition, the Rook being the best piece to keep the draw in hand, is often preserved for an ending which looks unpromising.

It is clear that endings with several pawns will occur most frequently, and they will therefore require the closest study. It will, however, first be necessary to become conversant with endings in which one side possesses but one pawn, by no means an unusual case.

Compared with the difficulties of a game of chess, or of chess generally, it cannot be said that these endings are particularly hard. The limited number of units also limits the number of possible variations, these being neither long nor very complicated. And yet innumerable mistakes are made in these endings, and they are exceptionally serious, being irreparable. It is quite surprising how principles, established for at least a quarter of a century, are still *terra incognita* to not a few otherwise brilliant players. Diag. 63 is an example, one of many, of inferior play in a Rook and pawn ending.

No. 63. White to play.

Salve *v.* Burn
St. Petersburg, 1909

Without analysing each move, or showing why many of the moves played are faulty, we shall merely quote the moves as played in the game by two famous masters, and the moves which subsequent analyses have proved to be correct : 1 R—B 7 *ch*, K—K 1 (the King, as will be seen later on, should have gone to Q B 1) ; 2 R— K R 7, R—Q 6 (2 ... R—Q R 6 ; would secure the draw) ; 3 K—K 6, R—K 6 *ch* (3 ... K—Q 1 ; is better) ; 4 K—Q 6, R—Q R 6 ; 5 R—R 8 *ch*, K—B 2 ; 6 R—B 8, R—R 3 *ch* (6 ... R—Q 6 ; draws) ; 7 R—B 6 (7 K—Q 7, would win), 7 ... R—R 1 (7 ... R—R 5 ; would draw) ; 8 R—B 7 *ch*, (8 K—Q 7, would still win) 8 ... K—K 1 ; and the game ended in a draw.

This game was played in 1909, a considerable time ago, since when the theoretical knowledge of that branch of the art, which interests us at the moment, has made great strides. But let us examine the sixteenth game in the championship match of 1935. The play went : 1 R—B 8 *ch*, K—Kt 7 ; 2 R—Kt 8 *ch*, K—B 8 ; 3 R—B 8 *ch*, K—Kt 8 ; 4 R—Kt 8 *ch*, R—Kt 7 ; 5 R—Q R 8, R—Kt 6 *ch* ; 6 K—Q 4, P—R 6 ; 7 K—

No. 64. White to play.

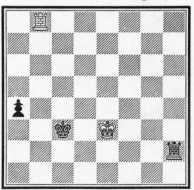

Dr. Alekhine *v.* Dr. Euwe
Match, 1935

B 4, K—Kt 7 ; 8 R—R 8, R—B 6 *ch* ; and White resigned. But he could have secured a draw by 1 R—Q R 8, K—Kt 6 ; 2 K—Q 3, P—R 6 ; 3 R—Kt 8 *ch*, K—R 7 ; 4 K—B 3. Four moves only were required to save the situation, whereas, in this game between world champions, White lost in eight ! And what can one say of chess editors, myself included, who, in publishing this game, failed to notice the mistake, the discovery of which must be credited to Dr. Euwe himself ?

How can one account for such a state of things ? Is it because these endings have been the subject of most exhaustive studies, so that it is quite possible to establish a series of typical positions, with the units distributed in various ways in relation to each other, in each case the line of play being indicated and leading to a definite and unalterable result ? Each one of these positions is representative of a type, although they may appear to have individual characteristics, and the slightest slip leads to a result which is contrary to reality.

Artistic and artificial studies are best suited for the mastering of the technique necessary for this type of end games. If, then, they occur in practical play, there is no room left for fancy and imagination : either the player knows all about it or he does not, either he follows the lines pre-indicated, or he loses his way.

Considerations of space preclude all these classified positions from being given, nor can we give the analysis of most of them. I shall give those which I consider essential from a practical point of view and shall particularly stress the main processes by which a win or a draw can be secured.

It would be a mistake to think that an extra pawn in a Rook ending ensures victory in all cases. It is therefore necessary to know the essential characteristics which lead to one or the other result.

Although there exists a great difference between the

values of a pawn on a R file and those in the centre, there are processes applicable to all. Let us first examine these.

It would be superfluous to stress the necessity for both sides to select the best possible posts both for the pawns and especially for the pieces. For the Rook, we know it already : the best square is the one affording the greatest possible freedom of action. We have seen that, in order to stop an adverse passed pawn or to support the advance of its own, the Rook is best placed behind the pawn. It cannot, however, be said that this would in all cases ensure the desired result. Too much depends on other circumstances, and the Rook being posted differently does not of necessity compromise the game. The Rook behind the passed pawn merely constitutes a favourable factor which it is useful to preserve. In the same way, it is clearly desirable to keep the King in the vicinity of the passed pawn : the reverse often has catastrophic consequences. Conversely, the adversary must try to keep the hostile King away. To cut off the King is the task for which the Rook is particularly fitted and which it will constantly be required to perform. A distance of one rank between the King and his passed pawn is sometimes, but not often, sufficient to ensure a win, which normally is assured when they are two ranks apart. Diag. 65 shows how this barrage can be set up. This is a particularly favourable position for White and the usual procedure for advancing the pawn and keeping the opposing King at bay is clearly illustrated here. 1 R—Q Kt 6, R—Kt 7 ; 2 P—Kt 5, R—Kt 8 ; 3 K—R 7, R—R 8 *ch* (if 3 ... K—B 2 ; 4 R—B 6 *ch*, K—Q 2 ; 5 K—Kt 6, R—Kt 7 ; 6 R—B 1, R—Kt 6 ; 7 K—R 6, R—R 6 *ch* ; 8 K—Kt 7, etc., or 3 ... R—Kt 7 ; 4 R—Kt 7 *ch*, K—B 1 ; 5 R—Kt 8 *ch*, K—B 2 ; 6 P—Kt 6 *ch*, K—B 3 ; 7 R—B 8 *ch*, K—Q 2 ; 8 Ṙ—B 1, etc.) ; 4 R—R 6, R—Q Kt 8 ; 5 P—Kt 6, K—B 1 (5 ... K—B 3 ; 6

No. 65. White to play.

de Rivière *v.* Morphy
Paris, 1863

R—R 2, R × P ; 7 R—B 2 *ch*, K—Kt 4 ; 8 R—
Kt 2 *ch*,) ; 6 R—R 2, R—Kt 6 ; 7 R—B 2 *ch*, K—Q 2 ;
8 P—Kt 7, R—R 6 *ch* ; 9 K—Kt 8, R—R 5 ; 10
R—Q 2 *ch*, K—K 2 ; 11 K—B 7, R—B 5 *ch* ; 12
K—Kt 6, R—Kt 5 *ch* ; 13 K—B 6, R—B 5 *ch* ; 14
K—Kt 5, R—B 8 ; 15 R—Q Kt 2, and wins.

In this example White had no difficulty in eliminating
the hostile Rook's pressure, after the 9th move, by a
direct attack against the King. It would have been
different had the black Rook, as befits a Rook, moved
as far as possible, therefore 9 ... R—R 8. In this
case White must employ a manœuvre which it is necessary to know and to remember, for it is an obligatory
process and of practically universal application in such
cases. The correct continuation, accordingly, is : 10
R—Q 2 *ch*, K—K 2 ; 11 R—Q 4 (the King has been
driven back two ranks), 11 ... R—R 7 ; 12 K—B 7,
R—B 7 *ch* ; 13 K—Kt 6, R—Kt 7 *ch* ; 14 K—B 6,
R—B 7 *ch* ; 15 K—Kt 5, R—Kt 7 *ch* ; 16 R—Kt 4,
and wins. It is now clear why the white Rook was
played to the fourth rank : it could interpose after a

check on the file.   On the fifth rank the Rook could
have been challenged by the black King from his K 3.
Another point is made clear : had the black King been
separated from the pawn by one rank only instead of
two, he could have attacked and ·captured the pawn by
... K—B 2 ; after the exchange of Rooks.

Having now a general knowledge of the winning
manœuvres applicable more or less in all Rook and pawn
endings, we must now differentiate between endings
with outside pawns on either R file and central pawns.
There is a material difference in that we lack room for
manœuvring on one side of the R P, and all the forces
are on the other side, whereas in the case of all other
pawns both sides are available, the play being in consequence much more varied.   Speaking generally, it is
more difficult to win with a R P, and it is necessary to
understand the manœuvres in either case and in which
way they differ from one another.   But at all times the
seventh rank provides the critical square for the pawn,
because the question whether the game is won or merely
drawn is decided there.   As long as the pawn has not
moved beyond the sixth rank, there are still opportunities for manœuvring.   Beyond that point, the result
of the end game is usually settled.   The utmost cir-
cumspection is therefore needed before advancing the
pawn to the seventh rank.

Examine the position : White : K at Q R 8, R at
Q Kt 4, pawn at Q R 7, Black : K at his Q B 1, R at
Q R 7.   White wins by the manœuvre already known
to us : 1 R—B 4 *ch*, K—Q 2 ; 2 K—Kt 7, R—Kt 7 *ch* ;
3 K—R 6, R—R 7 *ch* ; 4 K—Kt 6, R—Kt 7 *ch* ; 5
K—R 5, R—R 7 *ch* ; 6 R—R 4, followed by P—R 8
(Q).   If, however, Black has the move in this position,
he secures the draw by playing 1 ... R—Q B 7, avoiding
all danger, because his King cannot be driven from the
Q B file ; and yet the position appears to be in White's
favour, for his King is in front of his pawn and the

Rook is behind it. But the defending King is not sufficiently far away and the win depends on the move. This illustrates the drawback of the R P.

Let us reverse the situation and place the Rook in front of the pawn. The result depends entirely on which King is nearer to the pawn : if the white King can attack the adverse Rook, the win is easy. But what happens if he cannot do so ? Examine the curious position in Diag. 66. Black, with the move, can draw the game, but he must exercise great caution in order to avoid the many pitfalls which the stronger party has at his disposal in many endings with a R P. It is good

No. 66. Black to play and draw.

Study by Seyboth

to remember them : 1 ... K—B 4 ; 2 K—Q 7, K—Kt 3 ; 3 R—Kt 1 *ch*, K—B 4 (the first trap ! If 3 ... K × P ; 4 K—B 7, and Black is lost. Also after 3 ... K—R 3 ; 4 K—B 7, R × P *ch*; 5 K—B 6, with a similar mate); 4 R—Kt 7, R—R 1 (and not 4 ... K—Q 4 ; 5 R—Kt 5 *ch*, K—B 5 ; 6 R—Q R 5, K—Kt 5 ; 7 R—R 1, and White wins as he has gained a move and is thereby able to get nearer to the Rook) ; 5 K—B 7, R—R 1 (note that an insignificant move such as 5 ... R—K Kt 1 ;

would lose after 6 R—Kt 1, R—Kt 2 *ch* ; 7 K—Kt 8, R—Kt 1 *ch* ; 8 K—Kt 7, R—Kt 2 *ch* ; 9 K—R 6, R—Kt 3 *ch* ; 10 K—R 5, R—Kt 7 ; 11 R—B 1 *ch*, followed by 12 R—Q R 1, R—Kt 1 ; 13 K—Kt 6, etc.) ; 6 K—Q 7, R—R 1 ; etc.

Thus the King can, in this case, make up for the Rook's unfavourable position and secure the draw.   But suppose that the white Rook is confined at Q R 8 : then the position of its King is of little importance and the game is generally drawn.   As soon as the King gets near the pawn, the Rook checks and drives him away, returning then to Q R 8 to prevent the opposing Rook from moving away.   The defending King, however, must not leave his second rank, otherwise the white Rook checks and the pawn queens.   Even then there are exceptional cases which it is well to remember ; all the squares on Black's second rank are not equally favourable.   For instance, with the black King at his K B 2, K 2 or Q 2, White has the following line of play : 1 R—R 8, and if 1 ... R × P ; 2 R—R 7 *ch*. The black King must therefore avoid these three squares, and only four squares are available to him : Q Kt 2, Q B 2, K Kt 2 and K R 2.

White's difficulty, with a pawn at R 7 and a R at R 8, is that there is no possibility of gaining a *tempo*, as his King has no means of avoiding checks.

Is the pawn too far advanced ?

Let us imagine the pawn is not yet at Q R 7 and examine the following position : White : K at Q R 7, R at Q R 8, pawn at Q R 6, Black : K at his Q B 2, R at Q R 8.

The only possible way to win is to force the black King to leave his Q B 2 so that the white King may leave a free passage for his pawn.   As 1 R—Q Kt 8, will not do on account of 1 ... R × P *ch* ; the Rook must take a roundabout way : 1 R—R 8, R—R 7 ; 2 R—R 1, (threatening R—B 1 *ch*,) R—Q B 7 ; 3 R—Q Kt 1,

R—B 6 ; 4 R—Kt 7 *ch*, K—B 1 ; 5 K—Kt 6, R—Kt 6 *ch*; 6 K—B 6, R × R ; 7 P × R *ch*, K—Kt 1 ; draw. Thus if the black King has reached his Q B 2 or can reach it on his first move, the game is drawn. This is not surprising, for Black's position fulfils the two essential conditions : his King is not too far away from the pawn and his Rook occupies the most favourable post. We have seen a similar result in Diag. 64.

Let us now examine the same position with the black King at his Q 2 and White to play (otherwise 1 ... K—B 2 ;). If the black King is not to reach his Q B 2, the white Rook must be on the Q B file, and therefore the position is : White : K at Q R 7, R at Q B 8, pawn at Q R 6, Black : K at his Q 2, R at Q Kt 8. Again, White fails to force a win. After 1 K—Kt 7, R—Kt 8 *ch* ; 2 K—R 8, R—Q R 8 ; 3 P—R 7, R—Q Kt 8, White cannot free his pawn. It is clear that the white Rook is needed on the Q Kt file, and White must play 1 R—Kt 4. If Black can reply 1 ... K—B 2 ; we are back again to the drawing position which we have already seen. White can only win if the black King is as far as his K 2, e.g., 1 R—Kt 2, K—Q 2 ; 2 K—Kt 7, and the pawn gets through. The reason is that it is not only necessary to keep the black King from his Q B 2, but also to prevent a check by Black on the Q Kt file, which requires two moves.

There only remains to diagnose positions in which the R P is not so far advanced.

We shall now look at a position in which the pawn is still on the second rank and the opposing King far away, and find out whether White can achieve anything. White : K at Q R 1, R at K Kt 1, pawn at Q R 2, Black : K at his K R 4, R at Q R 1. We perceive at once that the pawn cannot advance without the support of its own Rook, as otherwise the King is exposed to consecutive checks. But as soon as the white Rook leaves its post, the black King approaches the pawn and

reaches a position which ensures the draw, e.g. : 1
K—Kt 2, R—Kt 1 *ch* ; 2 K—B 3, R—Q R 1 ; 3
K—Kt 3, R—Kt 1 *ch* ; 4 K—B 4, R—Q R 1 ; 5
R—Q R 1, K—Kt 3 ; 6 P—R 4, K—B 2 ; 7 P—R 5
(7 K—B 5, K—K 2 ; 8 K—B 6, R—B 1 *ch* ; 9 K—Kt 7,
R—B 7) ; 7 ... K—K 2 ; 8 P—R 6, K—Q 2 ; 9 P—R 7,
K—B 2 ; 10 K—Kt 5, K—Kt 2 ; draw. It is clear
that the win is very difficult and can be secured only
when the opposing forces are very badly placed.

The win is easier in the case of other pawns, although
even then it is not always a foregone conclusion. There
are positions where the draw is a certainty, and others
which can be won by subtle and well-considered play.

We shall again start with positions in which the pawn
has reached the seventh rank, because this is the object
in view and, in any event, it must get there if the game
is to be won. It is essential to be conversant with
possibilities arising from this position in order to conduct
the preceding stage with assurance and foresight.

Note first the essential points of the defence. The
King's best position is in front of the adverse pawn ; if
he cannot get there, he must not stay on the same side
as his Rook, or they would become mutually obstructive
in their manœuvres. As the Rook should at all times
preserve the greatest possible freedom of action, it
should be on the wider side, in other words, if the
pawn is on the K side, the Rook should manœuvre on
the Q side and *vice versa*, his King being of course
on the opposite side, whenever he cannot be in front
of the pawn. This remark, clear as it is as a matter
of principle, can also be proved to be correct by a simple
analysis. Supposing our Rook is on the K R file
operating against a white pawn at K 7. In order to
prevent this pawn from queening, we must give repeated
checks to drive the King away from his pawn, after
which the Rook returns to his first rank, stopping the
pawn. Only the Rook lacks the space necessary to

succeed in this manœuvre, for after 1 ... R—R 2 *ch* ;
2 K—B 8, R—R 1 *ch* ; 3 K—Kt 7, and the Rook can
neither check nor return to K 1 because of 4 K—B 7.
Now imagine that against this same pawn at K 7 the
black Rook is at its Q R 2, and the white King at his
Q 7. There follows : 1 K—Q 8, R—R 1 *ch* ; 2 K—
B 7, R—R 2 *ch* ; and the King cannot leave the pawn.
Then again, the narrow space at the disposal of the
defending King is not without its advantages, for we
know that the nearer he can remain to the pawn, the
greater the chances of a draw. If the defending King
is at two files distance from the pawn, the stronger side
usually wins. With an interval of three files the win
is certain. This can never happen if the defending
King is on the correct side, namely, the narrower one.
When the defending pieces are correctly distributed,
there are always chances of a draw. If the wrong formation has been adopted, a draw cannot be expected,
except against faulty play.

If the pawn has already reached the seventh rank,
even a favourable position of the defending pieces cannot ensure a draw, unless the stronger forces are badly
placed : if they are posted in a proper and natural way,
they nearly always win. For instance, in the following
position : White : K at Q 7, R at K B 1, pawn at K 7,
Black : K at his K Kt 1, R at Q R 1, White wins, for
he will post his King at K Kt 6, in order to interpose
R—B 6 if checked horizontally, thus forcing Black to
play ... R—K 1. Now the Rook is immobilized in
front of the pawn, the worst possible position. The
win is not difficult ; White plays R—K 1 and K—B 7.
The sequence of the moves would be as follows : 1 ...
R—R 2 *ch* ; 2 K—K 6, R—R 3 *ch* ; 3 K—K 5, (3
K—B 5, K—B 2 ;) 3 ... R—R 4 *ch* ; 4 K—B 6, R—
R 3 *ch* ; 5 K—Kt 5, R—R 4 *ch* ; 6 K—Kt 6, R—R 3 *ch* ;
7 R—B 6, R—R 1 ; 8 R—Q 6 or K 6, and wins.
This win is possible only if the white King can reach

K Kt 6 and so, if the black King were at his K Kt 2, the game would be drawn. The reason for this result is not far to seek. The King is only one file away from the pawn : if he were at his K R 2 or K R 1, White would win without difficulty. Even with the black forces in this most favourable position, White would win, with the "move," by 1 R—Kt 1 *ch*, K—R 2 ; 2 R—Kt 4, a well-known stratagem which the French call "the Bridge."

Now place the black King at his K 1 in front of the pawn, the win is no longer possible (except when a mate can be forced), e.g., with the white King at Q 6, R at K 1 and pawn at K 7, and the black King at his K 1 with the Rook at its Q R 7, there is no way of avoiding a perpetual check or the loss of the pawn : here the black King occupies the most favourable post. It is therefore necessary, before advancing the pawn to the seventh rank, to drive the opposing King away from his privileged position.

Let us examine the course of events when the defending King is placed in front of the pawn before it has reached the seventh. Philidor's famous position (Diag. 67) is a case in point. Observe first of all that White

No. 67. Black to play and draw.

Philidor

cannot win by exchanging Rooks, for in that case, exchanging Rooks let us say at K Kt 6, Black has an easy draw, as we already know. He must therefore proceed by advancing the pawn : 1 ... R—Q R 3 ; 2 P—K 5, R—Q Kt 3 ; 3 R—R 7, R—B 3 (the importance of the Rook being on the "longer side" is manifest) ; 4 P—K 6, R—B 8 ; 5 K—B 6, R—B 8 *ch* ; with perpetual check or winning the pawn. It is seen here that the defending Rook remains on its third rank until the pawn reaches it ; only then does it post itself behind the pawn, the surest means of obtaining the draw. This is obtainable also by placing the Rook behind the pawn before it has reached the sixth rank, or, alternatively, a move later, but it is far more difficult. It is necessary that the Rook should be able to occupy the farthest file, in this case the Q R file (and even then it would not work in the case of the Q P), e.g., 1 ... R—Q R 3 ; 2 P—K 5, R—Q Kt 3 ; 3 R—R 7, R—Kt 8 ; 4 K—B 6, R—K 8 ; 5 K—K 6, K—B 1 (the King proceeds to the "shorter side") ; 6 R—R 8 *ch*, K—Kt 2 ; 7 R—K 8, R—Q R 8 (the essential manœuvre in this type of ending : preserve the opportunity for horizontal and vertical checks, keeping to the outside ranks or files, in other words, utilizing the angle Q R 8—Q R 1— K R 1) ; 8 R—Q 8, R—K 8 ; 9 K—Q 6, K—B 2 ; and draws.

In the following position, which is favourable for White, he cannot nevertheless force a win : White : K at Q 7, R at K 8, pawn at K 5, Black : K at his K Kt 2, R at K 8, e.g. : 1 ... R—Q R 8 (1 ... R—Q 8 *ch* ; would also draw, but more laboriously : 2 K—K 7, R—Q R 8 ; 3 R—Q 8, R—R 2 *ch* ; 4 K—K 8, R—R 3 ; 5 R—Q 7 *ch*, K—Kt 1 ; 6 K—K 7, K—Kt 2 ; 7 P— K 6, R—R 8 ; etc.) ; 2 R—Q B 8, R—R 2 *ch* ; 3 R—B 7, R—R 1 ; P—K 6, K—B 3 ; 5 R—Kt 7, K—Kt 2 ; 6 K—K 7, R—R 8 ; 7 R—Q 7, R—R 1 ; 8 K—Q 6 *dis ch*, K—B 1 ; 9 P—K 7 *ch*, K—K 1 ;

10 K—K 6, R—R 3 *ch*; 11 R—Q 6, R—R 1; 12 R—Kt 6, R—B 1; and as Black has another file at his disposal, he secures the draw.   Without it he would be lost.

It is clear that the detail work which applies to end games always has as a foundation some principle of universal application.   It is thus easy to understand why in otherwise similar positions the Q P might win where the K P would draw and *vice versa*, and why against a K P the Rook must operate on the Q side, whilst against a Q P it must remain on the K side.

The reader should now be able to judge the play in examples 63 and 67, why mistakes were made and why other moves were superior.

In Diag. 68 the black Rook is badly placed : it will no doubt work its way to the other wing, but as the hostile Rook already occupies the K R file, the requisite

No. 68.   Black to play.

Dr. Lasker

number of files is not available, and Black will lose, the Rook needing a space of three files in order to secure a draw with certainty.   1 ... K—B 1; 2 R—R 8 *ch*, K—Kt 2; 3 K—Q 7, R—K Kt 8; 4 P—Q 6, R—

Kt 2 *ch* ; 5 K—K 6, R—Kt 3 *ch*; 6 K—K 7, R—
Kt 2 *ch* ; 7 K—B 6, R—Q 2 ; 8 K—K 6, R—Kt 2 ;
9 P—Q 7, and wins. Little would be needed here to
give Black a draw ; with the white Rook at K Kt 7
instead of K R 7, Black could play his Rook to K R 8.
These things are not flights of imagination, nor due to
chance : they are logical facts resting on the nature of
things.

Here is another example (Diag. 69), one of many.
Black has a simple draw as follows : 1 ... R—R 2 *ch* ;
2 K—Q 6, R—R 3 *ch* ; 3 K—K 5, R—R 7 ; 4 K—
Q 6, R—R 3 *ch* ; 5 K—Q 7, R—R 2 *ch* ; 6 K—B 8,
R—R 1 *ch* ; 7 K—B 7, R—R 2 *ch* ; 8 K—Kt 6, R—R 7 ;
9 R—K 4, K—B 1 ; 10 K—B 6, K—K 1 ; 11 K—Q 6,
R—R 2 ; 12 R—K R 4, R—R 3 *ch* ; 13 K—K 5,

No. 69. Black to play.

Dr. Tarrasch *v.* Swiderski
Nuremberg, 1906

R—R 8 ; draw. White cannot break through, nor
can he advance the pawn, for the two black pieces are
in the best possible position and on the correct side.
But reverse the position with the black King at his
Q B 1 and his Rook at K R 7, the white King at his

K 7 and his Rook at Q 4, and Black must lose as he
cannot now execute the same manœuvre : 1 ... R—
R 2 *ch* ; 2 K—B 8, R—R 1 *ch* ; 3 K—Kt 7, R—K 1 ;
4 K—B 7, R—R 1 ; 5 P—K 7, R—R 2 *ch* ; 6 K—B 8,
R—R 1 *ch* ; 7 K—Kt 7, R—K 1 ; 8 K—B 7, and wins.
As in a previous example, the black Rook has not sufficient space for the necessary checks. The opposing
King can attack it and come back for the protection of
his pawn.

Reverting now to positions in which the defending
pieces and especially the King occupy unfavourable
posts, we shall devote little attention to them as they
do not present any characteristics worthy of special
mention. As we have had occasion to observe, if the
defending pieces are unable to reach their proper positions by the time the pawn enters the seventh rank, the
game is lost, whereas it would, in the other case, be
nearly always drawn as we have already seen. The
problem is simply whether the defending King is cut
off from the pawn and whether this barrage can be
maintained until the decisive moment. This barrage
can be set up on a file as well as on a rank, in this case
whenever the King is behind the pawn and is to be
prevented from occupying one of the adjacent squares.
This is not always easy, for the pawn can queen only
with the assistance of the Rook, but as soon as the Rook
moves the adverse King comes up to the pawn.

Take the position in Diag. 70. The black King is
far away from the pawn, which is, however, not far
advanced. How can this pawn move forward without
allowing the hostile King to advance ? Let it be said
now that the protection of the pawn by a Rook on a
rank is bad policy, for the Rook can always be attacked
by the King. In the present example the white Rook
cannot move to K 4. But if Black had the move, he
would play 1 ... K—B 3 ; 2 R—K 4, K—B 4 ; 3
R—K 3, K—B 5 ; 4 R—K 1, K—B 4 ; and, by means

of the attack on the Rook, the same position is obtained, but with White to move. Why these complicated manœuvres? White's correct policy is to support the advance of the pawn by placing the Rook behind it, but without allowing the black King to get nearer to the pawn. Therefore the white King must move into

No. 70. White to play and win.

Grigoriev

opposition (in this case at Q 5). This manœuvre is carried out as follows : 1 K—B 3, R—B 1 *ch* ; 2 K—Q 4, R—Q Kt 1 ; 3 K—B 4, R—B 1 *ch*; 4 K—Q 5, R—Q Kt 1 (4 ... R—Q 1 *ch* ; 5 K—B 6, R—B 1 *ch* ; 6 K—Kt 7, R—B 6 ; 7 R—Q Kt 1, K—K 3 ; 8 P—Kt 4, etc.) ; 5 R—Q Kt 1, K—B 3 (it is now seen that the black King must lose a *tempo* and approach the pawn by a roundabout way, and we all know the value of a *tempo* in an end game. Were the white King not in opposition at Q 5 Black's King would have a free passage) ; 6 P—Kt 4, K—K 2 ; 7 K—B 6, K—Q 1 ; 8 R—Q 1 *ch*, and wins (8 ... K—B 1 ; 9 R—K R 1,).

Were this manœuvre not available or the pawn still further back, or the defending King in a more favourable position in relation to the white King, the win would be impossible, for the protection of a pawn on a rank leads, as has been pointed out, to nothing.

The example in Diag. 71 differs but little from the

No. 71. White to play and draw.

Chéron

preceding one, and yet the result is not the same. The King's prescribed manœuvre is not available, for if he tries to take the opposition at K 7, Black's Rook will attack the pawn.   If then White plays R—Q Kt 1, protecting the pawn, Black's reply ... R—Kt 6 ; blockades it, forcing the adverse King to retrace his steps, leaving the way clear for his rival. If the white King does not move so far away from his pawn, we have the same result : 1 K—B 2, R—B 1 *ch* ; 2 K—Q 3, R—Q Kt 1 ; 3 K—B 3, R—B 1 *ch* ; 4 K—Q 4, R—Q Kt 1 ; 5 R—Q Kt 1, K—B 3 ; 6 P—Kt 4, (6 K—Q 5, K—K 2 ; 7 K—B 6, R—Kt 6 ;) 6 ... K—K 3 ; 7 K—B 5, K—Q 2 ; with a drawn result. The white Rook's preliminary manœuvre in the preceding example is now clear : the defending King's position is not a matter of indifference. Let us now try to protect the pawn on a rank. The fourth rank is not favourable because of the imminent attack by ... K—Kt 3—Kt 4. Let us be

content, for the moment, with the third rank : 1 R—B 3,
R—K R 1 ; 2 P—Kt 3, (2 P—Kt 4, R—Q Kt 1 ;
3 R—B 4, K—Kt 3 ; 4 K—Kt 2, K—Kt 4 ; 5 R—B 4,
K—B 3 ; 6 K—Kt 3, K—K 4) 2 ... R—R 7 ; 3
P—Kt 4, R—R 5 ; 4 R—Kt 3, K—B 3 ; 5 P—Kt 5,
K—K 3 ; 6 K—Kt 2, (6 P—Kt 6, R—R 1 ;) 6 ...
K—Q 2 ; draw. The pawn cannot queen without the
assistance of the King.

These examples teach that the Kt P has this characteristic : that there is but one file on one side, which is
manifestly insufficient for manœuvres even by the King.
A Kt P, sufficiently advanced, that is up to the 6th or
7th rank, always wins, up to the 5th rank nearly always.

Finally, here is a position (Diag. 72) in which the
King is behind the pawn. Black, with the move, draws

No. 72. Black to play and draw.

Horwitz and Kling

as follows : 1 ... R—Kt 3 ; 2 P—K 7, (2 R—K R 8,
R × P ; 3 R—R 5 *ch*, K—Kt 5 ;) 2 ... R—B 3 *ch* ;
3 K—Kt 7, R—Kt 3 *ch* ; 4 K—R 7, K—B 3 ; 5 R—
B 8 *ch*, K × P. This pretty manœuvre is possible only
because, in either case, the black King attacks the hostile
Rook when his own Rook is attacked — White has

insufficient space.   Imagine the same position one file
further to the left and White would win for none of
the preceding manœuvres is available : 1 ... R—R 3 ;
2 R—K R 8, (2 P—Q 7, R—K 3 *ch* ; 3 K—B 7, K—
Q 3 ; 4 R—K R 8, R—K 2 *ch* ; 5 K—B 1, R×P ;)
2 ... R×P ; 3 R—R 5 *ch* ; and wins.

Space, lines, the "geometrical idea," these are the
fundamentals of the art of end game play.

Rook and Two Pawns *v.* Rook

With a Rook and two pawns against a Rook, the win
is not only easier, but it is practically a foregone conclusion.   It is customary to resign before the event,
and these endings occur very rarely in practical play
except in such rare cases where there are chances of a
draw.   It would, however, be a mistake to take for
granted that the win is always simple : on the contrary,
it is not seldom very laborious, requiring time and an
immense fund of patience.   The following end game
(Diag. 73) is a case in point.   It requires no less than
30 moves to prove a win.   1 R—R 8, R—R 6 ; 2
R—Q Kt 8, K—Kt 3 ; 3 R—Kt 5, R—Q B 6 ; 4

No. 73. White to play.

Steinitz *v.* Dr. Zukertort
London, 1883

R—K 5, R—R 6 ; 5 P—R 4, R—Kt 6 ; 6 P—R 5 *ch*,
K—R 3 ; 7 R—K B 5, R—Q R 6 ; 8 R—B 3, R—R 8 ;
9 K—Kt 3, R—Kt 8 *ch* ; 10 K—R 4, R—R 8 *ch* ;
11 R—R 3, R—K Kt 8 ; 12 R—R 2, R—Q R 8 ;
13 P—Kt 5 *ch*, K—Kt 2 ; 14 R—K B 2, R—R 8 *ch* ;
15 K—Kt 4, R—Kt 8 *ch* ; 16 K—B 5, R—K R 8 ;
17 P—R 6 *ch*, K—R 2 ; 18 R—B 4, R—K Kt 8 ;
19 R—K 4, R—B 8 *ch* ; 20 K—Kt 4, R—Kt 8 *ch* ;
21 K—R 5, R—R 8 *ch* ; 22 R—R 4, R—K Kt 8 ;
23 R—R 2, R—Kt 6 ; 24 R—R 2, R—R 6 *ch* ; 25
K—Kt 4, R—Kt 6 ; 26 R—R 7 *ch*, K—Kt 1 ; 27
R—K 7, R—Kt 3 ; 28 K—B 5, R—Kt 4 *ch* ; 29
R—K 5, R—Kt 1 ; 30 P—Kt 6, and wins.*

No doubt Black might have resigned earlier and the
ending contains no *finesse* at all and any experienced
player would have played it more or less in the same
manner.   A similar win is brought about in the next
example (Diag. 74), which closely resembles the preceding
position.   1 ... R—B 8 *ch* ; 2 K—Kt 5, R—B 2 ;
3 P—R 5, R—R 2 ; 4 R—Kt 5, R—Kt 2 *ch* ; 5 K—

No. 74.   Black to play.

Dr. Lasker *v.* Dr. Tarrasch
Match, 1908

*In the game as actually played, Black won.

B 4, R—B 2 ; 6 P—Kt 5, K—Kt 2 ; 7 K—B 5,
R—B 2 *ch* ; 8 K—Kt 4, R—R 2 ; 9 P—R 6 *ch*, K—Kt 3;
10 R—Kt 6 *ch*, K—R 2 ; 11 K—R 5, R—R 4 ; 12
R—Kt 7 *ch*, K—Kt 1 ; 13 R—K 7, R—Kt 4 ; 14
K—Kt 6, R—Kt 3 *ch* ; 15 K—B 5, R—Kt 4 *ch* ; 16
K—B 6, R—Kt 1 ; 17 P—Kt 6, R—R 1 ; 18 R—K 5,
K—R 1 ; 19 K—Kt 5, R—K Kt 1 ; 20 R—Kt 5,
R—K 1 ; 21 P—R 7, and White wins. Note the
extreme care taken in advancing the pawns, always
reserving the possibility of interposing sometimes the
Rook, sometimes a pawn in answer to a check.

Almost the only way in which the defending party
can secure a draw, is when his King can find a secure
post amongst the pawns and cannot be dislodged, while
the opposing King is far away from the pawns and cut
off by the Rook, e.g. : White : K at K B 7, R at K B 3,
pawns at Q 3 and Q B 4, Black : K at his Q 5, R at
K 4. 1 ... R—K 8 ; 2 R—B 6, K×P ; 3 P—B 5,
K—Q 5 ; 4 P—B 6, K—Q 4 ; etc. Again, if it is
White's move : 1 K—B 6, R—K 1 ; 2 K—Kt 6,
R—K 8 ; etc.

The win is more difficult when the pawns are not
united, and these positions are particularly interesting,
as, for instance, Diag. 75, where there is no win : 1 K—
Kt 3, R—Kt 5 *ch* ; 2 K—B 3, K—Kt 4 ; 3 R—Kt 8 *ch*,
K—R 5 ; 4 R—Q B 8, R—Kt 6 *ch* ; 5 K—B 2, R—
Kt 4 ; 6 R—K R 8, K—Kt 5 ; 7 R—R 1, P—R 5 ;
8 K—Kt 2, P—R 6 *ch* ; 9 K—R 2, K—R 5 ; 10
R—Q B 1, R—R 4 ; 11 R—Q Kt 1, P—B 5 ; 12
R—Kt 8, R—Q B 4 ; 13 R—R 8 *ch*, K—Kt 5 ; 14
R×P, P—B 6 ; 15 R—Kt 3 *ch*, K—B 5 ; 16 R—Kt 8,
and draws. The sacrifice of a pawn is more or less
compulsory, but the defender must make sure that the
resulting end game with one pawn should not be lost.
The draw is more difficult to obtain if Black plays 8 ...
R—Kt 1 ; and the position requires then the utmost
precision. It can nevertheless be forced, e.g. : 8 ...

No. 75. White to play.

Marshall *v.* Rubinstein
San Sebastian, 1911

R—Kt 1 ; 9 R—R 4 *ch*, K—Kt 4 ; 10 R—R 7, R—Kt 1 ;
11 R—Kt 7 *ch*, K—B 5 ; 12 R—Q R 7, R—Kt 7 *ch* ;
13 K—R 3, K—B 6 ; 14 R × P, P—B 5 ; 15 R—R 8,
R—Kt 7 ; 16 R—R 6, K—B 7 ; 17 R—R 6, R—Kt 2 ;
18 R—R 8, etc.

If isolated pawns offer fewer chances of a win than
do united ones, these chances are considerably increased
when they are far apart. This is easily understandable,
for the adverse King cannot exert his defensive powers
against both pawns at the same time, and we have
virtually two endings with a passed pawn each, of which
one at least can easily be disadvantageous for the defence.
Only in exceptional cases can drawing chances obtain,
as in the following example (Diag. 76). Here, from
the very beginning, both pawns are held up, the King
cut off and the Rook reduced to the defensive. White
must give up a pawn, remaining with a drawn position
with the remaining pawn : 1 ... R—R 5 ; 2 R—B 3 *ch*,
K—Kt 3 ; 3 K—B 2, R × K R P ; 4 K—K 2, R—R 5 ;
5 K—Q 2, R—R 3 ; 6 K—B 2, R—B 3 ; 7 R—Q 3
(the Rooks must not be exchanged and the barrage set

No. 76. Black to play.

Gothenburg *v.* Stockholm
Correspondence game

up against the King be lifted) ; 7 ... K—B 2 ; 8 K—
Kt 3, K—K 2 ; 9 K—Kt 4, R—Q 3 ; etc.

When there is a pawn on either wing, the question
is whether one of them can be given up, obtaining
thereby a winning position with the remaining pawn.
Such positions are not worth analysing. More interesting are the cases in which one side has two pawns and
the other side only one. The win appears to be easier
than with a single extra pawn, for the attacker has
threats both numerous and varied : it is not only a case
of queening a pawn after exchanging the other, but
there are chances of winning the adverse pawn or even
of sacrificing the Rook against the pawn, thus obtaining
the superior end game with two pawns against the
Rook, and, as in all cases, the player who has the
superiority in material has of course the better chances.

Everything depends, however, on the nature of the
position. First of all, the Kings : whether the defending
King has been able to hold up the pawns, whether he
is near or amongst them in one of the favourable positions
which we have already seen : whether the Rook which

guards the single pawn has space for manœuvring and
has preserved its activity ; finally whether the pawns
are sufficiently advanced and not likely to fall : all these
considerations must be cleared up, in order to be able
to decide on one or the other plan of campaign, either
for attack or defence.

For instance, in Diag. 77, the white Rook defends
its own pawn and attacks Black's K B P which restricts

No. 77. White to play.

Dr. Alekhine *v.* Dr. Euwe
Match, 1935

the black King's movements. Furthermore, the black
pawns are unfavourably placed, for White's King can
occupy his K B 4, the best possible post. To reach
this square is for White the crucial point in his plan of
defence. White's best play is 1 K—K 3 ; for 1 …
R—R 5 ; is useless on account of 2 R—B 4, and if,
on the other hand, 1 … K—Kt 4 ; there follows 2 R × P.
Black must therefore play 1 … P—B 4 ; 2 K—B 4,
R—R 5 *ch* ; 3 K—Kt 3, K—B 3 (3 … K—Kt 4, 4
R—Kt 7 *ch*,) ; 4 R—Q Kt 7, K—K 4 ; 5 R—Kt 5 *ch*,
and the King is tied to the defence of the K B P and
cannot enter his fifth rank because of R—Kt 4 *ch*. It

is interesting to note that, in the actual game 1 K—K 5,
was played, and Black, instead of taking advantage of
this mistake with 1 ... R—R 5 ; 2 R—B 4, P—B 3 *ch* ;
played 1 ... P—B 3 *ch*; which led to a speedy draw after
2 K—B 4, R—R 5 *ch* ; 3 K—Kt 3, P—B 4 ; 4 K—R 4,
K—B 3 ; 5 R—Q Kt 7, etc.

How can the average player hope to avoid such
mistakes ?   Not by memorizing all the known positions,
all the published games and their analyses, the usual
procedure or the measures employed, but by a thorough
understanding of available means and their essential
point.   Misjudging this led to the faulty play in the
last example.

EXERCISES

In Diag. 78 Black has the advantage, for his King

No. 78.

Dr. Euwe *v.* Dr. Alekhine
Match, 1935

is closer to the pawns from which the white King is
cut off.   What is the result and how is it obtained with
White to play ?   In Diag. 79 White is a pawn down,

No. 79.

Dr. Tarrasch *v.* Schlechter
Match, 1911

but his own pawn is so far advanced that he has the advantage. What is the result with Black to play, and how is it obtained ?

ROOK AND SEVERAL PAWNS

Endings with Rooks and pawns are, together with pawn endings, the very essence of end game play. Pawns and Rooks are predestined for this phase of the game.

When besides the Rook there is one pawn, or possibly two, these positions are of a type and can be studied thoroughly. That is why many composers have devoted much attention to artistic and artificial endings which afford a fruitful field for study.

Endings with several pawns cannot be treated in the same way and books devoted to composed endings and not to practical play give hardly any space to these endings, which have for them no interest.

The contrary is the case here : these endings from practical play are of the greatest interest for our purpose, and it is good to be able to refer to actual games from master practice.

It is, however, impossible to compile exact *data* relating to the particular pawns and their particular positions which would win or draw, or to give rigid and immutable precepts leading to a win or to the saving clause of a draw.   Nor is this to be deplored : instead of trying to remember a large number of rules, which are by no means unvarying in their application, the student must follow his own judgment, his own inspiration, relying on general principles, which he will deduce from the best and most characteristic games from master practice.

As was the case with the Queen endings, when there are, besides the Rook, a number of pawns still on the board, it is first necessary to analyse the position up to a certain point.   This is not necessary in the case of one pawn : there the advantage is obvious and is seen at a glance ; nothing more is needed than to ascertain the quickest and most certain way to win.   Such simple cases can occur also with several pawns ; for instance, one side is a pawn ahead, and there is no need for analysis unless the opponent has an advantage to offset the pawn. But where the balance in material is maintained, the characteristics of the position must be ascertained with the utmost precision : only thus can it be established which side has the advantage and what line of play must be selected.

All the elements of the position must be reviewed in turn : first of all, the Kings : which of the two is the better placed, the more active, the nearer to the centre or to the battlefield, which of them can penetrate the hostile pawn formation, protect a passed pawn, defend a weak one, etc.   Then come the Rooks : freedom of action, space, restriction of the opposing King, etc. But all this must be examined in relation to the pawns : we have not before us an empty board, but there is a pawn formation which cannot change quickly and suddenly as that of the pieces.   We must therefore concentrate on the pawns and note their weaknesses and strength. As always, a backward and isolated pawn, without proper protection, presents the outstanding weakness, whereas a passed pawn, or even the chance of obtaining one, forms a precious advantage. If, generally speaking, a compact pawn formation is desirable, a passed pawn is of far greater importance and gives the greatest promise of victory. The more distant this passed pawn, the more dangerous it is ; not only is the Rook kept away from the main field of battle, but also the King will be unable to get across and win it ; he would not have the time to return to the centre or the other wing. Another point : such pawn must be well forward or able to advance. If the pawn is still far away from the queening square, the adverse Rook will immediately occupy a position close in front, forcing its own Rook to get behind the pawn for its protection. Even an extra pawn is, in such circumstances, of little value or even a handicap, if it monopolizes the services of the Rook. Then the question of "the move" is an important one. On it will depend the activity or otherwise of the pieces on either side. Finally, the essential point of the whole position must be found as well as the line of play best adapted to its exigencies.

In Diag. 80, White's superiority needs no emphasizing. His pieces are more active and both his pieces and pawns better placed. Black is almost in a stalemate position, for he has but one move available, ... R—Q 2 ; and back again. On the other hand, White has no means of improving his situation still further, for all his forces are in the best possible positions. What is the alternative ? He must either admit that his judgment in distributing his forces was wrong and leads to nothing, in which case he must try to re-group them, e.g., by R—K 2—Q R 2—R 7 or 8, or else he must decide that, having obtained the best possible position, he must exploit it to the utmost and break through somehow.   At the very least, he must give this method

No. 80.   White to play.

Forgács *v.* Dr. Bernstein
Coburg, 1904

due consideration and submit it to a searching analysis. Incidentally, this course is the most logical : having started a process of strangulation, it would be unnatural to stop half-way and to give the adversary time to breathe.
Let us try : 1 P—Kt 5, P × P ; 2 K × P, and now we shall examine the results of a passive resistance by Black : 2 ... R—Q 2 ; 3 P—R 6, P × P *ch* ; 4 R × P, K—Kt 2 ; 5 R—Kt 6 *ch*, K—B 2 ; 6 K—B 5, R—Q 1 ; 7 R—R 6, K—Kt 2 ; 8 R—B 6, R—Q 2 ; 9 K—K 6, R—R 2 (9 ... R—Q 1 ; 10 R—B 7 *ch*, K—Kt 3 ; 11 R—Q 7) ; 10 R—B 4, R—R 3 ; 11 R—B 7 *ch*, K—Kt 3 ; 12 R—B 7, and wins.   Next a more active line of defence by Black must be tested : 2 ... R—K 1 ; 3 R × P, (3 R × R, K × R ; 4 K—Kt 6, K—B 1 ; draw) 3 ... R—K 5 ; 4 R—Q 7 *ch*, K—B 1 ; 5 K—Kt 6, R—Kt 5 *ch* ; 6 K—B 5, R × P ; 7 P—Q 6, R—K R 5 ; 8 R—Q 8 *ch*, K—B 2 ; 9 R—K R 8, and wins.   There may be some special *finesses* available to

either side, but the general line indicated must be correct ; White's superior position warrants this, and the Q P, once it becomes a passed pawn, is sufficiently far advanced to make a win certain. Note the essential point : the decision is brought about, not by the pawns on the flank—they are soon exchanged—but by the weakness of Black's backward pawn and the superior position of the white pieces.

Let us now see whether the alternative plan provides equally promising chances : 1 R—K 2. It is clear that Black cannot allow this Rook's irruption at Q R 7 or Q R 8. He would soon have no moves left. He has, however, the resource : 1 ... R—K B 1 ; with the intention of driving off the hostile King. The reply 2 P— Kt 5, is indicated. If then 2 ... K—Kt 1 *dis ch* ; 3 K—Kt 4, P×P ; 4 K×P, R—B 3 ; White wins by 5 R—K 6, R×R ; 6 P×R, K—B 1 ; 7 K—Kt 6, P—Q 4 (7 ... K—K 2 ; 8 K×P) ; 8 P×P, P—B 5 (8 ... K—K 2 ; 9 K×P, and after making two Queens, White mates at K B 8) ; 9 P—R 6, P×P ; 10 K—B 6, P—B 6 ; 11 P—Q 6, P—B 7 ; 12 P—Q 7, and wins. The following continuation is no better : 2 ... P×P ; 3 K×P, R—K R 1 ; 4 R—K 6, R—R 3 ; and if 5 R×R, P×R *ch* ; 6 K×P, K—B 3 ; 7 K—R 7, K— B 2 ; 8 P—R 6, and wins. Here again the play may be improved, but it is clear that the first method affords more security and the better chances. In the actual game, the continuation was 1 R—K 2, R—K B 1 ; 2 R—K 6, already resigning himself to a draw, without any further effort. After this gift of two important *tempi*, it is now Black's turn to try to win : 2 ... K— Kt 1 *dis ch* : 3 K—Kt 6, R—B 5 ; with an attack on two pawns. White now tried 4 P—Kt 5, P×P ; 5 R×P, P—Kt 5 ; but Black's pawn ensured the draw. It was White's inconsistency, his inability to decide on a definite plan, which deprived him of a win.

Here is a more difficult position (Diag. 81), as the

result cannot be foreseen by an exact analysis : it is not
unlike a complicated middle game position, where the
only guidance is that of positional judgment.   White is
clearly superior, for he has a distant passed pawn in

No. 81. Black to play.

Dr. Alekhine *v.* Dr. Euwe
Match, 1935

view whilst Black can only obtain one in the centre,
near to the opposing King, while his own is far away.
It could be queried whether the game could be saved
at all.   Is there anything that could be tried ?   If not,
Black loses quite simply as in the actual game : 1 ...
R—Kt 6 ; 2 P—Kt 5, P—Kt 4 ; 3 K—K 2, P—K 4 ;
4 K—Q 2, P—B 3 ; 5 K—B 2, R—Kt 5 ; 6 K—B 3,
R—Q 5 ; 7 R—R 6, K—Kt 3 ; 8 R×P, R×P ; 9
R—R 6, R—Q 5 ; 10 P—Kt 6, and wins.   In the
course of these nine moves, Black has obtained no
counter-chances at all and has even allowed the opposing
King to make his way to the Queen's wing, in order
to support the action of his Rook and two pawns.   In
the light of this continuation, not a very lengthy one, it
appears evident that Black's strategy was faulty.

What could he have done ?   Whatever he might have

tried, could have had no worse sequel. Therefore, he should have tried to create a passed pawn : 1 ... P—K 4 ; 2 K—K 2 (2 P—Kt 4, P—K Kt 4 ; 3 P—Kt 5, P—B 3 ; 4 R—R 6, R—R 6; 5 K—K 2, P—B 4 ; 6 K—Q 2, P—K 5 ;), 2 ... P—B 4 ; 3 K—Q 2, R—B 5 ; 4 P—Kt 5, P—K 5 ; and Black will have a passed pawn.

It would be impossible here to give a detailed analysis of all the possible variations in this position ; they are numerous and complicated and the greatest authorities are at variance on the subject. What is important to us is the plan based on the essentials of the position. The first step is therefore to establish what these essentials are, and to shape the play accordingly.

Here is another position (Diag. 82) which is, from this point of view, equally interesting. Black is a

No. 82. White to play.

Dr. Lasker *v.* Lövenfisch
Moscow, 1925

pawn ahead, although it is blockaded by the Rook. But the Rook can be driven off so that the pawn can make headway. What counter-chances has White ? His advantage lies in his King's position amidst the black pawns. We see at once that, as in the preceding

example, he must obtain a passed pawn, which will be
the more effective, because on a distant file, safe from
interference by the hostile King.   How is this to be
achieved ?   It will not be too easy, but if we remember
the means by which a passed pawn can be secured, we
shall soon find the proper method.   1 P—B 5, K P × P ;
2 P—K 6, P × P *dis ch* ; 3 K × P, and the R P queens.
Black will then be two pawns ahead, passed and united.
But White must take the risk, as otherwise his game is
lost without any complications.   A player cannot be
expected to be able to calculate such complicated variations, comprising, as here, some fifteen moves.   But
the same applies to the adversary, who, being a pawn
up, may be expected to see more clearly than his
opponent, who deems his game to be already lost.
Such end game play demands the utmost precision, as
is well illustrated in the present example, for White
began with 1 K—B 6, and the sequel was : 1 ... K—
Kt 4 ; 2 R—R 1, P—R 5 ; 3 P—B 5, K P × P ; 4
P—K 6, P × P ; 5 K × Kt P, (he had perhaps intended
to play 5 K × K P, but noticed in time that this would
lose at once by 5 ... P—R 6 ; 6 K—B 6, R—R 3 *ch* ;)
5 ... P—B 5 ; 6 P—R 5, P—B 6 ; 7 P—R 6, P—K 4 ;
8 R—K 1, P—R 6 ; 9 R × P *ch*, K—B 5 ; 10 R—K 1,
P—R 7 ; 11 P—R 7, R—R 1 ; 12 K—Kt 7, P—B 7 ;
13 R—Q R 1, K—Kt 6; 14 R—K B 1, P—R 8 (Q) *ch* ;
15 R × Q, R × R ; and White resigns (16 P—R 8 (Q),
R—Kt 8 *ch* ; and ... P—B 8 (Q) *ch*).   Had not White
lost a *tempo*, he would have secured the draw, as the
black pawn would have been at its Q R 4 at the time of
the break-through, and the principal manœuvre 6 ...
P—B 6; could not have been effected (7 R—K B 1,).
One *tempo* has lost him the game !   This often occurs
in end games, in which the result, as we well know,
often depends on "the move."   If we conceive an idea,
its realization must not be postponed for a single move,
especially one which effects nothing.   From the last

example, we learn the importance of the passed pawn which can, at times, hold its own against three on the other side.

As to the importance of "the move," it is well illustrated in Diag. 83.   Were it Black's move, he would at

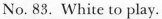

No. 83. White to play.

Dr. Alekhine *v.* Capablanca
Match, 1927

once play ... R—R 3 ; and the white Rook would be at a disadvantage in having to give the R P lateral protection.   But with the move White plays 1 P—Q R 5, R—R 3 ; 2 R—R 4, and now Black's Rook is unfavourably posted : it lacks space and freedom, and whenever it moves away, the white R P takes another step forward.   The win is not difficult.   Black can only prevent White's King from going to the assistance of his R P by assuming the opposition.   This cannot be done, for White's Rook has any number of moves, whilst the black Rook has none.   If, on the other hand, Black's King makes for the adverse pawn, the white King plays havoc with the pawns on the other wing, as, indeed, did happen in the actual game : 2 ... K—B 3 ; 3 K—B 3, K—K 4 ; 4 K—K 3, P—R 4 ; 5 K—Q 3,

K—Q 4 ; 6 K—B 3, K—B 4 ; 7 R—R 1, K—Kt 4 ;
8 K—Q 4, R—Q 3 *ch* ; 9 K—K 5, R—K 3 *ch* ; 10
K—B 4, K—R 3 ; 11 K—Kt 5, R—K 4 *ch* ; 12 K—
R 6, R—K B 4 (note Black's efforts to liberate his Rook,
but it is too late) ; 13 P—B 4, R—B 4 ; 14 R—R 3,
R—B 2 ; 15 K—Kt 7, R—Q 2 ; 16 P—B 5, P × P ;
17 K—R 6, P—B 5 ; 18 P × P, R—Q 4 ; 19 K—Kt 7,
R—K B 4 ; 20 R—R 4, K—Kt 4 ; 21 R—K 4, K—
R 3 ; (21 ... K × P ; 22 R—K 5 *ch*) 22 K—R 6,
R × R P ; 23 R—K 5, R—R 8 ; 24 K × P, R—K Kt 8 ;
25 R—K Kt 5, R—K R 8 ; 26 R—K B 5, K—Kt 3 ;
27 R × P, K—B 3 ; 28 R—K 7, and wins.   It will be
noticed how far the black King is from the main battlefield.   This enables White to propose an exchange of
Rooks on several occasions ; he was also able to give
up the pawn temporarily in order to gain a pawn on
the other wing.

The knowledge of these things should help the student
in his own practice.

The remedy shown above may not at all times be
efficacious, but it must be tried.   To attain a passed
pawn as distant as possible is one of the surest remedies.

We see this principle applied in Diag. 84.   White is
in a critical position : he has isolated pawns, two of
them doubled, and those pawns which might become
united are threatened by the black Rook.   The situation
looks desperate, the issue decided.   The best policy is
to make things difficult for the adversary, to place
obstacles in his way so as to make his victory a precarious one, for often the result hangs by a thread and
depends perhaps, as we have seen, on one single move.
Here he can obtain a passed pawn either at K R 5 or
at Q 5 and so he plays 1 R—K R 8, R × P *ch* ; 2 K—
Kt 2, K × P ; (2 ... K—Kt 2 ; 3 R—Q 8,) 3 R × P,
P—B 3 ; 4 R—R 7, K—K 4 ; 5 P—R 6, R—Q R 6 ;
6 R—K 7 *ch*, K × P ; 7 P—R 7, R—R 1 ; 8 K—Kt 3,
P—B 4 ; 9 P—B 4, P × P *ch* (a quicker way to win

No. 84. White to play.

Dr. Alekhine *v.* Bogoljubow
Match, 1934

would be 9 ... P—Kt 5 ; obtaining another passed pawn) ; 10 K × P, P—B 5 ; 11 K × P, P—B 6 ; 12 R—Q 7, R—R 1 (the plausible 12 ... R—B 1 ;* yields only a draw because of 13 R—Q B 7, R—B 1 *ch* ; 14 K—Kt 6, K—Q 5 ; 15 K—Kt 7, R—Kt 1 ; 16 P—R 8 (Q), R × Q ; 17 K × R, P—Q 4 ; 18 K—Kt 7, K—Q 6 ; 19 K—B 6, etc.) ; 13 K—Kt 6, K—B 3 ; 14 R—K Kt 7 (14 R—Q R 7, P—Q 4 ; 15 K—Kt 7, R × P *ch* ; 16 K × R, P—Q 5 ;), 14 ... P—B 7 ; 15 R—Kt 8, P—B 8 (Q); 16 R × R, Q—K Kt 8 *ch*; and wins.

Black has won, but how difficult it has been owing to White's passed pawn, and how often he could have gone astray and by a mere inadvertence missed the win which appeared so easy and certain ! That is precisely the power of the passed pawn—all may depend on one move.

Another means of defence consists in the sacrifice of the Rook against as many pawns as possible, including of course the dangerous passed pawn and then to queen one of one's own pawns. We already have had an example in which a single surviving pawn sufficed to

*This is the actual continuation played in the game.

secure the draw. This procedure is even more effective
when employed by the attacking side. But it is usually

No. 85. White to play.

Bogoljubow *v.* Dr. Alekhine
Match, 1934

a last resource, for with pawns against Rook it is often
difficult to foresee the final result many moves ahead,
whereas for the defender, this is as good a method as
any other, and preferable perhaps on account of its
complications and the chances which it offers.

Diag. 85 provides a good illustration. Here White
conceded a draw when he had a forced win by 1 R—
K 5 *ch*, K—B 5 ; 2 R × P, R—Q R 3 ; 3 R × P, R × P ;
4 R—R 8, P—Kt 6 ; 5 R—B 8 *ch*, K—Q 6 ; 6 R—
Q Kt 8, K—B 7 ; 7 P—B 5, and the three pawns win
against the Rook.

Yet another method is to give up one or more pawns
in order to obtain an overwhelming position of all the
remaining forces, but it can be applied only where the
opposing King is badly placed. We have already seen
a position of this type in Diag. 22 in which the concentrated power of King, Rook and passed pawn was directed
against the defending King on the edge of the board.

In Diag. 86 we have an example of the same process securing the draw.

Black's position is difficult : his R P is attacked and hard to defend. If this pawn falls, White obtains a distant passed pawn with every chance of a win. Generally speaking, three pawns against two, with a Rook on either side, are not sufficient to win ; but the pawns must be in opposition on the same files. This is not the case here, and the K R P will have a free run to its queening square, especially as the white pawn formation is compact and without weakness. Against this, his King is a little restricted in movement. Should Black succeed in keeping him imprisoned, for instance by placing his own King at his K B 6, he can frustrate White's every attempt to win. The plan is now formulated, and it remains to put it into execution. 1 ... P—R 4 ; 2 R—K R 7, P—K 5 ; 3 K—K 2, P—B 4 (the first sacrifice—White's King must not be permitted to settle at K 3 and, from there, to move to K B 4) ; 4 R—R 6 *ch*, K—K 4 ; 5 R × P, R—R 7 *ch* ; 6 K—B 1, P—K 6 (another sacrifice opening the way for his King ; Black

No. 86. Black to play.

Kashdan *v.* Dr. Alekhine
Folkestone, 1933

even forgoes creating a passed pawn at his K 6) ; 7
P × P, K—K 5 ; 8 K—Kt 1, R—K 7 ; 9 R—R 4 *ch*,
K—K 4 ; (if 9 ... K × P ; 10 R—K B 4, safeguarding
his King and queening the R P) 10 R—R 8, K—B 3 ;
11 R—B 8 *ch*, K—Kt 3 ; 12 R—K 8, K—B 2 ; 13
R—B 8, R × K P ; 14 K—B 2, R—R 6 ; 15 P—R 4,
K—B 3 ; 16 R—B 6 *ch*, K—B 2 ; 17 R—B 2, R—Kt 6 ;
18 R—K 2, K—B 3 ; 19 R—K 3, R—Kt 5 ; 20
K—B 3, R—R 5 ; and draws, as the black Rook guards
the fourth rank and prevents the King from penetrating
the pawn position. The passed pawn on the R file is
useless, and we have an ending of two pawns against
one which cannot be won.

This example illustrates the difficulties inherent in
endings where the pawns are all on one side. They
are difficult to win, even with an extra pawn. All
depends on the steadiness of the defender. He must
avoid creating weaknesses such as isolated pawns. He
must even strive to exchange as many pawns as possible,
especially outside ones. The attack is no less arduous.
These endings belong to the most difficult chapters of
end game play and often last as long as the Q endings.

The next example (Diag. 87) requires as many as
52 moves. We must refrain from analysing them.

White here appears to have a very bad game : his
pawns are isolated, two of them being doubled. He
therefore already suffers from the disabilities which, as
a matter of course, his adversary would try to inflict
upon him. Yet, the game ended in a draw after the
sacrifice of another pawn, leaving him two pawns to the
bad. The reason lies in the black King's inability to
attack the white pawns, because a Rook bars the way.
The continuation was : 1 R—R 1, P—Kt 4 ; 2 P—R 3,
K—Kt 2 ; 3 R—R 5, K—Kt 3 ; 4 K—Kt 2, P—R 4 ;
5 R—Q B 5, P—B 3 ; 6 R—R 5, R—Kt 6 ; 7 R—
Q B 5, P—K 4 ; 8 R—B 6, K—B 4 ; 9 R—R 6,
R—Kt 5 ; 10 R—B 6, R—K B 5 ; 11 R—R 6, P—

No. 87. White to play.

Eliskases *v.* Bogoljubow
Match, 1939

Kt 5 ; 12 R P × P *ch*, P × P ; 13 P × P *ch*, R × P *ch* ;
14 K—B 3 (now the ending with two pawns against
one cannot be won), 14 ... R—Kt 5 ; 15 R—R 3,
K—Kt 4 ; 16 R—K 3, R—Q 5 ; 17 K—Kt 2, P—K 5 ;
18 R—K 2, K—B 5 ; 19 R—R 2, P—B 4 ; 20 R—
R 8, R—Q 7 ; 21 R—K 8, R—K 7 ; 22 R—Q R 8,
R—Q 7 ; 23 R—K 8, R—Q 2 ; 24 R—Q R 8, R—Q 4 ;
25 R—K 8, R—Q 7 ; 26 R—K 7, R—Q 1 ; 27
R—Q R 7, K—Kt 4; 28 R—R 5, K—B 3 ; 29 K—
B 1, P—B 5 ; 30 K—K 2, R—Q Kt 1 ; 31 R—R 6 *ch*,
K—B 4 ; 32 R—R 5 *ch*, K—Kt 5 ; 33 P—B 3 *ch* (in
order to create doubled pawns, which eliminates all
possibility of a win for Black), 33 ... P × P *ch* ; 34
K—B 2, R—Kt 7 *ch* ; 35 K—B 1, R—K R 7 ; 36
R—Kt 5, R—R 4 ; 37 R × R, K × R ; 38 K—B 2,
K—Kt 5 ; 39 K—B 1, K—B 4 ; 40 K—B 2, K—K 5 ;
41 K—B 1, K—K 6 ; 42 K—K 1, P—B 7 *ch* ; 43
K—B 1, a "book draw."

Black's play, it must be confessed, was not very convincing, and his error consists in not having found
just the right plan. As often happens, his very first

move is at fault. He should have placed his Rook at his K Kt 4 in order to immobilize the adverse King at B 1 ; he then could have advanced his own King to his K R 6 or to the Q side and offered to exchange Rooks, whenever the white Rook threatened to hinder this plan. Black would then have many threats such as advancing his P to R 6 or to bring his K to B 4, threatening ... K—B 5. If then White replies with R—Q R 4, then ... K—K 3 ; R—R 6, P—K 5 ; wins easily.

If this example has no other merit, it is most instructive in that it shows how important it is in an end game to conceive a proper plan : failure to find the right idea easily throws away all chances of a win, even in a position where there appears to be no difficulty at all.

EXERCISES

Here is an extremely interesting end game from the

No. 88.

Reshevsky *v.* Dr. Alekhine
"Avro" Tournament, 1938

"Avro" tournament in Holland (Diag. 88) : White to play, who wins ?

No. 89.

Dr. Euwe *v.* Dr. Alekhine
Match, 1937

Diag. 89 shows a very difficult ending. It is Black's
move, what result ? The game was drawn after the
following moves : 1 ... P—B 4 ; 2 R—Kt 6 *ch*, K—B 2 ;
3 R—K R 6, P—B 5 ; 4 R × P, R—B 6 ; 5 R—Q Kt 5,
P—B 6 ; 6 K—Q 2, R—B 7 *ch* ; 7 K—K 3, P—Kt 7 ;
8 K—B 4, R—B 5 *ch* ; 9 K—K 3, R—B 7. Annotators
have pointed out that Black missed a win on two occasions ; he could have obtained it on the first move by
1 ... R—B 6 ; (instead of 1 ... P—B 4 ;) and on the
third move (instead of 3 ... P—B 5 ;). Are they right,
and what could be the continuation ?

TWO ROOKS

Endings in which each side has two Rooks differ
considerably from those shown in the last section, for
a new factor intervenes, namely, the concentration of
the tremendous and threatening power of these mighty
pieces, which gives the problem an entirely different
aspect. All things being equal, the player will prevail
who first succeeds in uniting the efforts of both Rooks
in an important direction : at the very least he will

nullify any other advantages which his opponent may
have.   Thus in Diag. 90 the ending is clearly in Black's

No. 90. White to play.

Dr. Lasker *v.* Eliskases
Moscow, 1936

favour because of his united passed pawns on the Q side.
Yet this will not be the deciding factor, but the *liaison*
established between the Rooks.   Either player can
effect it, but as White has the move the advantage will
in fact be his.   He is a pawn down, but "the move"
prevails over this disadvantage in material and it can
rightly be said that he has sacrificed a pawn for "the
move" in order to obtain the co-ordination of his Rooks.
As the Rooks become united on the seventh rank, the
importance of the whole manœuvre is clearly evident.
1 R—Q B 1, K—R 1 ; (faulty strategy : Black could
still secure the draw by speeding up the advance of his
passed pawns : 1 ... P—Q R 4 ; 2 R (B1)—B 7, P—R 5 ;
3 R × P *ch*, K—R 1 ; 4 R × P *ch*, K—Kt 1 ; 5 Q R—
Kt 7 *ch*, K—B 1 ; and White can neither inflict a mate
nor advance his pawns, because Black's pawns are too
swift.   As is nearly always the case, advanced passed
pawns provide the best resource.   An attempt by Black

also to double his Rooks would be abortive : 1 ...
R—K 1 ; 2 P—R 3, P—K R 4 ; 3 R (B 1)—B 7,
R—K 8 *ch* ; 4 K—R 2, R (K 8)—K 7 ; 5 R×P *ch*,
K—B 1 ; 6 Q R—B 7 *ch*, K—K 1 ; 7 R×P, and White
wins all the pawns and keeps his K Kt P protected)
2 R (B 1)—B 7, R—K Kt 1 ; 3 R×R P, P—R 3 ;
4 P—R 4, P—Kt 5 ; 5 R (R 7)—Kt 7, (the K R must
keep the Q P under observation ; this is why, on the
first move, the Rook went to Q B 1 and not to K 1)
5 ... P—Kt 6 ; 6 K—R 2, R—Q 7 ; 7 R×Q Kt P,
R—K 1 ; 8 R (Kt 3)—Kt 7 (back again, whilst Black
cannot achieve the doubling of his Rooks), 8 ... R×P ;
9 R×Kt P, R—Q 1 ; 10 R—R 7 *ch*, K—Kt 1 ; 11
R×P, R—K 6 ; 12 R (R 6)—R 7, P—Q 5 ; 13
R (R 7)—Q 7, R (K 6)—K 1 ; 14 P—R 5, P—Q 6 ;
15 P—R 6, R×R ; 16 R×R, R—K 3 ; 17 R×P,
and wins.

The right method against two united Rooks is clearly
shown in the following position from a game Rubinstein
—Capablanca, Berlin, 1928. The position was as
follows : White : K at K Kt 1, Q at K B 3, R at Q Kt 7,
R at K B 1, and pawns at K 3, K B 2, K Kt 2, K Kt 5;
Black : K at his K Kt 1, Q at K B 1, R at Q R 1, R at
Q B 1, and pawns at Q R 2, K 3, K B 2, K Kt 2. The play
was: 1 ... P—R 4 ; 2 R—Q 1, P—R 5 ; 3 R (Q 1)—
Q 7, P—R 6 ; 4 R×P, P—R 7 ; 5 R×P *ch*, (5 R×Q
ch, R×R ;) 5 ... Q×R ; 6 R×Q *ch*, K×R ; 7 Q—
B 6 *ch*, K—Kt 1 ; 8 Q—Kt 6 *ch*. The power of the
distant passed pawn !

ROOK *v.* QUEEN

The Queen nearly always wins against the Rook and
not by checkmating, but by separating the Rook from
the King and then winning the Rook. Only in exceptional circumstances can a draw be the result, mainly
on the edge of the board where a stalemate frequently
becomes possible.

Much more difficult is the win by the Queen against
Rook and pawn. Two likely cases : a pawn very far
advanced which forces the opposing King to keep in
touch with it, leaving the Queen to carry on the contest
single-handed : or a pawn on its original square, in
which case the defending King hides behind it, whilst
the Rook keeps the adverse King away, staying in front
of the pawn and under its protection.

Against two Rooks, the Queen is often powerless :
the most she can hope for is a draw, for the two Rooks
can mate without the help of the King, where the Queen
could only give useless checks. If there is a pawn on
the same side as the Rooks, they practically always win.
The Queen is unable to stop such a pawn even with the
help of the King, and a sacrifice is useless ; there will
always be a Rook left for the win.

In Diag. 91, Black allows his opponent to make a

No. 91. White to play.

Dus-Chotimirsky *v.* Znosko-Borovsky
St. Petersburg, 1905

second Queen, keeping in exchange two Rooks on the
seventh. In the contest between these heavy pieces,
the Rooks emerge victorious, in spite of White's passed

pawn on the Q side. The pawn soon falls, and the checks come to an end after a fresh and extensive journey across the board by the black King : 1 P—Kt 7, R—Q 8 *ch* ; 2 K—K 2, R (Q 6)—Q 7 *ch* ; 3 K—B 3, R × R ; 4 P—Kt 8 (Q), R (B 8)—B 7 ; 5 Q × P *ch*, K—B 3 ; 6 Q—R 4 *ch*, K—K 4 ; 7 Q—B 4 *ch*, (or 7 K—Kt 3, R × Kt P ; 8 Q × P, R × P ; but not 7 P—Q Kt 4, R × P *ch* ; 8 Q × R, R × Q *ch* ; 9 K × R, K—Q 4 ;) 7 ... K—Q 4 ; 8 K—Kt 3, R × Kt P ; 9 Q—B 7, R × P ; 10 Q—Q 7 *ch*, K—B 5 ; (the beginning of the King's pilgrimage, the object of which is not only to escape from a perpetual check, but also to participate in the Rook's attack, and which will culminate—who would have thought it ?—at K Kt 8 !) ; 11 Q—Q 4 *ch*, K—Kt 6 ; 12 Q—Q 1 *ch*, K—R 6 ; 13 Q—Q 3 *ch*, K—R 7 ; 14 Q—B 4 *ch*, K—Kt 8 ; 15 Q—Q 3 *ch*, K—B 8 ; 16 Q—B 3 *ch*, K—Q 8 ; 17 Q—Q 3 *ch*, R (Kt 7)—Q 7 ; 18 Q—Kt 3 *ch*, K—K 8 ; 19 Q—Kt 1 *ch*, K—K 7 ; 20 Q—Kt 3, P—K 4 ; (threatening ... P—B 5 *ch* ;) 21 Q—Kt 5 *ch*, K—K 8 ; 22 Q—Kt 1 *ch*, R—Q 8 ; 23 Q—Kt 4 *ch*, K—B 8 ; 24 Q—Kt 5 *ch*, K—Kt 8 (the journey's end) ; 25 Q × P, R × P *ch* ; 26 K—R 3, R—K B 8 ; 27 K—R 4, R × P *ch* ; 28 K—Kt 5, R—Kt 7 *ch* ; 29 K—B 6, P—R 4 ; 30 K × P, P—R 5 ; 31 Q—R 8, R—Kt 5 ; 32 K—K 6, K—Kt 2 ; 33 Q—Kt 2 *ch*, R—B 7 ; 34 Q—Kt 7 *ch*, R—K 5 *ch* ; 35 K—B 6, P—R 6 ; 36 Q—Kt 7 *ch*, R—Kt 5 ; 37 Q—Kt 7 *ch*, K—Kt 8 ; 38 Q—Kt 1 *ch*, R—B 8 ; 39 Q—Kt 6, P—R 7 ; 40 P—K 4 *dis ch*, K—Kt 7 ; and White resigned.

If such a co-ordination of the Rooks cannot be accomplished or occurs on unimportant ranks or files, their *rôle* is insignificant and becomes a *quantité négligeable*, and particularly so when they are pitted against a mobile Queen, soundly supported and able to penetrate into the enemy camp, commanding lines and especially dangerous diagonals. Then the Queen becomes

invincible and overcomes a purely passive resistance by
winning pawns and reducing the adversary's mobility.
His only chance then, besides having his Rooks doubled,
is to open up important lines and to obtain passed
pawns. Failing this, he is lost. Such an example is
shown in Diag. 92, in which Black does nothing to
increase the effectiveness of his Rooks or their mobility :

No. 92. White to play.

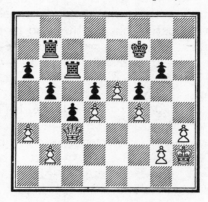

Kmoch *v.* N.

1 P—K Kt 4, R—Q 2 (probably Black fears 2 Q—B 3,
with an attack on the Q P and a threat of penetrating
into the enemy camp *via* K R 5 after an exchange of
pawns. But 1 ... P—Kt 5 ; 2 R P × P, R (B 3)—Kt 3 ;
would give Black far better chances. His Rooks would
be doubled and directed against the white King's vulnerable position, whilst the passed Q B would bid fair
to become a terrible weapon) ; 2 K—Kt 3, K—K 2
(one would expect 2 ... K—K 3 ; with the idea of
doubling Rooks on the K R file) ; 3 K—R 4, K—K 3 ;
4 K—Kt 5, R—Q 1 ; 5 Q—Kt 4, (by his lackadaisical
moves Black has allowed the hostile pieces to occupy

the best possible positions for the attack. Compare the
respective positions of the Kings as well as the activity
of the Queen with the disconnected formation of the
Rooks. This example is valuable in illustrating what
should not be done) 5 ... R—K Kt 1 ; 6 P—Q R 4,
Kt P × P ; 7 Q—Kt 7, R (Kt 1)—Q B 1 ; 8 Q—Kt 7
(and now the white Queen runs amuck) ; 8 ... R (B 1)—
B 2 ; 9 Q × P *ch*, K—K 2 ; 10 Q—Kt 7 *ch*, K—K 1 ;
11 Q—Kt 8 *ch*, K—K 2 ; 12 P × P, (there is nothing
to be done against the two united passed pawns) 12
... P—R 6 ; 13 P—B 6 *ch*, K—Q 2 ; 14 Q—B 7 *ch*,
K—Q 1 ; 15 Q—B 8 *ch*, and Black resigns.

EXERCISES

In Diag. 93 White plays and wins. How ? Find
the way and explain the principles.

No. 93.

Philidor

In Diagram 94 pay no attention to the Bishops and
consider the ending as a contest of two Rooks against

No. 94.

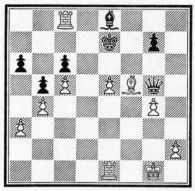

Reshevsky *v.* Botvinnik
"Avro" Tournament, 1938

Queen : Black has the move.   What is the result, and why ?

THE BISHOP AND THE KNIGHT

The superiority of the Bishop over the Knight has become an accepted fact. And yet these pieces are exchanged, especially in the opening, with such light-heartedness, and without any apparent advantage to either player, that one is tempted to look upon this claim as purely abstract. There are so many positions in which the Knight is more effective than the Bishop, there are so many players who prefer the Knight, because they handle it admirably and achieve success with infinite delicacy and lightness of touch that, for all practical purposes, these pieces become equal. In their friendly rivalry, the Knight and the Bishop emphasize each other's capacity and deeper characteristics, and for that reason it is best to study them together.

These characteristics are revealed in the end game more clearly than in any other phase of the game, and so the Bishop's superiority is here more clearly marked.

A Knight is more or less unable to stop a passed pawn or to give a threatened pawn adequate protection : on account of its short range, it can nearly always be driven from a position which is essential for the performance of its duties. A Bishop, on the other hand, on account of its long range is admirably adapted to fulfil either task to perfection. Again, a powerful piece can pursue a Knight, which cannot escape as can a Bishop. Where the Knight plays a poor part, the Bishop fights as an equal.

However, besides the Bishop's fine qualities, the end game also shows up its defects, chief of which is its inability to control squares of the opposite colour. A full half of the board remains, for the Bishop, *terra incognita*. And so it can easily happen that, in an ending, a Bishop remains entirely useless, and that then a Knight is greatly superior : it is therefore necessary, instead of speaking of Bishops in general, to make a distinction between Bishops of one or the other colour : in an end game there are nearly always a good and a bad Bishop, the wrong and the right Bishop. They are two distinct pieces, and it is by no means a matter of indifference whether the end game phase is reached with Bishops of the same or of opposite colours. But each Bishop is an admirable complement of the other, and both together they control, between them, the whole board and nearly equal two Rooks in power except for the fact that, unlike the Rooks, they cannot engineer double threats. No square escapes their influence and they can put up an impassable barrage. They are not simply two Bishops but a pair of Bishops, whereas the Knights always remain two single Knights. This latter is perhaps the weakest combination of any two pieces, which fact is emphasized by their inability to inflict a mate, whilst a Bishop and Knight can mate with a certain amount of difficulty and two Bishops much more easily. Two Knights in combination do not substantially increase their field of action and can, in certain circumstances, impede each other : when they guard each other, they are, so to speak, rooted to the spot, and can be extricated only with difficulty.   Neither can move without the other being lost, unless it moves with a check or a threat to a more valuable unit.   That is why a Bishop and Knight are to be preferred to two Knights, although the combination, as a team, is not particularly effective, and inferior certainly to the two Bishops.   At the same time, the Bishop and Knight, in spite of their marked dissimilarity, agree fairly well and, with skilful handling, can be a dangerous weapon. Without increasing each other's powers, they make up for their mutual and natural defects.   The Knight will threaten the squares which are inaccessible to the Bishop whilst the Bishop, by means of his long range, will control each square which the Knight cannot reach. They divide the task in hand : the Bishop undertakes far-reaching strategic plans, leaving short tactical diversions to its comrade.   The Knight revels in imaginative combinations, whilst the Bishop rather tends to positional solidity.   Justifying its name, the Bishop is solid and restful ; the Knight is by nature a more restless and disquieting piece.

The Bishop also rectifies one of the Knight's main defects : the Knight cannot gain a *tempo* : as the colour of its squares changes with every move, it is always on a square of the same colour on either odd or even moves. It can ramble across the whole board, make a large number of moves, but if it started from a black square there will be no variation in the colour on either even or odd moves.   He cannot therefore return to the original square except in an even number of moves and cannot bring about the same position with a change in "the move," which, in an ending, can be of paramount importance.   This is where the Bishop steps in.   It can return to the original square in two moves instead of one and thus, at will, revert to the original position, with the other side to play.

With regard to the Bishop, if it is weak in the middle game and without the control of an important open diagonal, it can usually recover its full power, by being given some other objective.   In an ending its weakness is nearly always irremediable.   With such a Bishop, the end game must at all cost be avoided.   The Knight, on the other hand, can hardly ever be entirely worthless, as it changes its objectives of its own accord.   Thus it can conceivably be superior to a Bishop ; saving some exceptional cases, there cannot be endings in which any kind of Bishop must be superior to a Knight.   Existing distinctions are not due to hazard or to tactical subtleties : they depend on characteristics of a general nature which are easy to understand and to which we shall revert later.   Their effect can be foreseen and correctly assessed.   As in most cases, endings with Bishop and Knight are won or lost, not by inferior play, but by defective preparation ; failing rightly to appreciate the *rôle* of a Bishop and a Knight in a certain ending, a player lightheartedly embarks upon it and suffers the consequences.

Before analysing endings with Bishop and pawns against Knight and pawns, which form the third major group of end games (pawn endings and endings with Rooks and pawns being the first two), we shall review very shortly the simplest endings with these pieces : the mates and the fight with or against one pawn.   The weakness of these pieces is illustrated by the fact that they cannot mate without the help of another piece, besides the King.   We must therefore examine the mate with two Bishops, Bishop and Knight, and two Knights.

THE MATE WITH TWO BISHOPS

This mate is very easy : it affords no greater difficulty than that with the Rook ; it can be effected in, at most,

18 moves. A mistake to avoid is to give way to a natural tendency to keep the Bishops as close as possible to the adverse King, forgetting that they are equally effective at long range, where they are immune from attack. It must also be remembered that this mate can be effected in a corner, any corner, and, whilst it is easy enough to force the King into the required position, the final stage requires a certain amount of precision, if the agony is not to be unduly prolonged and a stalemate is to be avoided.

According to the author, the mate in Diag. 95 requires

No. 95. White to play and win.

Berger

18 moves : the following solution is shorter, and illustrates more clearly the action of the Bishops and the technique of this end game : 1 B—R 3, K—K 4 ; 2 K—Kt 2, K—Q 5 (diagonal opposition) ; 3 B—Kt 3, K—K 5 ; 4 K—B 3, K—B 6 ; 5 B—Q 6, K—K 5 ; 6 B—K 6, K—K 6 ; (horizontal opposition) ; 7 B— Q 5, (reducing the black King's territory by one diagonal) 7 ... K—K 7 ; 8 B—B 5, K—K 8 ; 9 B—B 4, K—Q 8 ; 10 B—B 2, K—B 8 ; 11 B—K 2, K—Kt 8 ; 12 K— Kt 3, (in order to effect the mate, the King must be

posted at Q Kt 3 or Q B 2) 12 ... K—B 8 ; 13 B—K 3 *ch*, K—Kt 8 ; 14 B—Q 3 *ch*, K—R 8 ; 15 B—Q 4 mate.

THE BISHOP AND KNIGHT MATE

This mate is much more difficult and takes many more moves : there are positions in which as many as 40 moves are required. It can be effected only in a corner which is determined by the colour of the Bishop, which must be the same as that of the corner square. The process comprises two phases : first the King must be driven to the edge of the board and it is nearly always impossible to prevent him from reaching the wrong corner where the mate cannot be effected ; the King must then be driven into the required corner. In the first phase, it is necessary to know the manner in which the action of the pieces must be co-ordinated. The best method is : the Bishop in direct opposition to the King, and the Knight on the square behind the Bishop on the diagonal, so that the King is unable to move up to the Bishop in order to attack it, e.g. : B at K 4, Kt at Q 3, the hostile King at his K 3. Another method of placing the pieces is as follows : The Bishop is so posted that it cuts off the hostile King from the major part of the board, whilst the Knight, from a square of the same colour as the Bishop, prevents the King from escaping *via* the two squares of the opposite colour, e.g. : B at K Kt 6, Kt at Q 5, the hostile King at his K B 6. By a combination of these two methods, the King is driven towards the edge in the shortest possible time.

In the second phase the danger of a stalemate looms large over the proceedings.

There are many mating formations, but the white King must always be at Kt 6 or B 7, the Bishop must threaten R 8, standing at Kt 7 or anywhere on the long diagonal, and the Knight must attack the adjacent square

Kt 8 or R 7, and must therefore mark time at Q 7, B 6 or R 6.

Let us analyse the two phases mentioned, beginning with the second, in order to see how the ultimate object is achieved. Imagine the following position : White : K at Q B 6, Kt at Q B 7, B at Q R 7, Black : K at his Q B 1. 1 Kt—Q 5, (1 Kt—K 6 stalemate) 1 ... K—Q 1 ; 2 B—B 2, K—K 1 (2 ... K—B 1 ; 3 B— Kt 3, K—Q 1 ; 4 B—B 7 *ch*, K—B 1 ; the wrong move ; 5 Kt—Kt 6 mate, and not in the corner) ; 3 K—Q 6, K—B 2 ; (3 ... K—Q 1 ; 4 Kt—K 7,) 4 K—K 5, K—Kt 3 ; 5 K—B 4, K—R 4 (leaving the fatal corner); 6 K—B 5, K—R 3 ; 7 Kt—B 4, (guarding K Kt 6 and K R 5) 7 ... K—Kt 2 ; 8 K—K 6, K—R 3 ; 9 B—R 4, (it is now clear why the Bishop retired to K B 2 on the second move) 9 ... K—Kt 2 ; 10 B—K 7, K—R 3 ; 11 K—B 7, K—R 2 ; 12 B—B 8, K—R 1 ; 13 Kt—R 5, (the Knight must be enabled to attack K R 7) 13 ... K—R 2 ; 14 Kt—B 6 *ch*, K—R 1 ; 15 B—Kt 7, mate.

And now let us set up a position with the King in the centre and see how he can be forced into a corner. It must be remembered that the Knight's main task is to guard the squares which cannot be attacked by the Bishop, and that it is a case of preventing the King from escaping from a restricted territory rather than of ceaseless threats, and finally, that the attacking King must move closer to his rival whenever the pieces have obtained the requisite formation. Imagine the following position : White : K at Q 1, B at Q 2, Kt at Q B 2, Black : K at his Q 1. 1 Kt—Q 4, K—K 2 ; 2 B—B 4, K—B 3 ; 3 K—K 2, K—K 2 ; 4 B—K 5 (the ideal formation for the pieces : the author prescribes here 4 K—B 3, but the line of play in the text demonstrates the method more clearly), 4 ... K—Q 2 ; 5 K—K 3, K—K 2 ; 6 K—K 4, K—Q 2 ; 7 K—Q 5, K—K 2 ; 8 Kt—K 2, (the Knight is intended to deprive the black

King of a flight square at K Kt 3), 8 ... K—Q 2 (8 ...
K—B 2 ; 9 Kt—B 4,) 9 B—Q 6, K—Q 1 ; 10 K—K 6,
K—B 1 (10 ... K—K 1; 11 B—B 7,); 11 B—Kt 4,
(guarding Q R 5) 11 ... K—B 2 ; 12 Kt—Q 4, K—Kt 2;
13 K—Q 7, K—Kt 3 ; 14 K—Q 6, K—Kt 2 ; 15
B—R 5, K—R 3; 16 B—B 7, K—Kt 2; 17 K—Q 7,
K—R 3 ; 18 K—B 6, K—R 2 ; 19 Kt—K 6, K—R 3 ;
20 B—Q 8, K—R 2; 21 B—Kt 6 *ch*, K—R 1; 22
Kt—B 7 *ch*, K—Kt 1 ; 23 B—B 5, K—B 1 ; 24 B—
R 7, and we arrive at the preceding position with Black
to play, which is more advantageous for White : 24 ...
K—Q 1 ; 25 Kt—Q 5, etc. The only difficulty is
really the necessity of not wasting any moves and to
effect the mate in the prescribed number of moves, as
otherwise the game will end in a draw.

THE MATE WITH TWO KNIGHTS

A mate with two Knights is possible, but it cannot
be enforced. In the position : White : K at Q Kt 6,
Kts at Q B 6 and Q B 7, Black : K at Q R 1 ; it is clear
that Black on his last move must have played ... K—R 1 ;
and that he could equally well have played ... K—B 1.
Another position : White : K at Q Kt 6, Kts at K 7
and Q B 6, Black : K at his Q Kt 1. Black must play
... K—R 1. Now the Knight at K 7 must move up
to give mate, which requires but two moves, Kt—Q 5,
and Kt—B 7. But after the first move, Black is stalemated and White cannot carry out his plan. In order
to force a mate with two Knights, the adversary must
have a pawn, which will make the necessary moves to
avoid stalemate. And so, the player who remains with
two Knights must on no account capture all the opposing
pawns : he must leave one, being thereby generous, not
to his opponent, but to himself. At the same time, not
every pawn can ensure victory : if it is too far advanced,
it will queen before mate is effected and win the game
after all. How many moves are at our disposal to effect

the mate ?   Presuming that the opposing King is in a
semi-stalemate position at his Q R 1, the attacker's
King at Q Kt 6, the Knight at Q 6, a check must
now be given by the other Knight at Q B 6 followed
by mate in two by the Kt at Q 6 after Kt—Kt 5—B 7.
We have therefore three moves.   Supposing the black
pawn is at its K B 6, there is no time to effect the mate.
There is sufficient time if the pawn is at its K B 5, for
then 1 Kt—Q 4, P—B 6 ; 2 Kt—B 6, P—B 7 ; 3
Kt—Kt 5, P—B 8 (Q) ; 4 Kt—B 7 mate.   With the
pawn at its K Kt 5 this would not be possible, as the
pawn would queen with check.

However, the pawn's position is not the only important
point.   With the Knight at K Kt 3, it would reach
Q B 6 in three moves instead of two.   With the King
in a stalemate position at K R 8, matters would again
be different.   The King must therefore be driven into
the proper corner.   The defender will try his hardest
to reach the (for him) more favourable corner and to
push forward his pawn as far as possible ; on the contrary, the owner of the two Knights will try to stop the
pawn's progress by placing one of the Knights in front
of it and to drive the King into the corner best suited
for that Knight's manœuvres, and to place his pieces in
the manner which will in the quickest time lead to a
mate.   These manœuvres require delicate handling and
need some twelve moves or so.

The following example illustrates the method em-
ployed : White : K at K 4, Kts at Q 3 and K R 3,
Black : K at his Q B 5, pawn at K R 5. 1 Kt (Q 3)—
B 4, K—B 4 ; 2 K—Q 3, K—B 3 ; 3 K—B 4, K—Q 3 ;
4 K—Q 4, K—B 3 ; 5 Kt—Q 3, K—Q 3 ; 6 Kt—B 5,
K—B 3 ; 7 Kt—K 4, K—Kt 4 ; 8 K—B 3, K—B 3 ;
9 K—B 4, K—Kt 3 ; 10 Kt—B 3, K—B 3 ; 11 Kt—
Q Kt 5, K—Kt 3 ; 12 Kt—Q 4, K—R 4 ; 13 K—Kt 3,
K—Kt 3 ; 14 K—Kt 4, K—R 3 ; 15 Kt—Kt 3, K—
Kt 3 ; 16 Kt—R 5, K—R 3 ; 17 Kt—Q B 4, K—Kt 2 ;

18 K—B 5, K—B 2 ; 19 Kt—Kt 6, K—Kt 2 ; 20 Kt—Q 5, K—R 3 ; 21 K—Kt 4, K—R 2 ; 22 K—R 5, K—Kt 2 ; 23 K—Kt 5, K—R 2 ; 24 Kt—Kt 4, K—Kt 2 ; 25 Kt—R 6, K—R 2 ; 26 Kt—B 5, K—Kt 1 ; 27 K—B 6, K—B 1 ; 28 Kt—Kt 7, K—Kt 1 ; 29 Kt—Q 6, K—R 2 ; 30 K—Kt 5, K—Kt 1 ; 31 K—Kt 6, K—R 1 ; now the desired position is reached and White can play for the mate 32 Kt—Q Kt 5, K—Kt 1 ; 33 Kt—R 7, K—R 1 ; 34 Kt—B 4, P—R 6 ; 35 Kt—B 6, P—R 7 ; 36 Kt—Q 5, P—R 8 (Q) ; 37 Kt—B 7 mate.

With the pawn at K Kt 5 the manœuvre would fail. Interesting as this example is, it is of small practical value as these endings are of very rare occurrence. A. Troitzky, who has made a special study of this ending and is a recognized authority on the subject, counts only six in the whole of master practice.

Minor Piece and Pawn

There is no call to study positions in which a minor piece has to contend against a pawn. As the piece cannot effect a mate, all it has to do is to stop the pawn and secure the draw by an exchange. The Bishop effects this without any difficulty, because of its long range. The same does not apply to the Knight, which must be quite near in order to achieve the same result. At the same time, the "Knight's combination" can be useful here, and is rarely seen to such advantage as in an end game. Two questions have to be answered here : has the distant Knight sufficient time to reach the pawn which is on its way to the queening square ? This is a simple calculation, but it is at the end of this journey that the "Knight combination" frequently occurs ; then, can a Knight, already in close proximity to the pawn, really bar the way or deny it access to a certain square, or will it be driven away by the hostile King supporting his pawn ?

It must be said at once that the Knight's task is more difficult when dealing with a R P, for then its radiation is curtailed and it can manœuvre only on one side of the pawn so that, if the pawn has already reached the seventh rank, it cannot be stopped. In the case of other pawns the Knight's wheeling manœuvres are successful. Examine the position : White : K at Q R 5, P at Q Kt 5 ; Black : K at his K R 8, Kt at K R 7. The play is : 1 P—Kt 6, Kt—B 6 ; 2 P—Kt 7, (2 K—Kt 5, Kt— K 4 ; 3 P—Kt 7, Kt—Q 2 ; 4 K—B 6, Kt—Kt 1 *ch*; 5 K—B 7, Kt—R 3 *ch* ; 6 K—Kt 6, Kt—Kt 1 ;) 2 ... Kt—K 4 ; 3 K—Kt 6 (3 P—Kt 8 (Q), Kt—B 6 *ch*;), 3 ... Kt—Q 2 *ch* ; 4 K—B 7, Kt—B 4 ; 5 P—Kt 8 (Q), Kt—R 6 *ch* ; winning the Queen.

More interesting are positions in which a pawn, supported by a minor piece, has to force its way to the queening square against the opposition of an adverse minor piece. It will here be a question of interrupting the defending Bishop's diagonal or of driving off the defending Knight. In examining the correct means to apply, we shall see that each case, be it with a Knight or a Bishop on the defending side, presents its own particular difficulties. If the corner square is not of the same colour as the attacking Bishop, the pawn cannot queen, if the hostile King has had time to occupy that square. There are no means of driving him out, as can easily be seen. In this case, the defender does not even need to have a minor piece.

When the two minor pieces are Bishops of opposite colours, the game is automatically drawn. Their paths do not cross and the defender's diagonal cannot be blocked. Even in the extreme case in which the defending Bishop is on the wrong diagonal, the game is drawn, provided the defending King has succeeded in occupying in the path of the pawn a square of the opposite colour to that of the attacking Bishop. He cannot by any means be dislodged. That is why most games with

Bishops of opposite colours end in a draw, even when there are many pawns on the board. One side or the other may win one, or even two pawns, but all to no purpose, the pawns cannot queen.

When the R P which has already reached the seventh is guarded by a Knight, it cannot queen provided the defending King has already occupied the corner square in front of the pawn. This was already known many years ago, as is shown in the following position by Ercole del Rio (1750) : White : K at Q R 1, Black : K at his Q B 5, Kt at Q Kt 5, pawn at Q R 7. White plays K—Kt 2—R 1, etc., and draws the game, as the black King cannot move up on account of stalemate. Matters would be entirely different were the black pawn at its Q R 6, for then 1 K—Kt 1, K—Kt 6; 2 K—R 1, Kt—B 7 *ch* ; 3 K—Kt 1, P—R 7 *ch* ; would force the win.

Even when a piece and a pawn ahead, the advance of hostile pawns requires the greatest vigilance. It is part of the charm and difficulty of end game play that attention must not be relaxed at any time, especially in endings which are catalogued and classified, but in which the smallest deviation from the straight path may alter the whole situation. In end games "near enough" is inadmissible.

The other method, which we have seen before, of obtaining a draw with a R P is also effective when there is a Knight in the opposite camp. In this case the King is shut in at R 8 with his own pawn at R 7, whilst the opposing King guards the outlet from B 7 or B 8. The presence of the Knight does not interfere with this plan, but it is necessary to pay attention to the colour of the squares available for the Knight. As we have mentioned before, the Knight cannot gain a move, and the colour of its squares alternates with every move ; therefore it is important, when the Knight deprives the opposing King of one of these squares, that in order to win it should do so without check.

This also has long been known and was shown in an example by Salvio in 1604 : White : K at Q R 8, Kt at K Kt 1, pawn at Q R 7, Black : K at his Q B 2.   If White has "the move" the game is drawn.   But White wins if "the move" is Black's.   1 Kt—K 2, K—B 1 ; 2 Kt—B 4, K—B 2 ; 3 Kt—Q 5 *ch*, K—B 1 ; 4 Kt— K 7 *ch*, K—B 2 ; draw.   But if, instead, 1 ... K—B 1 ; 2 Kt—K 2, K—B 2 ; 3 Kt—B 4, K—B 1 ; 4 Kt—Q 5, and the King must relinquish his post of observation and let the prisoner escape.   The Knight's inability to gain a *tempo*, the peculiarity of its manœuvres, alternately on white and black squares, is clearly demonstrated in examples of this kind.   But, again, had the pawn been less advanced and still been at Q R 6 (the white King at Q R 7, the black King at his Q B 2), the game is easily won irrespective of "the move." 1 Kt—K 2, K—B 1 ; 2 Kt—Q 4, K—B 2 ; 3 Kt— Kt 5 *ch*, K—B 1 ; 4 K—Kt 6, K—Kt 1 ; 5 P—R 7 *ch*, K—R 1 ; 6 Kt—B 7 mate, or 1 ... K—B 1 ; 2 Kt— K 2, K—B 2 ; 3 Kt—B 3, K—B 1 ; 4 Kt—Kt 5, K—Q 2 ; 5 K—Kt 7, and wins.

We shall now pass on to endings with a pawn and Bishops of the same colour or with a Bishop opposing the Knight.

In order to stop the adverse Bishop from stopping our passed pawn, our own Bishop must block up the diagonal and drive its rival away, but not, however, on to another and equally important one.   This manœuvre seems simple, but it cannot at all times be effected, so that the result is sometimes a win, sometimes a draw. In the following position : White : K at K B 8, B at Q B 6, pawn at K 7, Black : K at his Q 3, B at K R 4, White plays 1 B—K 8, B—Q 8 (with the choice of two diagonals aiming at K 1) ; 2 B—Kt 5, B—R 4 ; 3 B—B 4, (3 B—K 2, B—Kt 3;) B—Kt 3; 4 B—B 7, and wins.   This result depends on a number of subtle points. For instance, with the black King at his K B 3, the game would be drawn, for the white Bishop could not go to K B 7, and so, with the move, Black could avoid the worst danger by 1 ... K—K 4 ; and after 4 B—B 4, K—B 3 ; thwarting all his adversary's plans. Again, supposing that one of the diagonals which our Bishop must utilize be very short, and for this we move the whole position one square to the left (pawn at Q 7), the game would also be a draw, but for a different reason. Our Bishop will be unable to change diagonals on the second and third move as in the preceding example, e.g., 1 B—Q 8, B—Q 7 ; and now the white Bishop should play to Q R 5. But this square is guarded by the opposing Bishop. If 2 B—Kt 6, Black does not recapture, but answers 2 ... B—Kt 5 ; and White cannot continue with 3 B—B 5, because the Bishop can now be taken. If, on the contrary, we move the position one square to the right, with Black's Bishop at K R 3, it would be Black who would suffer from the shortness of the diagonal on which his Bishop has to manœuvre : White plays 1 B—B 4, on his first move and wins at once.

Knight endings are no more difficult, but they are based on different *data*. The Knight cannot be effective at long range and must be near the pawn ; it must be the opponent's task to drive it away, but he must be on the watch against the Knight forking the King and the new Queen.

In Diag. 96, a position from tournament play, the win was achieved in the following manner : 1 K—B 7, Kt—B 2 ; (1 ... Kt—Q 3 *ch* ; 2 K—B 8, followed by 3 Kt—B 7) ; 2 Kt—K 6, Kt—Kt 4 ; 3 K—B 8 (3 P—Q 8 (Q), Kt—Q 3 *ch*) ; 3 ... Kt—Q 3 ; 4 Kt—Q 8, and wherever the black King moves, 5 Kt—B 7, or Kt—Kt 7, wins. The secret of this win is to place the King in proximity to the pawn but on a square of the colour which avoids a fork.

In the contest between Bishop and Knight, it happens that the Knight is able to debar the Bishop from the

No. 96. White to play.

Möller *v.* Englund
Hanover, 1902

peaceful occupation of its diagonal, but not without subtle play, e.g. : White : K at K 7, Kt at K 4, pawn at K B 6, Black : K at his Q B 8, B at Q Kt 6.   Here White wins because one of the Bishop's diagonals is very short and can be controlled by King and Knight. 1 Kt—Kt 5, (threat 2 Kt—K 6,) 1 ... B—Kt 1 ; 2 Kt—B 7 (threat 3 K—B 8, e.g., 2 ... K—Q 7 ; 3 K— B 8, B—R 2 ; 4 Kt—Kt 5, B—Q 6 ; 5 Kt—K 6, B—Kt 3 ; 6 Kt—B 4, B—B 7 ; 7 K—K 7, B—Kt 6 ; 8 Kt—K 6,) 2 ... B—R 2 ; 3 Kt—R 6, B—Kt 3 (now the Bishop is on a short diagonal with only two available squares, White's K R 5 and K Kt 6, which can be simultaneously attacked by the Knight from K B 4, the actual object of its manœuvres) ; 4 Kt—B 5, K—Q 7 ; 5 Kt—R 4, B—R 4 ; 6 Kt—Kt 2, followed by 7 Kt—B 4. It is seen how uncertain are the chances of a win ; with one square more on the diagonal, nothing fatal could have happened : or, with the defending King a little nearer, the Knight's operations would have failed.

In the case of the R P there are additional *finesses* sometimes at the expense of the Bishop.   In Diag. 97

No. 97. White to play and draw.

Loyd

the Bishop, by a piquant suicide, presents its side with an unhoped-for draw.   1 B—Q 7, P—R 7 ; 2 B—B 6 *ch*, K—Kt 8 (2 ... Kt—B 6 *ch* ; 3 K—K 2,); 3 B—R 1, K × B (3 ... Kt—Kt 7 *ch* ; 4 K—K 2, Kt—B 5 *ch* ; 5 K—K 1,); 4 K—B 2, draw.   We already know this position, and it is clear that 4 K—B 1 would be un-pardonable, as it would lose after 4 ... Kt—B 4 ; 5 K—B 2, Kt—Kt 6 ; 6 K × Kt, K—Kt 8 ; etc.   It is always essential to take into account the colour of squares which the Knight patronizes, and not to allow it to approach the King *without check*.   The King must occupy a square of the same colour as the Knight's actual square.   Who would think of such things in the opening or the middle game?   In the end game it is essential to do so at all times.

Normally a weak defensive piece, the Knight can stop a pawn protected by a Bishop, provided it is near enough and posted on a square of the opposite colour : the Knight cannot then be dislodged.   It is too late to think of winning; the Bishop's powers against a Knight should have been utilized earlier, when the Knight was still away.   Although it cannot force the capture of a

Knight on an open board, a Bishop of either colour can restrict the Knight so that it is deprived of all mobility. In the following position : White : K at K Kt 5, B at K B 7, pawn at K 5 ; Black : K at his Q 1, Kt at Q R 4, White's first move wins : 1 B—Q 5, and the Knight has no move. Only the King can impede the pawn's progress. 1 ... K—K 2 ; 2 K—B 5, K—Q 2 ; 3 K—B 6, K—K 1 ; 4 P—K 6, K—B 1 ; 5 P—K 7 *ch*, K—K 1 ; 6 K—K 6, followed by 7 B—B 6 mate.

In this illustration the Knight is on the edge of the board, but a similar effect can be obtained in the centre. For example, a Knight at Q 4 is temporarily immobilized by a Bishop at Q 7. In such cases the whole contest centres round the Bishop's efforts at restraining the action of the Knight, preventing its getting nearer to the pawn, causing it to waste many moves in order to reach its object by roundabout ways. In addition, the Bishop can lose a *tempo*, which, as we have seen, the Knight is unable to do.

EXERCISES

In Diag. 98 White plays and wins. Find the win and explain White's manœuvres.

No. 98.

Centurini

In Diag. 99 White wins even without the move ;
give the continuation with Black to play.

No. 99.

Marks

Bishop and Pawns

When there is one Bishop left on either side, each
accompanied by a number of pawns, it is necessary first
to proceed to an analysis of the position on the lines
which should, by now, be familiar to us.   The relative
position of the Kings, the pawns and, especially, the
Bishops, is investigated, in order to establish which side
has more space and more mobility, which Bishop may
be deprived of freedom and remain shut in.   To this
is added one characteristic which does not occur in the
case of the Rooks, the colour of the Bishops.   Both
Bishops may be perfectly free and yet one of them remains
useless and the other very powerful.   If the opposing
pawns are on squares of the opposite colour, our Bishop
can undertake nothing and will, to the end, remain a
bad Bishop, whereas a good Bishop is on squares of the
same colour as the adversary's pawns.   It is extremely
bad play, when exchanging pieces for the end game, to
preserve a bad Bishop, whatever piece remains on the

opposite side ; a Knight proves far stronger than such a Bishop, and, to an even greater extent, a good adverse Bishop.   Another characteristic of these endings is the readiness with which a Bishop can be sacrificed to advantage.   We have already seen that a Queen can practically never be sacrificed against pawns, the Rook sometimes against several pawns, but a Bishop can frequently be given up for a single pawn, if the way is thereby cleared for an advanced pawn.   If a pawn has reached Q Kt 6, what could be simpler than to sacrifice the Bishop for a pawn at Q R 6 ?   This threat makes the position of the defending Bishop still more awkward : not only must it guard pawns which have not the protection of another pawn, but the possibility of such a sacrifice is ever present and the mere threat often impedes its every movement.

Generally speaking, these endings are not of frequent occurrence nor are they particularly interesting, being much easier to handle than Rook endings.   A single Bishop cannot set up an impassable barrage for the opposing King, who can therefore easily penetrate into the enemy camp ; then a bad Bishop can never threaten anything of particular moment : therefore, the counter-attacks, which in Rook endings so often redress the balance, do not happen in the case of Bishops.

We shall give only one example of an ending with Bishops of the same colour (Diag. 100).   Here the white Bishop is manifestly the stronger of the two : Black's Bishop not only is a "bad Bishop" (all the white pawns are on black squares), but it is shut in, and has to guard all the pawns, especially the Q R P. All it can do is to mark time at Q Kt 2 and Q B 1. White's difficulty consists in his inability to penetrate into the adverse lines, as the position is blocked.   The game ended in a draw after 1 P—K 4, P—Q 5 ; and there is no possibility of a break through.   Subsequent analysis proved that there are chances of a win for White

if he first places his King at Q 4, preventing ... P—Q 5 ;
and only then advances the K P.   He would thus obtain
a passed pawn at K 5.   Then, attacking the B P with
his Bishop, he would play P—Kt 5, obtaining, with this
sacrifice, yet another passed pawn, which would have
forced a win.

No. 100. White to play.

Dr. Lasker *v.* Bogatyrtschuk
Moscow, 1935

It would lead too far to investigate how this plan
could be carried out and whether it would really be
effective : it is sufficient for our purpose to indicate the
probable line of play as it explains sufficiently well the
line of action of a Bishop when opposed to another of
the same colour.

We have already remarked that Bishops of opposite
colours are the combination of pieces most likely to lead
to a draw.   Amongst the many reasons for the truth
of this assertion is the fact that in most cases the pawns
on either side are on squares of opposite colours and
the Bishops are both either "good" or "bad."

With Bishops of opposite colours this question is unimportant : their ways do not clash : the one cannot

blockade the other, nor can there be repeated attacks on
a weak pawn which commit the adverse Bishop to the
defence : with Bishops of opposite colours, neither of
them can defend whatever the other attacks.   Their
action develops quite independently : each one moves as
if the other did not exist.   The fate of the battle depends
solely on the respective positions of the Kings and the
pawns.   An extra pawn is rarely sufficient to win, but
with the superior position, the extra pawn may become a
dangerous passed pawn and bring in other advantages.

In Diag. 101 the position after two moves becomes

No. 101. White to play.

Nimzowitsch *v.* Capablanca
Riga, 1913

an ending with Bishops of opposite colours.   Black has
an extra pawn in addition to other advantages : the
possibility of obtaining a passed pawn on the K side
and the unfavourable factor for White of having doubled
and isolated pawns on the Q side.   The pawn at Q B 2
in particular will require to be protected : therefore the
white King can be tied to its defence.   Finally, White's
Q R P cannot be held and, if it moves forward, it will be

attacked by the black King who threatens to invade White's territory via his Q B 5 or Q Kt 4—Q R 5. All this is still vague ; let us see with what consummate mastery Black accomplishes his task : 1 B × K B P, R—Q 8 ; 2 B—K 5, R × R *ch* ; 3 K × R, B × P ; 4 P—Q R 4 (in order to advance this pawn to its fifth, where it can be guarded by the Bishop ; Black crosses this plan in a manner both astute and elegant), 4 ... K—K 3 ; 5 B—Kt 8, P—Q R 4 ; 6 K—K 1 (6 B—B 7, P—Kt 4 ; refuting the advance of White's Q R P, for after an exchange Black would obtain a passed pawn on the Q R file), 6 ... K—Q 4 ; 7 K—Q 2, B—Q 2 ; 8 B—B 7, K—B 3 ; 9 B—Q 8 (9 B × P, P—Kt 3 ; winning the Bishop ; very probably White had not foreseen this charming manœuvre by Black, and he now remains yet another pawn down), 9 ... P—Kt 3 ; 10 P—B 4, K—Kt 2 ; 11 K—B 3, B × P ; 12 K—Kt 2, B—Q 2 ; 13 K—Kt 3, B—K 3 ; 14 K—B 3, P—R 5 ; 15 K—Q 3, K—B 3 ; 16 K—B 3, P—Kt 5 ; 17 B—R 4, P—R 4 ; 18 B—Kt 3, P—R 6 ; 19 K—Kt 3, B × P *ch* (again very attractive play) ; 20 K × P (this is a useless pawn, which could not win with a white-square Bishop. If 20 K × B, P—R 7 ; 21 B—K 5, P—R 5 ; 22 K—Kt 3, P—Kt 6 ; 23 P × P, P—R 6 ;) ; 20 ... P—Kt 4 ; 21 P—B 3, K—Q 4 ; 22 B—B 2, B—K 7 ; 23 K—Kt 3, B—Q 8 *ch* ; 24 K—Kt 2, K—B 5 ; 25 K—B 1, B—B 6 ; 26 K—Q 2, P—Kt 5 ; 27 P × P, P × P ; 28 B—R 4, B—K 5 ; 29 B—B 6, B—Kt 3 ; 30 B—R 4, P—Q Kt 6 ; 31 B—B 6, P—R 5 ; 32 K—K 3, P—Kt 6 ; 33 P × P, P—R 6 ; 34 K—B 2, B—B 4 ; 35 P—Kt 4, B × P ; 36 K—Kt 3, K—Q 6 ; and White resigns.

After losing a second pawn, White fought a desperate battle against the passed pawns on either wing. Black jealously kept his K R P, of which the queening square corresponded to the colour of his Bishop, and gave up his Q R P without regret, as, with a white-square Bishop, it could not be made to queen.

KNIGHT AND PAWNS

Endings with Knights are usually lively, because they readily adapt themselves to unforeseen combinations. They may be more difficult. First of all there is no absolutely safe square as is the case with the Bishop, when the King only needs to seek squares of the opposite colour. Then the Knight, lacking the Bishop's long range, takes much more time to stop or to win a pawn ; each pawn, especially when more distant, presents a more serious danger than in any other ending. The most exact calculation is needed to ascertain whether a Knight really has the time to collect a pawn on the other side of the board and to return usefully to the main battlefield. The question of time in this type of end game assumes a particularly important character.

In Diag. 102, after the speedy elimination of the

No. 102. Black to play.

Znosko-Borovsky *v.* Dr. Seitz
Nice, 1930

Rooks, there is a keen contest between the distant pawns on either wing, Black's on the Q side and White's on the K side. The pawns are equal, but Black must have spent a great deal of time in regaining a pawn which he had lost.   This gives White a considerable advantage, whereby he will be able not only to stop the adverse passed pawns, but ultimately to win them, whilst Black's Knight will have to rush to the other side to prevent White from obtaining a fresh Queen.   It is important to note that in all endings in general, whoever is the first to effect a capture, or to emerge from a series of exchanges, has the advantage, for time is an essential factor in the end game, and in Knight endings it is invaluable.

1 ... R—Q 1 (quite rightly Black wants to get his forces into play ; by this temporary sacrifice of a pawn, which he will soon recover, he even obtains two united passed pawns on the Q side, whilst the adverse Knight strays from the centre of the struggle.   If he had saved his pawn by 1 ... P—B 4, his pieces would remain too passive after 2 Kt—B 6, P—R 3 ; 3 R— Q 1) ; 2 Kt × B P, R—Q 7 ; 3 P—K 3, R×P ; 4 P—Q R 3, Kt—R 4 (the K R P cannot be saved) ; 5 Kt×P, Kt—B 5; 6 K—Kt 1, (the threat was 6 ... Kt×P *ch* ; if 6 K—B 3, P—B 4 ; threatening ... Kt—Q 7 *ch*;) 6 ... P—Kt 4 ; 7 Kt—B 6, R—Kt 6 ; 8 P—K R 4, (the treasure hunt on both sides.   If instead 8 P—Q R 4, P—Kt 5) 8 ... R × R P (as always, preserving the Rook would afford chances of a draw) ; 9 R × R, Kt × R; 10 P—R 5, (now the real battle begins.   The white King would not be in time to stop the Kt P, and if 10 Kt—Q 5, Kt—B 5 ; Black can stop the K R P without having weakened his pawns) 10 ... P—Kt 5 ; 11 Kt—Q 5, P—Kt 6 ; 12 Kt—B 3, Kt—Kt 4 ; 13 Kt—R 4, (a very important move, the Knight not only stops the two pawns, but also prevents the adverse King from approaching) 13 ... Kt—Q 3 ; 14 P—R 6, P—B 3; 15 P—R 7, Kt—B 2 ; (the pawns are equal, but there is a difference.   The white King can easily reach and capture the black pawns, whilst the black King can retaliate only with considerable loss of

time and with the Knight out of play) ; 16 K—B 1,
K—Kt 1 (16 ... K—Kt 2 ; 17 Kt—B 5 *ch,*); 17 K—K 2,
K—B 2 ; 18 K—Q 3, K—Q 1 ; 19 K—B 3, K—K 2 ;
20 Kt—B 5, (to stop the black King for the time being,
as if 20 ... K—B 1 ; then 21 Kt—K 6 *ch*, K—K 2 ;
22 Kt—Kt 7, K—B 1 ; 23 Kt—B 5,) 20 ... Kt—R 1 ;
21 Kt × R P, K—B 2 ; 22 Kt—B 5, K—Kt 2 ; 23 Kt—
Q 7, Kt—B 2 (if 23 ... P—K 5 ; 24 K × P, P—B 4 ;
25 K—B 4, K × P ; 26 P—Kt 4, P × P ; 27 Kt—B 6 *ch*,
K—Kt 3; 28 Kt × P,) ; 24 K × P, K × P (this loses
forthwith, but the game can no longer be saved, e.g.,
24 ... P—B 4 ; 25 K—B 4, K × P ; 26 K—Q 5,
P—K 5 ; 27 K—K 6, K—Kt 3 ; 28 P—Kt 4, P × P ;
29 Kt—K 5 *ch*, Kt × Kt ; 30 K × Kt, and wins.   Thanks
to his having made the first capture, White is always
ahead of his adversary : note that his King was able to
afford a double journey, from the K side to the Q side,
and back again to the centre) ; 25 Kt × P *ch*, K—Kt 3 ;
26 Kt—K 4, K—B 4 ; 27 P—B 3, K—K 3 ; 28 K—B 4,
Kt—R 3 ; 29 P—Kt 4, Kt—B 2 ; 30 K—B 5, Kt—R 3 ;
31 K—B 6, Kt—B 2 ; 32 Kt—B 5 *ch*, K—B 3 ; 33
K—Q 5, and Black resigns.

In order to gain a better understanding of the characteristics of the Kt end game, it is good to imagine the same
ending with any other piece.   In the example just shown,
a Bishop or a Rook could stop the white R P and, at
the same time, take part in the contest in other quarters ;
the pawn, on the other hand, would require the support
of its own pieces before it could advance.   Against a
Knight, a passed pawn can fight its own battle and is in
need of no support : it is not immobilized by the Knight;
on the contrary, the Knight suffers this disability.   The
Knight's attack is ineffective, for the passed pawn escapes
simply by advancing, and the Knight must lose much
time in returning to the attack.

Another example (Diag. 103) shows the contest
between a distant pawn and a centre pawn, and we are

quite prepared to see the R P win. But the reduced
material renders the win problematical, nor does the

No. 103. White to play.

Dr. Lasker *v.* Nimzowitsch
Zürich, 1934

presence of the Knight make the task easier. 1 K—B 1,
K—B 3 ; 2 K—Q 2, K—K 4; 3 K—K 3, P—K R 4;
4 P—R 3, P—R 4 ; 5 Kt—R 3, Kt—B 7 *ch* ; 6 K—
Q 3, (White fears the threat ... Kt × P ; and eschews
6 K—Q 2, and yet, as demonstrated by Alekhine, this
sacrifice would not then secure the win : 6 K—Q 2,
Kt × P ; 7 P × Kt, K × P ; 8 K—B 3, P—Kt 4 ; 9
Kt—B 2 *ch*, etc. Therefore the black Knight would
have to return to its Q 5, and it is not clear how Black
would have realized the plan which now succeeds so
well, namely to play his Knight to its K 4, without
allowing the white King to occupy his K B 4) 6 ...
Kt—K 8 *ch* ; 7 K—K 2, Kt—Kt 7 ; 8 K—B 3, Kt—
R 5 *ch* ; 9 K—K 3, Kt—Kt 3 (what wanderings a
Knight can undertake across the chessboard !) ; 10
Kt—Kt 5, K—B 3 ; 11 Kt—R 7 *ch*, K—Kt 2 ; 12
Kt—Kt 5, K—B 3 ; 13 Kt—R 7 *ch*, K—K 2 ; 14
Kt—Kt 5, Kt—K 4 ; 15 K—Q 4, K—Q 3 (at last

Black has succeeded in reaching the desired position, but still the win is by no means forced) ; 16 Kt—R 3, P—Q R 5 ; 17 Kt—B 4, P—R 5 ; 18 Kt—R 3, P—Kt 3 (the pawn takes two moves to get to Kt 4, so that the break through is effected with the Knight away at its K R 3 and not K B 4, whence it could give check); 19 Kt—B 4, P—Kt 4 ; 20 Kt—R 3, Kt—B 3 *ch* ; 21 K—K 3, K—B 4; 22 K—Q 3, P—Kt 5; 23 P × P *ch*, K × P (White's passed pawn is stopped by the opposing Knight, which takes part in the battle over the whole board, whereas the white Knight, occupied as it is in stopping the R P, is out of action : such is the difference between distant and central pawns) ; 24 K—B 2, Kt— Q 5 *ch* ; 25 K—Kt 1, (25 K—Q 3, Kt—K 3; 26 K— B 2, K—B 5) 25 ... Kt—K 3 ; 26 K—R 2, K—B 5 ; 27 K—R 3, K—Q 5 ; 28 K × P, K × P ; 29 P—Kt 4, K—B 6 ; 30 P—Kt 5, K—Kt 7 ; and Black resigns, for if 31 P—Kt 6, K × Kt ; 32 P—Kt 7, Kt—B 4 *ch* ; or again 31 Kt—B 4 *ch*, Kt × Kt ; 32 P—Kt 6, Kt—K 3 ; 33 K—Kt 5, Kt—Q 1 ; and the end is brought about by a Knight combination, a worthy termination to a Knight ending.

What precision such an end game demands, what calculations ! But all our basic principles are found there, although each single piece requires their special application.

Bishop *v.* Knight

End games in which Bishop and Knight battle for supremacy with the help of their respective pawns are most exciting, and demand of a player a keen sense of position, the ability to build up a strategic plan and a certain amount of imagination for tactical opportunities. These fall mostly to the Knight, and in order to minimize its natural failings, it is always important to keep the Knight dynamically free. The contrary obtains in the case of the Bishop : its strength is shown at its best in vast strategical conceptions. But above all it is necessary to foresee in good time which of the two pieces will prove the stronger in a particular end game, which should for preference be kept, and which one it is wise to exchange as quickly as possible. In most of these endings the Bishop is clearly superior to the Knight. If it is a "good" Bishop, it will win more easily, whilst, against a "bad" Bishop, the Knight can even win. The Bishop can practically immobilize the Knight and undermine its supports which are so important for its safety and as a jumping-off ground for any aggressive action.

The task of assessing the relative value of a Bishop and a Knight is a formidable one and can easily warp a player's judgment of end game play. We have already learnt that a "good" Bishop is the one which is on squares of the same colour as the adverse pawns : reliance can be placed on such a Bishop. But would this notion justify its preference to any sort of Knight ? There may occur in an end game turns which could not be foreseen and which are disadvantageous. This would mostly be due to some important positional details being overlooked and which contain weaknesses quite outside the relative values of Bishop and Knight. To have given these values due consideration does not absolve us from the duty of taking the characteristics of the position into account. You may possess a splendid Bishop against a practically useless Knight and yet lose the game if your King is in a corner, away from the scene of operations which the opposing King has already reached. There is no doubt that the notion of the "good" Bishop is but an approximation and suffices at most for a general survey of the situation long before the end game actually begins. The case of the "bad" Bishop is clearer still ; it is almost without exception of the same colour as its own pawns, which forces him to adopt a purely defensive *rôle* and deprives him of all mobility.   On the other hand it happens but seldom that all our pawns are on squares of the same colour, and we must learn to distinguish between those which are of no importance as far as this appreciation is concerned, and those which are of moment, which present critical weakness or, on the contrary, can be used as a most potent weapon.   Nor must it be forgotten that, besides pawns, there are strong and weak squares, which play a most important part in the result of an ending according to whether we or our adversary will be able to occupy or control them.

Thus, we see, the question becomes complicated. But, for our general guidance, we must remember that in most cases the Bishop is stronger than the Knight. When in doubt, put your trust for preference in the Bishop.   Concerning the Knight, our adversary's or our own, we must clearly grasp the chances which the position affords.   The essential condition for the full deployment of its powers is, as we have said before, that the Knight has some *points d'appui* in the centre, on squares of the opposite colour to that of the adverse Bishop (which, *per contra*, indicates the value of this Bishop).

It could be claimed that, where this condition is not fulfilled, the Knight will prove unequal to its task.   No doubt the other characteristics of this strong piece—mobility, ability to attack critical points, etc.—remain valuable : but only in the circumstances described can a Knight prevail over a Bishop.

Let us examine Diag. 104.   At first sight one might think that Black's position is inferior on account of the doubled pawn and of the isolated pawn on the K side. But his King is in the centre and threatens to take an active part in the struggle.   His mainstay, however, is the Bishop's strong post, whence it dominates the board, attacks pawns and controls all the squares to which the Knight could move ; the Knight has no

No. 104. Black to play.

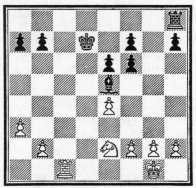

Tchekhover *v.* Dr. Lasker
Moscow, 1935

support and is therefore impotent. If Black's Bishop
were on white squares, the Knight would be splendidly
supported at Q B 3 ; in the present case it would be
under fire, there, by the Bishop. Furthermore, White
has no means of exploiting his opponent's weaknesses
on the K side, nor of obtaining there a passed pawn.
Black, on the contrary, will be able to start a lively
action on the Q side owing to his King's favourable
position. Whereas a Bishop could stop a passed pawn,
the Knight, a poor defensive piece, will succumb in-
gloriously, as soon as Black's passed pawn appears on
the Q side. White's game collapses with astonishing
readiness and speed. 1 ... R—Q B 1 (1 ... B × P ;
2 R—Kt 1,); 2 R × R (forced, unfortunately, for otherwise a pawn is lost in view of the threat ... R—B 7 ;
and if 2 Kt—B 3, B × Kt ; 3 P × B, K—B 3 ; and wins),
2 ... K × R; 3 P—Q Kt 3, K—B 2; 4 K—B 1, (White
has not the time to occupy Q 3 with his Knight, which
could guard against an irruption by the opposing King,
for after 4 P—Q R 4, K—B 3 ; 5 Kt—B 1, K—B 4 ;
6 Kt—Q 3 *ch*, K—Q 5 ; Black would win. It would

also be useless to post the Knight at Q B 4, from where it could be driven away at will by ... P—Kt 4 ;) 4 ... P—Kt 4 ; 5 K—K 1, B—Kt 7 ; 6 P—Q R 4, P × P ; 7 P × P (now White has an isolated pawn which can be defended neither by the too distant King nor by the Knight and which must therefore fall), 7 ... K—B 3 ; 8 K—Q 2, K—B 4 ; 9 Kt—B 3, K—Kt 5 ; 10 Kt—Kt 5, P—Q R 4 ; 11 Kt—Q 6 (an abortive attempt to make up on the other wing for the loss of the Q R P : it is the Knight's only chance of asserting its power, and if it fails nothing can retrieve the game), 11 ... K × P ; 12 K—B 2, B—K 4 ; 13 Kt × P, B × P ; 14 Kt—Q 8, P—K 4 ; 15 Kt—B 6, B—Kt 8 ; 16 P—B 3, B—B 4 ; 17 Kt—Kt 8, K—Kt 4 (the agile Knight, in the absence of support, is already in danger) ; 18 P—Kt 4, B—K 2 ; 19 P—Kt 5, P × P ; 20 Kt—Q 7, B—Q 3 ; 21 Kt—B 6, K—B 5 ; and White resigns, for after 22 Kt × P, there follows 22 ... B—K 2 ; and the Knight is in a trap. The futility of the Knight's manœuvres is clearly demonstrated here : even more remarkable is their slowness. The Knight moves about feverishly, but what a time it takes to cross the board, which the Bishop can take in its stride !

In the last example, there was hardly a fight, as the Knight was utterly unequal to its task. True, it was not only the Bishop's superiority which won the day, but also the King's favourable post, in close proximity to the weaknesses in the opposite camp. Nevertheless, there is no doubt that the Bishop is here the stronger piece in spite of the fact that the adverse pawns are on squares of the opposite colour. Its power is exerted against the Knight, debarring it from all the best squares, rather than against the pawns.

Let us now turn our attention to Diag. 105, where the Knight has the privileged position. There it can be well supported on the black squares at its Q Kt 4, Q B 5 and Q 4, which are inaccessible to the Bishop,

No. 105. Black to play.

Capablanca *v.* Reshevsky
Nottingham, 1936

which is of the same colour as most of its pawns. Besides, Black has two marked weaknesses, the isolated pawns on the Q Kt and Q files, which require constant protection by the Bishop and hinder its movements. Consequently, the white position must be considered by far superior and Black should have refused to enter upon such an end game.

Nevertheless, White wins only with a good deal of trouble. Black chooses a procedure which has long been familiar to us : he creates a distant passed pawn, which affords such counter-chances that White's win hangs by a thread, the Knight being, as we know, a poor defender.

1 ... P—Kt 4 ; 2 R P×P, B P×P ; 3 Kt—Kt 4, P×P ; 4 P×P, B—Kt 2 ; 5 P—Kt 4 (avoiding the creation of a passed pawn on the K R file), K—Kt 2 ; 6 K—K 2, K—Kt 3 ; 7 K—Q 3, P—R 4 ; 8 P×P *ch*, K×P (the intention is to attack the K B P as soon as the adverse King sets out to win the pawns at Q Kt 5 and Q 5) ; 9 K—Q 4, K—R 5 ; 10 Kt×P, (with the elimination of the Q P, the Bishop becomes stronger) 10

... K—Kt 6 ; 11 P—B 4, P—K Kt 5 ; (and not 11 ...
B × Kt ; 12 K × B, P × P ; 13 P × P, K × P ; 14 K—B 5,
etc.) 12 P—B 5, B—B 1 (Black cannot afford to
exchange his Bishop and to queen the pawn, because
White would also queen a pawn, then exchange Queens
and win with his extra pawn) ; 13 K—K 5, B—Q 2 ;
14 P—K 4, (14 Kt—B 6, does not work because of 14
... K—R 6 ; 15 Kt × B, P—Kt 6 ; and Black queens
first and wins the pawns by a series of checks) 14 ...
B—K 1 ; 15 K—Q 4, K—B 6 (better would be 15 ...
B—B 2 ; 16 Kt—K 3, K—B 5 ; or 16 K—K 3, B × Kt ;
17 P × B, K—R 6); 16 P—K 5, P—Kt 6; 17 Kt—K 3,
K—B 5 ; 18 P—K 6, P—Kt 7 ; 19 Kt × P *ch*, K × P ;
20 K—Q 5, K—Kt 5 ; 21 Kt—K 3 *ch*, K—B 5 ; 22
K—Q 4, and Black resigns, having no moves left.

It would be useless to verify whether each move in
this ending was the best available, that would be a
standard of perfection, to which we cannot as yet aspire.
The important point is to realize White's superiority
and on what it is based. The Knight here was stronger
than the "bad Bishop." And we have seen what a
poor part the Bishop had to play throughout this ending.
Had the Bishop been able to extricate itself from its
restricted position and to defend its pawns from the
front, it could have taken an active part in the contest,
for it would have been possible to move about and to
attack the weak points in the opponent's camp and to
reduce his mobility. But the win was, even so, much
more difficult than in the preceding example, which
shows that even against a "bad Bishop" a Knight's
task is no sinecure. In the present instance there was
even the additional handicap of two weak and isolated
pawns claiming the Bishop's protection, and yet it
needed little for Black to succeed in saving the game.

In Diag. 106 Black has a weak and isolated Q P, and
yet in spite of his "bad Bishop" and the power of the
opposing Knight, the game ended in a draw. With

defeat looming ahead, Black plays a purely defensive
game, which in itself is proof of the inadequacy of his
Bishop.   Such an ending should be avoided : it is,
however, superlatively instructive in showing how this
type of end game can be successfully defended ; the
play proves that it is by no means, as is often thought,
a dead loss.

No. 106. Black to play.

Flohr *v.* Capablanca
Moscow, 1935

1 ... K—K 2 ; 2 K—Q 2, K—Q 3 (releasing the
Bishop.   Black must anticipate the occupation by the
adverse King of his Q 4 with subsequent manœuvres
by the Knight to capture the Q P) ; 3 K—B 3, P—
Q Kt 3 (the black pawns occupy strong squares, not those
of the same colour as the Bishop, thus making up for
the Bishop's weakness and allowing it additional freedom
of action and, incidentally, depriving the Knight of future
strong points : most instructive) ; 4 P—B 4 (here 4
P—Q Kt 4 leads to nothing ; Black replies 4 ... B—Q 2 ;
and even if White succeeds in blockading Black's Q R P
it will be defended by the Bishop from the front and
not from the rear, which is of paramount importance) ;

4 ... B—Q 2; 5 Kt—B 3, P—B 3; (the same idea: restricting the Knight whilst restoring freedom to the Bishop) ; 6 K—Q 4, P—Q R 4 ; 7 Kt—Q 2 (a criss-cross journey, by which the Knight takes the place of the King at Q B 3) 7 ... B—B 1 ; 8 Kt—Kt 1, B—K 3 ; 9 Kt—B 3, K—B 3 (just in time to prevent the Knight's irruption into the black camp) ; 10 P—Q R 3, P—R 3 ; 11 P—K Kt 3, P—R 4 (this pawn is invulnerable because White's Kt cannot play to K Kt 3 or K B 4, occupied by pawns ; but Black must not lose sight of the fact that his adversary could try to advance his pawns to K Kt 4 and K B 5 and to establish his Knight at K B 4, from where it would attack the black Q P and K R P and, for a long time to come, force the Bishop to remain at its K B 2) ; 12 P—Q Kt 4, P × P ; 13 P × P, K—Q 3 ; 14 P—Kt 5 (threatening P—B 5, etc. If then ... B × P ; then Kt × P, and if ... B—B 2 ; Kt—K2—B 4) ; 14 ... P—Kt 3 ; 15 P—B 5, (a temporary sacrifice) 15 ... P × P; (not 15 ... B × P; 16 Kt × P, B—Q 2; 17 Kt × B P, B × P; 18 Kt—Q 5,) 16 Kt—K 2, B—Q 2 ; 17 Kt—B 4, B—K 1 (17 ... B × P ; 18 Kt × R P,); 18 Kt × Q P, B × P ; 19 Kt × Kt P, (19 Kt × B P, B—K 7;) 19 ... B—B 3; 20 Kt—B 4 *ch*, K—K 3; 21 Kt—Kt 2, B—Kt 4 (the Knight again makes for K B 4 and the Bishop prepares to prevent this by guarding the squares at its Q 6 and K 7) ; 22 Kt—Q 1, B—K 7 ; 23 Kt—B 2, B—B 8 ; 24 Kt—Q 3 (the struggle between Knight and Bishop ends on a peaceful note, all resources being exhausted) ; 24 ... B × Kt; 25 K × B, and we have the same position as in Diag. 43, which ends in a draw.

We see here that it is not possible to maintain all the pawns on squares of the same colour as the Bishop during the whole course of an end game : this would, in any event, create fresh weaknesses, or even holes (incidentally, the colour of weak squares must be taken into account also), and periodical tactical threats by the opponent have to be parried. The general tendency, however, must be as indicated and provide a basis for the appreciation of any position, especially where the pawns are numerous and occupy squares of both colours. Then the comparative values of the pawns have to be correctly assessed, their chances of attack, the danger of their being lost. This assessment is by no means easy : sometimes the loss of some pawns, or even one pawn, entails immediate and certain loss, when other pawns are gained with difficulty and their loss finds compensation elsewhere. Such pawn weaknesses often decide the fate of the game and upon their nature depends the superiority or otherwise of Bishop over Knight.

When such weaknesses occur, the whole problem takes on a new aspect, and the value of the several pieces must be judged in accordance with them. In Diag. 107

No. 107. White to play.

Znosko-Borovsky *v.* Sonja Graf
Margate, 1939

Black's chief weakness consists in her advanced Q Kt P, which is too far advanced and is disconnected from the Q R P, which in turn becomes weak. Their own King

cannot protect them, whilst the adverse King is able to
attack one or the other. In the present illustration,
the black-square Bishop can protect only one of these
pawns ; a white-square Bishop could guard another
pawn, but again not the two, whereas White's Knight
can attack both pawns consecutively and also guard its
own two pawns at Q Kt 2 and Q R 4, which, incidentally,
are not as weak as are Black's pawns. Either Bishop,
therefore, would in this case be equally inadequate,
although the white Bishop would be slightly the stronger,
because it would cut off the Knight, should it capture
the R P. Black would be better placed with a Knight,
and so, if White wins promptly, and without difficulty,
it is due to these weaknesses in the adverse pawn formation, and less to the superiority in this position of White's
Knight over the Bishop. 1 Kt—B 4, K—Q 4 ; 2 K—
Q 3, B—R 5 (the Q side pawns can no longer be
defended) ; 3 Kt × P, (if 3 P—B 3, B—K 8; guarding
the R P from the front and stopping the white
King from reaching Q B 3) 3 ... B × P ; 4 Kt × P,
and with two united passed pawns the game is easily
won.

In all these examples the positions were fairly open, so
that the Bishops, even when weak, had opportunities of
withstanding the Knight's attacks. In cramped positions, the Knight's powers increase, and it can, when
cleverly handled, thread its way amongst the pawns and
attack backward ones. If the pawns are on squares of
the same colour as their Bishop, the latter's activities
are restricted to such an extent that it can no longer
hold its own against the Knight. The Knight compels
it to remain strictly on the defensive, by attacking the
pawns from a square of the opposite colour and safe
from interference by the Bishop.

Diag. 108 illustrates this point. Most of Black's pawns
are on black squares, and the Knight has strong points
available at Q 5, K 6 and K B 5, whence it can easily

No. 108. White to play.

Dr. Tartakower *v.* Gromer
Paris, 1935

attack the most important pawns, those on the Q side, whilst the white pawns are on white squares and safe from attack by the Bishop. The win is obtained with astonishing ease and by perfectly straightforward play, because the position is blockaded and the Bishop can achieve nothing : 1 Kt—R 3, K—Kt 3 ; 2 K—Kt 4, P—R 4 ; 3 Kt—B 2, B—Kt 2 ; 4 P—R 4, P—Kt 3 (now this pawn is bound to fall) ; 5 Kt—R 3, B—R 3 ; 6 Kt—Kt 1, B—Kt 2 ; 7 Kt—B 3, B—B 3 ; 8 K—B 4, K—B 2 ; 9 K—B 5, K—K 2 ; 10 Kt—R 2, K—B 2 ; 11 Kt—B 3, K—K 2 ; 12 P—K 5, P × P ; 13 Kt × K P, B—Kt 2 ; 14 Kt—Kt 6 *ch*, K—Q 3 ; 15 Kt—B 4, B—R 3 ; 16 Kt—Q 5, B—Q 7 ; 17 Kt × P, B—B 8 ; 18 Kt—Q 5, B—Q 7; 19 Kt—B 6, (the Knight is quite unhindered in its neat evolutions in such a blocked position) 19 ... K—B 2 ; 20 K—K 6, B—Kt 5 ; 21 Kt—Q 5 *ch*, K—Kt 2 ; 22 K—Q 6, B—R 6 ; 23 Kt—B 6, B—Kt 5 ; 24 Kt—Q 7, B—R 6 ; 25 K—Q 5, and Black resigns.

The Bishop did not shine to advantage, roaming across

the board without achieving anything. If it had stayed within its own lines for the defence of the Kt P, it would have been practically stalemated and the white King would have penetrated to K 6. The Knight's work was incomparably more efficient, driving off the opposing King on the lines of the two Knights' mate.

In this example the Knight's superiority was un-doubted, there was, properly speaking, no fight. A more stubborn and also more attractive contest results where the two antagonists are in a position respectively to exert their full powers, and where it is difficult to decide which of the two is the stronger. In the course of such an ending it happens that they alternately appear to obtain the upper hand. When these pieces are handled according to their true characteristics, the play often becomes most attractive. The position in Diag. 109 is

No. 109. White to play.

Dr Euwe *v.* Botvinnik
Nottingham, 1936

extremely difficult and full of resources for either player.

The fact that White has doubled and isolated pawns deprives his extra pawn of all importance. It cannot break through. White's plan will evidently be to create a passed pawn on the K R file ; supported by the Bishop on the long diagonal it will assume an extreme importance. Meanwhile Black will try to obtain a passed pawn on the Q side and to create for the Knight the strong points which it lacks at present : the Bishop at Q B 3 for the moment hinders its every move. But it aims first of all at its Q Kt 5, and as soon as the white Q R P advances in order to prevent Black's ... P—Kt 4 ; the Knight can no longer be captured at its Kt 5, for a pawn there would win the game. On the other hand, the Knight at its K 4, supported by the King would enforce the draw : thus the chances are approximately even. But, all things being equal, the Bishop is always preferable to the Knight.

1 K—B 4, P—R 3 ; 2 P—Q R 4, (White is confronted with a difficult choice : he must allow his opponent to obtain a passed pawn at once by ... P—Kt 4 ; or to allow the Knight to settle at its Q Kt 5, a fine starting point for fruitful expeditions based on this strong square) 2 ... K—K 3 ; 3 P—R 4, Kt—Kt 5 ; 4 K—B 3, (the threat was ... Kt—Q 6 *ch* ; followed by ... Kt—K 4 ;) 4 ... Kt—Q 6 ; 5 B—Kt 7, Kt—K 4 *ch* (if now 6 B × Kt, K × B ; the game is drawn. But, had Black first played 5 ... P—K R 4 ; 6 K—K 2, Kt—K 4 ; 7 B × Kt, K × B ; he would have lost the game, as he would soon be in *Zugzwang*. Can you see the difference between these two lines of play ?); 6 K—K 2, (rightly playing for a win. He obtains a passed pawn on the K side, even though he must sacrifice all his Q side pawns in the process) 6 ... Kt × P ; 7 B × P, Kt—Kt 7 (this move is decidedly too ambitious and is expecting altogether too much from the Knight's acrobatic talent : its position at Q B 5 was invaluable as, from there, it could shut in the Bishop at its K 5 or Q 6. That is

why 7 ... P—Q Kt 4 ; 8 P × P, P × P ; is much superior,
as the two united passed pawns would maintain the
balance between the two sides); 8 B—Kt 7, (the Bishop
returns to the highway and again restricts the Knight's
mobility ; the difference in the action of the two pieces
stands out clearly in this example) 8 ... Kt × P ; 9
P—Kt 4, P—Q Kt 4 ; 10 P—R 5, P × P ; 11 P × P,
K—B 2 ; 12 B—R 1 (a hard struggle of three supported
pawns against three isolated ones), 12 ... Kt—Kt 3
(P—B 5 ; or P—Kt 5 ; 13 P—K 5) ; 13 K—B 3,
P—Kt 5 ; (a grave error which could seriously affect the
result of the game : now the white King has good
squares at his disposal amidst the pawns, namely at
Q B 4, Q Kt 3 and Q R 4. Black should have played
13 ... P—R 4;) 14 P—K 5, Kt—Q 2; (otherwise
P—K 6 *ch*,) 15 K—K 4, K—K 3 ; 16 P—R 6, Kt—B 1
(and now again the Knight in defending the pawn is
condemned to inactivity, whilst the Bishop enjoys full
freedom of action) ; 17 K—Q 3, K—Q 4 ; 18 P—
K 4 *ch*, K—B 3 ; 19 K—B 4, P—R 4 ; 20 P—K 6
(with 20 K—Kt 3, K—Kt 4 ; 21 P—K 6, P—R 5 *ch* ;
22 K—R 2, Kt—Kt 3 ; 23 P—R 7, K—B 3 ; White
would have good winning chances, as his opponent
would have to play without his Knight) ; 20 ... K—Q 3 ;
and the game was given up as drawn, e.g. : 21
B—Kt 7, Kt—R 2; 22 P—K 7, K × P; 23 K × P,
K—B 2; 24 K—Kt 5, K—Kt 3 ; 25 K × P, P—Kt 6 ;
26 K—R 4, P—Kt 7; etc. A charming ending which
throws a searching light on the two antagonistic
pieces.

EXERCISES

Here are two positions which, by a remarkable coin-
cidence, bear an astonishing resemblance. In Diag. 110
White has the move, in Diag. 111 Black.

No. 110.

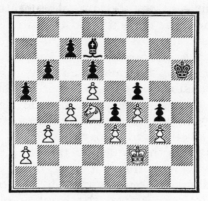

Botvinnik *v.* Eliskases
Moscow, 1936

No. 111.

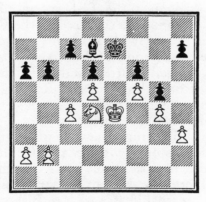

Dr. Tartakower *v.* Flohr
London, 1932

Give an appreciation of these two positions, indicate the course to follow and the result.

Bishop or Knight Against Rook

The Knight and the Bishop, when pitted against a Rook show the same capacity and the same shortcomings which we have noticed before. As the Rook is unquestionably the stronger, the minor pieces can hold their own in certain circumstances only. Even an extra pawn cannot ensure the draw ; but if full scope is given to the minor pieces' characteristics, the Rook may find it hard to prevail. The Knight requires strong squares, supported by well-guarded pawns, with a ragged pawn formation on the other side, so that he can attack the pawns successively without loss of time. The Bishop requires its pawns to be in compact formation, on squares of its own colour. Against the Rook it plays a frankly defensive *rôle*, in which it proves very effective provided it can be safeguarded against attack by hostile pawns, against which its own attacks are usually useless. The Knight, on the other hand, must always try diversions, or even real attacks against the pawns, which cannot be safeguarded, as against the Bishop, by simply moving to a square of the opposite colour. If the Rook supports a passed pawn, it nearly always wins : to counterbalance it, the weaker party must also have a passed pawn, which should be well guarded and sufficiently advanced. The absence of open lines for the Rook is also a factor in favour of the other side.

Let us examine a few positions.

In Diag. 112, the Knight has two united passed pawns, and yet it succeeds only with great difficulty in drawing the game, and it is not entirely clear that the draw could be forced. Here the Knight's shortcomings as a defensive piece are manifest : with a Bishop this ending could probably be won : it would guard the pawns and allow the King to take part in the common action. Here the Knight must passively allow the downfall of its own pawns. There is nothing better than to capture, in the meantime, as many pawns as possible to replace those

No. 112. Black to play.

Dr. Euwe *v.* Capablanca
Match, 1931

which fall to the enemy, and to create some strong
points : 1 ... P—K 5 *ch*; 2 K—B 4, (2 K × P, Kt—
B 6 *ch* ; the Knight fork combination is its most effective
weapon and must be exploited to the utmost) 2 ...
Kt—Kt 5 ; 3 R—Q Kt 5, Kt—Q 6 *ch* ; 4 K × P,
Kt × P *ch* ; 5 K—Q 4, P—B 4 (the object of the manœuvre : at last the Knight has the necessary strong
square in the centre) ; 6 R—Kt 2, Kt—Kt 5 ; 7 P—R 3,
Kt—B 3 ; 8 R—Q B 2, Kt—K 5 ; 9 P—Kt 4, K—B 3 ;
10 P × P, K × P (very bold : prudence dictates the recapture with the pawn, so as not to give the other side a
passed pawn; but Black chooses an active defence, the
best procedure with a Knight, and in allowing his adversary a passed pawn he himself obtains two united passed
pawns); 11 R—B 7, Kt—Kt 4; 12 R × Q R P, P—R 4;
(12 ... Kt × P ; 13 R × P, and White's passed pawn
wins, for the Q Kt P would soon fall) 13 R—R 3,
(protecting the K R P) 13 ... Kt—B 6 *ch* ; 14 K—Q 3,
(more interesting would be 14 K—Q 5, P—K Kt 4 ; 15
P—K 4 *ch*, K—B 5 ; 16 R × Kt *ch*, K × R ; 17 P—K 5,
P—Kt 5 ; or 16 R—R 8, P—Kt 5 ; with a probable

draw) 14 ... Kt—Kt 8 ; 15 K—Q 2, (again guarding the K R P) 15 ... P—K Kt 4 ; 16 R—Kt 3, P—R 5 ; 17 R × P, (17 R—Kt 5 *ch*, K—K 5; 18 R × K Kt P, is inadmissible because of 18 ... Kt—B 6 *ch* ;) 17 ... Kt × P ; 18 K—K 2, P—Kt 5 ; 19 R—Kt 5 *ch*, K—K 5 ; 20 R—Kt 4 *ch*, K—B 4 ; 21 K—B 1, K—Kt 4 ; 22 R—Kt 5 *ch*, K—Kt 3 ; 23 R—Kt 4, K—R 4 ; 24 R—Kt 5 *ch*, Kt—Kt 4 ; draw.

The Knight's exploits in this ending are remarkable. Too much, however, must not be expected from a Knight : if it drifts apart from its own forces, it may well be cornered by the Rook, which in such cases radiates its full powers. The Knight must either remain close to its King or else have the use of strong points : otherwise it is lost, and all the more surely if the board is bare.

In Diag. 113 White has a lost game, because Black has a passed pawn and because White requires too much time to bring to bear his pawn majority on the Q side. If, however, he were to succeed in rapidly advancing his pawns, he might escape by giving up his Knight and securing a draw with two pawns against the Rook.

No. 113. Black to play.

Louis *v.* Znosko-Borovsky
Broadstairs, 1921

But White engages his Knight in a risky adventure ; as
we have seen in the preceding example, the Knight is
not a defensive piece.   If he has to defend, he must
do so actively.   If, in the present instance, the Knight
is lost, it is because the board is denuded of pieces and
the Knight is thrown entirely on its own resources.
1 ... K—R 3 ; 2 P—R 4, K × P ; 3 P—Kt 4, K—Kt 5 ;
4 P—Kt 5, K—B 4 ; 5 P—R 5, K—K 5 ; 6 Kt—
B 5 *ch*, K—Q 4 ; 7 Kt—Q 7 (a double threat of capturing the K B P and advancing his own Kt P ; it would
seem that Black cannot afford to give up the K B P,
his best winning asset.   However, the Knight cannot
safely capture it) ; 7 ... R—Kt 2 ; 8 Kt × P *ch*, K—K 4 ;
and the Knight is lost in the middle of the board, an
unusual occurrence in practical play.   Two "echo"
variations—to employ a term dear to problemists—are
9 Kt—R 5, R—Kt 4 ; and 9 Kt—K 8, R—K 2.

Before leaving the subject of the Knight, let us
remember the examples of a pawn being promoted to a
Knight.   Here also the Knight had to remain close to
the King.

When considering endings with Bishop against Rook,
we immediately notice a basic difference, due to the
essential characteristics of these two pieces.

Having once conquered a long diagonal and found a
well-defended central square from which it can support
its own pawns and control the advance of the opposing
pawns, the Bishop quietly remains there : it seldom
moves about and is mostly satisfied with marking time.
In Diag. 114 White played badly : 1 P—R 6, R—Q 3 ;
2 P—R 7, R—R 3 ; 3 K—B 3, R—R 5 ; and the
game is drawn, because the Bishop is tied to the defence
of the R P and the King cannot move on account of
Black's passed Q B P, whilst the Rook has entire freedom of action, stopping the advance of the R P from
the rear.   He could have won the game by 1 K—B 3,
R—B 2 ; and only now 2 P—R 6, K—B 1 ; (2 ...

No. 114. White to play.

Dr. Bernstein *v* Rubinstein
Ostend, 1906

R—B 3 ; 3 P—R 7, R—R 3 ; 4 K × P,) 3 P—R 7,
R—B 1 ; 4 B—K 5, threatening B—Kt 8, shutting in
the Rook at its Q R 1, and winning the Q B P.   What
difference an inversion of moves can make !   This final
position with a pawn, supported by a Bishop, shutting
in a Rook is worth remembering.   It frequently occurs
in practical play and is one of the Bishop's most dangerous
weapons.   The Bishop can be employed also in cutting
off the Rook from the queening square, and it is difficult
to decide which is the worse evil of the two.

The position in Diag. 115 is the complement of that
given in Diag 18 ; Black has a won game, not only
because he has two united and very far advanced passed
pawns on the Q side, but also because he has an extra
pawn on the K side.   Thus, whatever the Rook undertakes, it cannot remedy all evils.   1 K—B 2, B × P ;
2 R—K R 1, B—K 4 ; 3 R × P, K—B 2 ; 4 R—R 1,
P—Kt 4 ; 5 R—K 1, K—B 3 ; 6 R—K Kt 1, K—Kt 3 ;
7 R—K 1, B—B 3 ; 8 R—K Kt 1, P—Kt 5 ; 9 P × P,
P—B 5 (the passed pawn becomes decisive, whilst
White's passed pawn is stopped ; the reason is that the

No. 115. White to play.

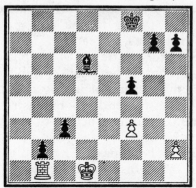

Fine *v.* Keres
"Avro" Tournament, 1938

white pieces are tied to the defence of Q Kt 1) ; 10
P—Kt 5, B—Q 5 ; 11 R—Q 1, B—K 6 (Black gives
up a second pawn in order to obtain a winning position,
Bishop at Q B 8 guarded by a pawn at Q Kt 7) ; 12
K×P, B—B 8 ; 13 R—Q 6 *ch*, K×P ; 14 R—Kt 6,
P—B 6 ; 15 K—Q 3, K—B 5 ; 16 R—Kt 8, K—Kt 6 ;
and White resigns.   The Rook must be given up for the
K B P and then the Q Kt P, supported by the Bishop,
wins easily.   The main point about this ending is that,
on account of Black's passed pawns on both wings,
White's King and Rook could not co-operate.   Each
piece by itself was unable to cope with the advance of
the pawns, supported as they were by the black pieces.

TWO BISHOPS *v.* TWO KNIGHTS OR KNIGHT AND BISHOP

After what was said about the weakness of a single
Bishop, restricted to squares of one colour, it is easy
to realize the importance of remedying this defect by
the presence of a second Bishop.   The contribution of
the two Bishops is extremely powerful and controls the

whole board.   They cannot be compared with the two
Rooks, for their efforts cannot concentrate on one object ;
but they are very strong in the end game, when they
work in two directions, threatening both wings.   The
two Bishops can literally tie up the opposing forces.   In
examples of the contest between two Bishops and other
minor pieces it may seem surprising that the adversary's
position in most cases tends to be restricted : but it is
the result of the preliminary action of the Bishops, which
is slow and methodical.

Against the two Bishops other combinations of minor
pieces, Knight and Bishop, or two Knights, are ineffective.

There are few examples of a win by two Knights
against two Bishops ; the most famous instance rather
demonstrates the weakness of the two Knights, which are
able to win only because of the gain of a pawn ; even
then the game should have been drawn, had it not been
for a blunder by the opponent, who had to lose a piece in
order to avoid being mated.   Here is the position in
question (Diag. 116).

No. 116.   White to play.

Dr. Lasker *v.* Tchigorin
Hastings, 1895

1 K—K 2, P×P ; 2 P—K 4, Kt—B 3 ; 3 B×P,
Kt—R 4 ; 4 B—K 3, P—B 5 ; 5 B—B 2, R—R 4 ;
6 R—Kt 1 *ch*, K—B 1 ; 7 R (R 3)—R 1, P—K 4 ;
8 R (R 1)—Kt 1, Kt—Kt 2 ; 9 R—Q Kt 4, R—B 2 ;
10 B—Kt 1, Kt—K 3 ; 11 R—Q 1, Kt (K 3)—Q 1 ;
12 R—Q 2, Kt—B 3 ; 13 R—Kt 5, R×P ; 14 P×P,
Kt (B 2)×P; 15 B—R 4, R—K Kt 2; 16 K—B 2,
R—Kt 3 ; 17 K—B 2, R—Kt 3 ; 18 R (Q 2)—Q 5,
R—R 8 ; 19 B—Q 8, Kt—Q 6 *ch* ; 20 B×Kt, P×B ;
21 R×Q P, R (R 8)—K Kt 8 ; 22 R—B 5 *ch*, K—K 1 ;
and White resigns. With 21 B—B 7, White would
probably have saved the game.

It would be a mistake to assume that two Knights
must of necessity lose against two Bishops. There are
positions in which the Knights deploy their full powers
and where the Bishops are restricted in their action. It
is the Bishops' drawback, that they require long open
diagonals with valuable objectives, where the Knights
can be effective at short range.

The position in Diag. 117 is an example of a difficult
win for the Bishops. It may be that it cannot be won at

No. 117. Black to play.

Botvinnik *v.* Flohr
Match, 1933

all, for Black has a doubled pawn ; he has to be content
with a passed pawn, which will eliminate one of the
Bishops ; and if White loses in the end through some
weak moves, they are the direct result of the difficulties
of the defence against the power of the two Bishops.
First of all Black liquidates the Q side pawns, in order
to give his white Bishop its full powers, at present rather
restricted ; 1 ... P × P; 2 Kt (B 3) × P, (it is understandable that White does not wish to have all his pieces
immobilized after 2 P × P, B × Kt P ; 3 Kt (Q 4) × P,
B—R 3 ; 4 K—K 3, and the Knights can hardly move ;
and yet this continuation would have been preferable)
2 ... P × P ; 3 Kt × B, P—R 7 ; 4 Kt—B 2, B—R 3 *ch* ;
5 K—K 3, K—K 2 ; 6 Kt × P (B 7), K × Kt; 7 K—Q 4,
(better would have been first 7 P—R 4, so as not to
lose another pawn) 7 ... B—B 8 ; 8 P—R 4, B × P ;
9 K—B 5, P—B 5 ; and wins.

This example can hardly be said to be representative
of transcending play, but it is an outstanding illustration
of the power exerted by two Bishops, when they succeed
in obtaining the command of important lines : it also
shows how insufficient the powers of a Knight are, when
on the defensive (the Knight at Q B 2 is literally stalemated by the advanced passed pawn) and how inadequate
the mutual protection of two Knights.   Remember this :
a Knight requires strong points ; without them, the
Knight is not safe and loses a great part of its strength.

The slow pressure exercised by the Bishops against a
close position is demonstrated in the following example
(Diag. 118).   Here the Bishops have ample space,
whilst the Knights are confined to the first three ranks.
Worse still, they can obtain no strong points in the
centre, which is frequently the case against two Bishops,
which can dominate the whole board.   The Knight at
its Q 2 is particularly badly placed : as soon as it moves,
the opposing Bishop is played to Q B 8, attacking the
Kt P, which in turn cannot move without weakening

No. 118. White to play.

Flohr *v.* Botvinnik
Match, 1933

the Q R P : we see how difficult the situation is for Black. The continuation was : 1 B—Q B 1, Kt—Kt 2 ; 2 P × P, Q P × P (2 ... B P × P ; 3 K—B 3, P—R 4 ; 4 B—Kt 5 *ch*) ; 3 K—B 3, P—R 4 ; 4 B—K 3, (three moves ago, this Bishop had no diagonals at its disposal ; now he commands two very important ones) 4 ... K—Q 3 ; 5 B—R 6, Kt—K 1 ; 6 P—Kt 4, P × P *ch* ; 7 B × P, Kt—B 2 ; 8 B—K 3, Kt—Kt 4 ; 9 K—K 2, Kt—B 2 ; 10 K—Q 3, P—B 4 (in order to obtain breathing space) ; 11 P × P, P × P ; 12 B × P, Kt × P ; 13 B—Q 2, (White is determined to keep his two Bishops) 13 ... Kt (Q 2)—B 3 ; 14 K—B 4, K—B 3 ; 15 B—Kt 6, P—Kt 4 *ch* ; 16 K—Q 3, Kt—K 2 ; 17 B—K 4 *ch*, Kt (K 2)—Q 4 ; 18 B—Kt 5, Kt—R 4 ; 19 B—B 3, Kt—Kt 6 ; 20 B—Q 2, K—Q 3 ; 21 B—Kt 4, Kt—B 3 ; 22 B—B 8, K—B 3 ; 23 B—K 1, P—K 5 *ch* ; 24 K—Q 4, Kt (Kt 6)—R 4 ; 25 B—B 5, K—Q 3 ; 26 B—Q 2, and Black resigns, for he has no moves. An extremely instructive ending, which well demonstrates the concentrated power of two Bishops, and the helplessness against them of the Knights, which move in various directions on the board, without any co-ordination.

If anything, the Bishops are even more valuable in compromised positions, in which their defensive powers shine to advantage.   In Diag. 119, the black pawns are extremely weak, and the Bishops lack important diagonals, whereas the white Knights not only have good attacking positions, but they boast of admirable strong points.   In addition, White has a distant passed pawn.   Nevertheless, White does not succeed in winning the game, for the Knights are handicapped by the fact that, as soon as they move, the Bishops would instantly gain freedom

No. 119. White to play.

Capablanca *v.* Dr. Alekhine
Match, 1927

of action, as their pawns would be able to move.   To afford the Bishops open lines would be dangerous, and White must rest content with maintaining his present advantageous position, and, for want of anything better, undertake aimless manœuvres.   1 P—R 3 *ch*, K—R 5 ; 2 Kt—B 5 *ch*, K—R 4 ; 3 K—Kt 3, (3 Kt—Q 6, B × Kt ; 4 P × B, P—Q 5 *dis ch* ; 5 Kt × B, P × B P ; and wins.   A simple tactical turn, due to the position

of White's King, which allows a discovered check)
3 ... B—Kt 5 ; 4 Kt—Q 4, K—Kt 3 ; 5 K—Kt 4,
P—B 4 *ch* ; 6 K—Kt 3, K—B 3 ; 7 Kt—B 3, B—B 4 ;
8 K—B 2, B—Kt 5 ; 9 Kt—K 5, B—Q 3 ; 10 Kt—B 3,
B—Kt 5 ; 11 P—R 4, K—Kt 3 ; 12 Kt—K 2, B—
Q B 1 (the attack against Q 5 is discontinued, and the
Q B takes advantage of the fact by regaining its freedom) ;
13 Kt—Kt 3, B—K 3 ; 14 P—R 5 *ch*, K—R 3 ; 15
K—K 2, B—K 2 ; 16 K—Q 2, B—Q 1 ; 17 Kt—Q 4,
(17 K—B 3, B—R 4 *ch* ; 18 K—Q 4, B—Kt 3 *ch* ;)
17 ... B—B 1 ; 18 K—B 2, B—R 4 ; 19 K—Q 1,
(19 Kt (Q 4) × P *ch*, B × Kt ; 20 Kt × B *ch*, K × P ;
21 Kt—Q 6, K—Kt 5 ; 22 Kt × K B P, K—B 6)
19 ... B—Kt 5 ; 20 K—K 2, B—Q 2 ; and so on.

We shall give one example only (Diag. 120) of the
struggle between two Bishops and Bishop and Knight,
an interesting one in that it ends in a draw, a rather rare
occurrence in this type of ending. This result here is
due to the fact that the white position is very compact ;
he is on the defensive, his King is unexposed, and the
pawns not advanced, so that the Bishops can find no

No. 120. Black to play.

Winter *v.* Kashdan
London, 1932

proper objective. Black succeeds in winning a pawn, but only by the exchange of one of his Bishops for the Knight, and remaining, as it happens, with Bishops on opposite colours ; thus the game is drawn in spite of the extra pawn. This gives us a precise indication concerning these endings : allow the exchange of the Knight, even with the loss of a pawn, but only against a Bishop of the same colour as your own ! A serious danger for the adversary ! All his efforts may be in vain, because he must avoid remaining with Bishops of opposite colours. This long end-game went as follows : 1 ... B—K B 3 ; 2 K—B 1, K—K 3 ; 3 K—K 2, P—Kt 5 ; 4 Kt—R 4, B—B 3 ; 5 Kt—Kt 6, B—Kt 4 *ch* ; 6 K—K 1, P—Kt 4 ; 7 B—B 7, P—K R 4 ; 8 P—Kt 3, B—Kt 2 ; 9 Kt—B 4, K—Q 4 ; 10 Kt—Q 2, B—B 1 ; 11 B—R 5, P—K 3 ; 12 B—Q 8, P—Kt 5 ; 13 P— K R 4, B—Q 3 ; 14 K—Q 1, B—Q 6 ; 15 K—B 1, B—K 7 ; 16 B—B 6, B—B 2 ; 17 B—K 7, P—K 4 ; 18 P×P, P—R 4 ; 19 B—B 6, B—Kt 3 ; 20 B—Kt 5, K×P ; 21 K—B 2, K—Q 4 ; 22 K—B 1, B—B 2 ; 23 K—B 2, K—B 3 ; 24 K—B 1, B—K 4 ; 25 K—B 2, K—Kt 4 ; 26 K—B 1, P—R 5 ; 27 K—B 2, B— Q B 6 ; 28 K—B 1, B—Q 6 ; 29 K—Q 1, B—Kt 7 ; 30 B—K 7, B—B 6 ; 31 B—Kt 5, K—R 3 ; 32 K— B 1, B—Kt 4 ; 33 K—B 2, B—Q 2 ; 34 K—B 1, B—K 3 ; 35 K—B 2, K—Kt 4 ; 36 K—B 1, B×P ; 37 Kt×B, P×Kt ; 38 P×P, B—K 8 ; 39 K—Q 1, B—B 6 ; draw.

Note that in this instance, the Bishop was the active piece, the Knight being reserved for the defence. The reverse can happen and is in accordance with the true nature of these pieces. The Knight must, however, be careful, lest the same fate befalls it as happened when it was pitted against the Rook.

POSITIONAL ANALYSIS
We now possess all *data* necessary to make a thorough

analysis of any end game position, no matter how complicated. A complete analysis is here even more important than in the middle game, where errors of judgment can still be remedied : in the end game all is final and irreparable.

The analysis of an end game position presents, however, some special characteristics, as compared with the middle game, due to the different object in view and the difference in value of the forces employed. As we have already analysed simple end game positions, we shall confine ourselves to a few more complicated endings, involving various combinations of pieces, which we have not yet studied, and this we shall do as briefly as possible in order to avoid repetition.

As has been seen before, this analysis comprises an exhaustive and consecutive study of the position of the King, the pieces and the pawns, taken, if necessary, in separate portions. We must get used to the idea that, in an end game, the pawns do not only form the skeleton of the position, but provide the most potent weapon : the pawn formation is the basis of a position, and on it depends the result of the game. The position of King and pieces must be analysed in their relation to the pawn skeleton. The King or a piece can be very well posted, and yet be entirely ineffective because of the relative formation of the pawns.

Take a simple position such as that shown in Diag. 121. *A priori* we realize that Black's position is superior because of his pawn majority on the Q side, where he has the chance of obtaining a passed pawn. In addition his Rook occupies an open file, while the white Rook is rather badly posted, with no great prospects for the future. Comparing the respective positions of the Bishops, preference may be given to the white Bishop, because it has more free space ahead, and because the black Bishop is on a square of the same colour as its pawns. But a more exhaustive examination

No. 121. Black to play.

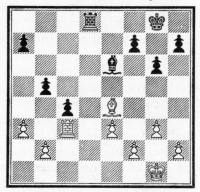

Marshall *v.* Capablanca
Match, 1909

demonstrates that the position of the black Bishop is ideal in that it supports the advanced Q B P, which will enable the other Q side pawns to advance as well. Thus is seen how necessary it is to examine the position of each unit most minutely, and not to be satisfied with approximation, with generalities, even when based on special end game principles (as here the colour of pawns and Bishop). Imagine the black Bishop to be on another diagonal and immediately White could get rid of his weakness (the pawn at Q Kt 2) by 1 P—Kt 3, or considerably ease his position first by 1 P—Q R 4. Now we see the importance of the Bishop at Black's K 3 : it is not only a defensive piece, but it contributes also to the attack. We have at the same time discovered the weakness in White's game, his Q Kt P, and at once Black's additional objective takes shape in our mind : the attack on the weak pawn. If Black merely advances the Q side pawns, he will obtain a passed pawn. But it would be an isolated one, and possibly may not be able to progress. As we know, it is rarely sufficient to exploit a single weakness ; it is important to create others ; Black's plan will then be twofold : advance of the Q side pawns and attack on White's Q Kt P. Another important point : who has the move ? If it is White, his King will have time to move to K 2 and to contribute powerfully to the defence. If it is Black, the white King will be driven to K Kt 2, away from the dangerous pawns. The power of resistance of White's position would then be considerably lessened.

We have spent little time on this analysis, and yet we have discovered not only the respective value of the two positions and their basic idea, but a whole plan has grown out of it, and we shall not be surprised to see the play shape as follows : 1 ... R—Q 8 *ch* ; 2 K—Kt 2, P—Q R 4 ; 3 R—B 2, P—Kt 5 ; 4 P × P, P × P ; 5 B—B 3, R—Kt 8; 6 B—K 2, (a belated manœuvre, for White can derive no benefit from his attack on the Q B P) 6 ... P—Kt 6 (6 ... P—B 6 ; 7 P × P, P—Kt 6 ; 8 R—Q 2, P—Kt 7 ; 9 B—Q 3, and the pawn is stopped. Pawn advances always require the utmost prudence); 7 R—Q 2, (and not 7 R—B 3, R × P ; 8 B × P, R—B 7 ; winning a piece by this ultimate *finesse*) 7 ... R—Q B 8 (threatening ... R—B 7) ; 8 B—Q 1, (White's position has now become very cramped. The advance of Black's Q side pawns would not have sufficed. He had a second string to his bow) 8 ... P—B 6 ; 9 P × P, P—Kt 7 ; 10 R × P, R × B ; and wins.

Let us examine another position, one, this time, with minor pieces (Diag. 122). We perceive at once the defects in Black's position : an isolated pawn at his Q 4, Bishops of the same colour, and the other pawns also on white squares. Against this, White has a strong Knight in the centre, guarded by the K P and safe from attack by the Bishop. Another important point : his King is already on the Q side, where the decisive battle is to be fought, whilst the adverse King is still on the K side. White has several means of exploiting his

No. 122. White to play.

Znosko-Borovsky *v.* Halberstadt
Paris, 1931

advantage : advance the Q side pawns, manœuvre the Knight so that it occupies one of the strong squares at Q 4, Q B 5 or Q R 5, all black squares, advance the King to the attack on the backward pawns (Black's Q R 3, Q Kt 2 or the isolated Q P). All these processes must be combined, but the most important point is to bring up the King as speedily as possible, for if White merely advances the pawns, the hostile King will rush to the threatened flank and redress the balance. The play went as follows : 1 K—Kt 2, K—B 1 ; 2 K—Kt 3, K—K 2 ; 3 P—Kt 5, (by this temporary sacrifice the white King forces a passage to the black squares ; Black must capture the pawn, otherwise, if he play 3 ... K—Q 3 ; there follows 4 P × P, P × P ; 5 K—Kt 4, Kt—Q 2 ; 6 K—R 5, and White has created a further weakness in Black's camp in the backward pawn at Q R 3, which sooner or later must fall) 3 ... P × P ; 4 K—Kt 4, B—Q 2 (4 ... K—Q 3 ; 5 Kt × P *ch*, K—B 3 ; 6 Kt—R 7 *ch*, K—B 2 ; 7 Kt × B, K × Kt ; 8 K—B 5, K—B 2 ; 9 B—B 2, P—Kt 3 *ch* ; 10 K— Q 4, K—Q 3 ; 11 B—Kt 3, and Black loses by

Zugzwang, the Bishop being here manifestly superior to the Knight) ; 5 K—B 5, P—Kt 5 (very astute : the Bishop takes a breather) ; 6 K—Kt 6, (realizing that the Kt P, being too far advanced, would fall in any event, whereas after 6 K × P, K—Q 3, the King can no longer invade black territory) 6 ... B—R 5 ; 7 K × P, Kt—Q 2 (threatening to fork K and B) ; 8 B—B 2, B × B ; 9 Kt × B, P—Kt 6; (a fresh tactical expedient); 10 P × P, Kt—B 4 *ch*; 11 K—B 6, Kt × P; 12 K × P, and White has won a pawn. He has a won game, for the black Knight is out of play. This position is instructive ; as in the preceding example in which Black exploited two weaknesses, the Q Kt P and the restricted position of the Rook, White in the same way works against the two weaknesses in Black's game, the Q P and the Q Kt P, relying on his own King's dominating position and his command of the black squares.

A last example (Diag. 123). White has a Queen

No. 123. White to play.

Yates *v.* Dr. Alekhine
Kecskemet, 1927

against R, Kt and pawn ; but he has two weak and isolated pawns on the Q side, whilst his adversary's

pawns are all very well placed and mutually supporting.
It is thus very difficult to pronounce an opinion on
the respective values of the two positions. We may
say at once that, in such cases, the result of the game
will largely depend on the degree of mobility and usefulness of which the Queen can boast. If the Queen
is shut in and idle, there will be no threats, and the
opposing pieces, working in concert, will become
troublesome. The more active the Queen is, the more
will the opposing pieces lose in importance. Here the
Queen's irruption on the K side may have been good at
the time, but now her action there has no future and it
is necessary to transfer her activities to the other wing,
after which the black Q side pawns will be attacked and
there will be threats of a perpetual check. At once it
becomes evident that only Black can win, for if he does
nothing and is content to defend the position, the white
Queen can achieve nothing. White should therefore
have played for a draw, and his first move ought to have
been Q—K 4, threatening Q—Kt 7 *ch*, or Q—B 6.
Instead of this, and guarding against ... Kt—B 5 *ch* ;
he actually played 1 P—Kt 3, R—Q 5 (threatening to
win a pawn by ... R—R 5) ; 2 P—R 3, R—K B 5
(a tactical turn : 3 P × R, Kt × P *ch* ; winning the
Queen. This shows that tactical opportunities play an
important part in end game play and often add interest
and liveliness to that phase of the game) ; 3 K—Kt 2
(a far-reaching mistake. He should have played 3
Q—Q 3, and if 3 ... R × P ; 4 Q—R 6, and, having
won the Q side pawns, White with a mobile Queen and
a passed pawn, could have held his own) 3 ... R × P
(the same stratagem once more) ; 4 Q—Q 3 (too late) ;
4 ... R—Q 5 ; 5 Q—R 6, R—Q 2 ; (just in time to save
the pawn). The Rook returns from its escapade, having
won a pawn, and with two extra pawns, Black has no
difficulty in winning the game. Quite apart from his
blunder on the third move, White erred in having

failed to grasp the nature of the ending and the proper *rôle* of his forces. Being one move late, the Queen could not effect anything useful and had perforce to remain inactive. It is this precision which is the first requirement in end game play and which constitutes its great difficulty.

THE CONCEPTION OF A PLAN AND ITS EXECUTION

Is it really necessary to conceive a plan in an end game ? Could one not play from move to move, following simply a general idea according to one's superiority or otherwise ?

To put this question is to answer it. We accept the necessity of formulating a plan in any other phase of the game : why should the end game be an exception ? It would be tantamount to claiming that the end game is not subject to the same laws of logic and comprehension as the rest of the game. It may be that the degree of precision which is required in end game play makes the execution of a plan more difficult than its conception, for the result depends on minute details—the move, the square, etc. But the fact remains that, in order to carry out a plan, it must first be conceived, it must have been thought out. If we automatically advance a passed pawn, or bring our King to bear on enemy weaknesses, we could not take into account the subtleties on which the success of our enterprise depends and would probably miss many an opportunity which might arise.

The question has been settled long ago in the minds of the great masters. Here, for instance, is Dr. Emanuel Lasker's opinion : "There can be no question of isolated moves in an end game. There the plan is of paramount importance, the plan and the development of the game built up on its basis. The preliminary moves and their order are of but secondary importance." Other great masters are of the same mind.

Examine Diag. 124. White has an extra pawn, a

No. 124. White to play.

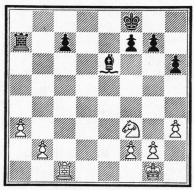

Capablanca *v.* Ragosin
Moscow, 1936

"strong" Rook on an open file, attacking a pawn on its original square, defended by a badly-placed Rook. It might be said, what could be simpler than to win this game ? And this is how Capablanca settles his plan of action : "White's plan is to prevent the advance of Black's Q B P, which might otherwise weaken White's Q Kt P, and to control the whole board up to and including the fifth rank. This can be accomplished by placing the King at K 3, the Rook at Q B 3, the Knight at Q 4, and pawns at Q Kt 4 and K B 4, after which White would advance his Q side pawns." The execution of this plan required five moves (1 Kt—Q 4, R—Kt 2 ; 2 P—Q Kt 4, B—Q 2 ; 3 P—B 4, K—K 2 ; 4 K—B 2, R—R 2 ; 5 R—B 3, K—Q 3 ;), then the next nine moves were made in preparation for the advance of the pawns (6 R—Q 3, K—K 2 ; 7 K—K 3, R—R 5 ; 8 R—B 3, K—Q 3 ; 9 Kt—K 2, P—Kt 3 ; 10 R—Q 3 *ch*, K—K 3 ; 11 K—Q 4, R—R 3 ; 12 R—K 3 *ch*, K—Q 3 ; 13 Kt—B 3, P—B 4 ; 14 P—Kt 5, R—R 1 ;) and only now did the advance of the pawns begin, which brought victory in another 15 moves.

Granted that it might have been possible to evolve a different plan, but it is precisely the omission of such preparations, by the neglect of safety measures, that chances of victory are allowed to slip. Even with a won position, as in the present instance, and when the player knows in which way victory may be achieved, it is still necessary to realize what position must be built up and secured as a starting point for the decisive manœuvre.

It is true that chances may be, and are spoilt by a single weak move, a slip, or the overlooking of a tactical *finesse* on the part of the opponent, but, nevertheless, the essential point is to establish a general line of play, and in this is shown the true mastery of the game. The elaboration of the right plan is a matter of practice and experience.

A famous ending with four Bishops was once won thanks to an extra pawn, and its consummation required nearly 30 moves. Here is the position (Diag. 125),

No. 125. Black to play.

Leonhardt *v.* Capablanca
San Sebastian, 1911

and here is how it was won by Black : 1 ... B—K 4 ;
2 P—Kt 5, P—R 3 ; 3 P—Kt 6, P—Kt 4 ; 4 P × P,
P × P ; 5 B—B 8 *ch*, K—B 3 ; 6 K—K 2, B—B 3 ;
7 K—B 1, B—Q 4 ; 8 K—K 2, B—B 5 *ch* ; 9 K—Q 2,
P—B 5 ; 10 B—Kt 4, B—K 3 ; 11 B—B 3, P—Kt 5 ;
12 B—K 4, P—Kt 6 ; 13 B—Q B 5, B—Kt 5 ; 14
K—K 1, P—B 6 ; 15 B—K 3, B—Q 3 ; 16 P—Kt 7,
K—K 4 ; 17 B—B 6, B—Kt 1 ; 18 K—B 1, B—R 4;
19 K—Kt 1, K—B 4 ; 20 B—Q 5, K—Kt 5 ; 21
B—K 6 *ch*, K—R 5 ; 22 B—Q B 5, B—Kt 5 ; 23
B × B, K × B ; 24 K—B 1, K—R 6 ; 25 B—Kt 1,
B—B 2 ; 26 B—R 7, K—R 7 ; 27 P—Kt 8 (Q),
P—Kt 7 *ch* ; and White resigns.

We perceive that Black's plan was to advance his
passed pawns as rapidly as possible, ignoring the Kt P
until it had reached the seventh and blockading it with
the K B. Then the King's advance, supporting the
pawns, forced the exchange of one of the Bishops. The
plan succeeded to perfection and the ending was univer-
sally admired. Dr. Tarrasch, however, severely criti-
cised its inception and maintained that Black should
have stopped the Q Kt P at Kt 5 by placing his K B
at its Q Kt 3 before the pawn could become dangerous,
and that he would have won both more easily and more
quickly.

In either case, it is clear that the win could be achieved
only by the advance of the black passed pawns. Thus
it is a clash of two plans, both effective, and not of a
number of haphazard single moves.

Let us examine one more position (Diag. 126). Who
has the better game ? White has two pawns on the Q
side against Black's isolated one. On the other hand
he himself has an isolated Q P. If he exchanges one
of the Q side pawns, he will, it is true, have a distant
passed pawn, but it will mean a second isolated pawn
against Black's compact formation of five united and
mutually protective pawns. The drawback for Black is

No. 126. Black to play.

Ratner *v.* Znosko-Borovsky
Paris, 1931

that his Q Kt P can forthwith be attacked by Kt—B 3,
and its defence by ... Kt—R 2 ; would not be a happy
one as, on a black square, it can at once be attacked by
the Bishop. Black also can attack the Q P, which,
however, can easily be defended by the Bishop, which
therefore must not be exchanged. Finally, White's
Q R P can be attacked also by the Bishop and guarded
by the white Knight after capturing the Kt P.

This practically concludes our analysis, which reveals
the characteristics of the position, its dangers, weaknesses and threats. Accordingly, Black conceives the
idea of bringing his King as speedily as possible to his
Q B 3, threatening the Knight which by then will be
at its Q Kt 5 ; the white R P will fall, his pawn at
Q Kt 4 will remain in the line of fire of Black's K B
and the black King will have a free passage to either of
White's isolated pawns. The game went as follows :
1 ... P—Q 4 ; 2 P—Q Kt 4, Kt—Q 3 ; 3 Kt—B 3,
K—K 1 ; 4 B—B 7, (White follows up his plan of winning the Q Kt P ; incidentally he frees his Bishop,
which otherwise would remain shut in after ... K—Q 2 ;)

4 ... Kt—B 5 ; 5 Kt × Kt P, K—Q 2 ; 6 B—B 4,
K—B 3; 7 Kt—B 7, (7 Kt—B 3, Kt × P ; or 7 P—
Q R 4, B × P ; and in either case a white pawn falls
because of the close proximity of the black King) 7 ...
P—K 4 (the hidden threat which endangers both white
pieces) ; 8 Kt—K 6, P × B ; 9 Kt × B, P × P ; 10
R P × P, Kt × P; (the pawns are now equal in numbers,
but the white King is far away from the Q side, whilst
Black's King, with the aid of the Knight, threatens the
two isolated pawns ; in the meantime the white Knight
roams aimlessly far afield.) 11 Kt—K 6, (seeking compensation on the K side) P—Kt 4 ; 12 Kt—B 8, P—R 3 ;
13 Kt—K 6, Kt—B 7 ; 14 P—B 4, P × P; 15 Kt × P,
Kt × Q P; (at last Black has won a pawn and owns a
passed pawn) 16 K—B 2, P—B 4 ; 17 Kt—Kt 2,
K—Q 3 ; 18 Kt—K 1, Kt—K 3 ; 19 K—K 3, P—
Q 5 ch ; and so on. And now the win presents no
difficulty at all ; it is, as it is called, merely a question of
technique. It is clearly a matter of winning the Q Kt P
and to create two passed pawns as far distant as possible
from one another, and in particular to see to it that the
sacrifice of the Knight does not lead to the loss of the
two pawns. It is not so much the plan but its execution which counts, and especially tactical combinations
on the other side which might ruin it. 20 K—Q 3,
K—Q 4 ; 21 Kt—Kt 2, P—R 4 ; 22 Kt—R 4, P—B 5 ;
23 P × P, Kt × P ch ; 24 K—Q 2, K—B 5 ; 25 Kt—B 5,
Kt—K 3 ; 26 Kt—Q 6 ch, K × P ; 27 K—Q 3, P—R 5 ;
28 Kt—K 4, P—R 6 ; 29 Kt—B 2, P—R 7 ; 30
K—K 4, K—Kt 6 ; 31 K—B 3, P—Q 6 ; 32 K—Kt 2,
P—Q 7 ; 33 K × P, K—B 7 ; 34 K—Kt 2, Kt—B 4 ;
35 K—R 2, Kt—K 5; 36 Kt—Kt 4, (a last threat of
the Knight's fork) 36 ... K—Q 6 ; and White resigns.

EXERCISES

In Diags. 127 and 128 analyse the position, evolve a

plan of action in both cases and trace the probable course of the play. White to play in both positions.

No. 127.

Flohr *v.* Lövenfisch
Moscow, 1936

No. 128.

Rioumin *v.* Capablanca
Moscow, 1936

TACTICAL OPPORTUNITIES
We have, on several occasions, noticed how tactical

opportunities, grafted on the general strategical scheme, can influence the course of play, sometimes ruining our plan, sometimes forcing us to alter it, or again adding to its effective execution.   It is necessary to foresee their incidence, whether they be to our adversary's advantage or our own, for they can retrieve a hopelessly lost game or accelerate the course of victory.

Contrary to popular belief, end games are full of subtle beauty, of charming turns and admirable *finessing*, which one might even prefer to the more blatant brilliancies of the middle game.   There is no doubt that end game play is not at all as rigid and arid as is commonly supposed ; it requires much more than simple and tiresome calculation.   In these finer points of end game play, the surprising fact is that all the forces, even the pawns and the King play their part, each unit according to its particular means and following its own particular trend, carrying out at the proper time unexpected manœuvres, going against the natural course of events.   We shall now examine a few examples illustrating the point, for such tactical opportunities are a necessary corollary to a strategical plan.

Quite naturally, the Knight is the piece *par excellence* to provide the greatest stock of such combinations. Here is a charming example (Diag. 129).   Black played 1 ... K—Kt 4 ; in the hope of easily drawing the game after 2 ... P—B 4.   In fact, the game would be drawn after a simple move such as 1 ... B—Q 3 ; but the move actually made gave the adversary the chance of a tactical combination and of winning the game by that means rather than by the profundity of his strategy.   White replied 2 Kt—K 5, threatening to capture the B P, which cannot be defended by ... K—B 3 ; because of the check by the Knight at Q 7, winning the Bishop.   After 2 ... P—B 4 ; there is another application of the Knight fork combination : 3 P—Q 6, P × P *ch*; 4 K—Kt 2, (an important move,

No. 129. Black to play.

Capablanca *v.* Alekhine
Match, 1927

which prevents any checks by the Bishop. If, instead,
4 K—K 2, B × Q P ; followed by ... K—B 5 ;) 4 ...
K—B 3 (if 4 ... B × Q P ; 5 Kt—B 7 *ch*) ; 5 Kt—
Q 7 *ch*, and wins. A whole series of forks by the Knight
on different squares, which, however, did not occur in
the game.

In the next example (Diag. 130) the Knight is not
the sole engineer of victory. Strictly speaking, it only
initiates the winning manœuvre, which is completed by
King and pawns. The adverse Knight joins in the
fray, with tactical turns of its own, though without much
success, and the whole makes a pleasing and harmonious
impression. The better to appreciate Black's extraordinary manœuvre, it must be realized that his normal
continuation 1 ... Kt—B 5 ; would not have won.
White replies Kt—R 2 and back to B 1, keeping the
adverse King away. The problem is how to deprive
the white Knight of access to the square Q B 1 and,
on the other hand, to open the way for the black King
towards White's Q B P. Here is the solution : 1 ...
Kt—Q 6 ; 2 Kt—Kt 3, (2 Kt × Kt, P—R 7 ; and if

No. 130. Black to play.

Marco *v.* Maróczy
Paris, 1900

2 Kt—R 2, K—K 7 ; 3 K—Kt 3, K—Q 7 ; 4 K × P, K—B 7 ; an admirable move by the King, winning the Knight) 2 ... Kt—K 8 *ch* ; 3 K—Q 1, K—Q 6 ; 4 K × Kt, K × P ; 5 Kt—R 1, K × Q P ; (and not 5 ... K—Kt 2 ; falling into the trap : 6 K—Q 1, K × Kt ; 7 K—B 1, K—R 7 ; 8 K—B 2, drawn. How attractive is this exchange of sacrifices !) 6 Kt—B 2 *ch*, K—B 6 ; 7 K—Q 1, (7 Kt × P, K—Kt 7; and the Knight is caught) 7 ... P—R 7 ; 8 K—B 1, P—Q 5 ; 9 Kt—R 1, P—Q 6 ; 10 Kt—B 2, P—B 4 ; and White resigns. Another pretty turn occurs here : 11 P × P, P—Kt 5 ; 12 P—B 6, P—Kt 6 ; 13 P—B 7, P—Kt 7 *ch* ; and mate next move. White requires but one move to queen also.

Diag. 131 illustrates a combination reminiscent of middle game play, but based on an idea essentially typical of the end game—the stalemate. Black, with the exchange and a pawn about to queen, seems to win forthwith. His first moves are more or less forced, but the final point is exquisite and had to be foreseen : 1 P—R 6 *ch*, K × P ; 2 P—K 7, R—Kt 1 ; 3 K—B 1,

No. 131. White to play.

Teichmann *v.* N.
Berlin, 1913

K—Kt 2; 4 P—K 8 (Q), R × Q; 5 K—Kt 2, R—K 7;
(5 ... R—Q R 1 ; 6 K—R 1, followed by Kt—K 1—
Q 3—B 1, etc.) ; 6 K—R 1, R × Kt ; stalemate. (If
6 ... K any ; 7 Kt—Kt 4, followed by Kt × P).

A most brilliant combination, based also on the
stalemate idea, is shown in Diag. 132. 1 R × Kt,

No. 132. White to play.

Bird *v.* Englisch
London, 1883

R—R 4 *ch* ; (1 ... R × R ; 2 Kt × P, R—Kt 2 ; 3 R × R,
K × R ; 4 Kt × R *ch*,) 2 K—Kt 1, R × R ; 3 Kt × P,
threatening mate or the loss of a Rook, but Black forces
a draw by 3 ... R—R 8 *ch* ; (Black could also play 3 ...
R—K 8 *ch*; 4 K—B 2, R (R 4)—R 8;) 4 K × R, (4 K—
B 2, R—K B 1 ;) 4 ... R—K 8 *ch* ; 5 K—R 2, R—R
8 *ch* ; 6 K × R stalemate.

The stalemate combination is a speciality of the end
game, and it often provides a last resource in an otherwise lost position. In Diag. 133 Black places his King

No. 133. Black to play.

Znosko-Borovsky v. Romih
Paris, 1938

in a stalemate position, but he has a free Rook : it can
then give a perpetual check, which it can do with impunity
as White cannot capture it—a combination which occurs
frequently and which it is well to remember : 1 ...
B—Kt 7 ; 2 R—Kt 7 *ch*, K—Kt 1 ; 3 R—Kt 5 *ch*,
K—R 1 ; 4 R—K Kt 8 *ch*, for if at once 4 R × B, the
black King has no move and his Rook can pursue the
white King with uninterrupted checks 4 ... R × P *ch* ;
5 K—B 5, R—Q 4 *ch* ; etc.

The King also lends himself to all kinds of tactical combinations by occupying an unexpected square, which however conforms to the real needs of the situation.

No. 134. Black to play.

Subarev *v.* Grigoriev
Leningrad, 1925

In Diag. 134 White has a distant passed pawn, against which Black has four united pawns and can force the creation of a well-advanced passed pawn. We already know how such a pawn is forced through, but in this example, the "slow motion manœuvres" of the black King are wholly delightful ! By straightforward and quite natural methods, both players would have obtained a new Queen, and there would still have been a difficult struggle to win with an extra pawn, whilst the line of play selected by Black leads to a clear-cut win in a few moves : 1 ... P—Kt 4 ; 2 P × P *ch*, K—Kt 3 (the point ! 2 ... K × P ; 3 K—K 6, P—B 5 ; 4 P × P *ch*, K × P ; 5 P—B 4, etc.) ; 3 K—K 6, P—R 5; 4 P × P, (thanks to Black's second move, this capture is effected without check, and the *tempo* thus gained prevents White from making a Queen at the same time as Black) 4 ...

P—B 5 ; 5 P—B 4, P—Q 6 ; and wins. Black will have queened by the time this pawn reaches the seventh.

Such subtleties are of frequent occurrence in end game play, and often essential for making the utmost of a position. Often they alone bring about the true result, where ordinary normal means would garble the account.

EXERCISES

In Diag. 135 White has the move : what is the result and how is it obtained ?

No. 135.

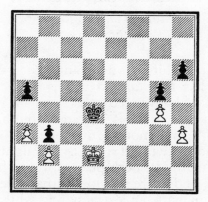

Ritterhaus *v.* N.
1925

In Diag. 136 Black has the move : What is the result ? In order to achieve it a *finesse* is necessary ; what is its nature ?

No. 136.

Haida *v.* Nimzowitsch
Marienbad, 1925

FALSE RESULTS

In endings, as in other parts of the game, weak moves are made which lead to missed opportunities ; that is but natural and requires no explanation.

There have occurred other and stranger cases where a drawn position has been given up as a loss, or a draw conceded when the game is won. This happens most frequently because a *finesse* is overlooked which would alter the complexion of things ; it also happens that a whole manœuvre escapes the player's attention—and that is why I have insisted on the necessity of practising positional analysis and the construction of a strategical plan as much as the search for tactical opportunities.

As no real guarantee can be given even then that no possible opportunities shall be missed, the only remedy against such a failing—a remedy which may not be to the adversary's liking—is not to agree on the result of an ending before all possibilities have been exhausted.

A *finesse* may occur at the very last moment, which we do not see now, but which we shall find when the time comes. It has become a habit to foresee everything, to make a move only when convinced that nothing untoward can happen later. The presumption is that one knows all and sees everything, and so a result is readily agreed without proof that it is inevitable. A great master may overlook a turn a few moves ahead, which the amateur may see at the proper time when the opportunity for it arises.

The first illustration (Diag. 137) was given up as a

No. 137.

Bogoljubow *v.* Dr. Alekhine
Match, 1934

draw, although the three united passed pawns win by force against a Rook. This surprising result was due to a misunderstanding ; it was thought that the same position had occurred three times, which was not the case. But the position in Diag. 138 was deliberately abandoned as a draw after the King and the Bishop had described a circle around the B P. 1 ... K—B 5 ; 2 B—Q 3, K—K 6 ; 3 B—B 1, K—B 7 ; 4 B—R 3, K—Kt 6. White was evidently unable to find the win, which is, however, neither difficult nor complicated. 1 ... K—B 5 ; 2 B—B 8, K—Kt 6 (2 ... P—B 7 ;

No. 138. Black to play.

Friedl *v.* Haida
Brünn, 1920

3 B—R 3); 3 P—B 5, P—B 7; 4 B—R 6, and
wins.

The position in Diag. 139 was also given up as a

No. 139. White to play.

Bogoljubow *v.* Sir George Thomas
Hastings, 1922

draw although it is, in fact, a win for White. It is

true that the win is not obvious and requires lengthy manœuvres with a pretty *finesse* at the end. Is it this *finesse* which escaped the players' attention ? One might think so, for without it the King's operations lead to nothing : 1 K—Q 5, R—R 4 *ch* ; 2 K—B 4, R—R 5 *ch* ; 3 K—Kt 3, R—R 6 *ch* ; 4 K—B 2, R—B 6 *ch* ; 5 K—Kt 2, and wins. It is fairly certain that, had White thought out this line up to the final point, he would have played it.

Still more surprising is the case of Dr. Tarrasch, the great analyst, who gave up as lost the position in Diag. 140, which actually is a draw.

No. 140. White to play.

Dr. Tarrasch *v.* Blümich
Breslau, 1925

What did he overlook ? The intermediate check by the Rook and its sacrifice ? Yet, it is quite a usual process. Possibly the great master, not seeing any way out, did not wish to play on as an average player would, and thus missed the chance which surely he would have seen one or two moves later. Here are the moves which secure the draw : 1 P—R 6, R—Kt 3;

(1 ... R—Kt 1 ; 2 K—Kt 4,) 2 R—R 5, P—R 7 ;
(2 ... R—Kt 1 ; 3 P—R 7, R—K R 1 ; 4 K—Kt 4,
P—R 7 ; 5 R—Kt 5 *ch*,) 3 P—R 7, R—Kt 1 ; 4
R—Kt 5 *ch*, R × R ; 5 P—R 8 (Q), with perpetual
check.

The next example (Diag. 141) is even worse. White

No. 141. White to play.

Nowarra *v.* Eliskases
Bad Oeynhausen, 1938

resigned, for he saw no defence against the terrible
threat ... Kt—B 6 *ch* ; followed by ... P—Q 7 *ch* ;
and if first B—B 6, then ... R—Kt 8 *ch* ; followed by
K × R. The sacrifice of the exchange would be no
remedy, for White would quickly be lost. But an intermediate check would have saved everything : 1 P—
R 3 *ch*, K—Kt 6 ; 2 B—B 6, and a long struggle would
follow with good chances of a draw.

These examples could be multiplied many times, but
those given here will suffice to prove that, if it is foolish
in the middle game to go on playing when at a real
disadvantage, in the end game it is wise, as well as
permissible, to hold out to the end.

THE TRANSITION STAGE BETWEEN THE MIDDLE AND END GAME

We have emphasized on several occasions that an end game is often lost, not because it was badly played, but because it was lost from the start. If such an ending is compulsory, there is nothing to be done, except to try to defend it as strenuously as possible. But to enter upon it of one's own free will is a mistake and almost a crime.

Two essential points must be elucidated before embarking on an end game : first, is it necessary to do so or is there any advantage to be gained by it ? In other words, the question for the stronger party is, whether his advantage can be better exploited in the end game, and for the weaker side, whether his inferior position will be more easily defended there.

Then there is the choice of various types of end games, which may be available. This means that, at the proper moment, there must be a revaluation of the position from the point of view of the end game, where, as we know, values change, weaknesses disappear or increase, strong pieces and strong squares lose some of their values, etc. It may be objected that this is very difficult. It is hard enough to conduct properly an end game with which we are actually faced; how can we foresee the value of an ending which has not even started ? But we have demonstrated that the end game is also subject to rules and principles of a general nature, upon which such a valuation can properly be based. No doubt an ending, which seemed to us to be advantageous, may contain *finesses* which we could not foresee ; it may be that tactical interludes may upset our general calculations. There is nothing to be done against this ; only practical experience will teach us to sense the shoals ahead ; let us be satisfied in the meantime in developing our capacity to judge an ending to come from a general point of view, with a proper regard to the characteristics which are familiar to us, and we shall have taken a good stride forward.

This phase of the game is one of the most difficult, for its characteristics and objects are less clear cut and pronounced.

In the revised edition of my "Middle Game in Chess" I have devoted a chapter to this subject. It deserves equal notice in a book treating of the end game, and I shall therefore quote some new examples elucidating the same question.

Take the position in Diag. 142 : Black has every incentive to embark upon an end game, for he is threatened with a strong K side attack and has a pawn majority on the Q side. On the other hand the white Knight would in this case be stronger than the Bishop, and it would be well to exchange it first of all. In any event, this disadvantage would find its compensation in the extra pawn on the Q side. Should this pawn disappear, the advantage would entirely be White's.

It is with such reflections that Black steers towards the end game ; there is, however, a surprise in store for

No. 142. Black to play.

Dr. Euwe *v.* Spielmann
Amsterdam, 1930

him, in the shape of a tactical combination which renders
the ending particularly awkward for him.

　1 ... P—B 6 ; 2 P × P, P × P ; 3 R × P, Q × R ;
4 Kt × B, Q—Q 6 ; (more or less forced in view of the
threat 5 Q—Kt 5 *ch*,) 5 Kt × R *ch*, R × Kt ; 6 Q × Q,
P × Q ; 7 R—Kt 1, R—B 7 *ch* ; 8 K—B 3, R × K R P ;
9 R—Q 1, P—Q 7 ; 10 P—K 4, K—Q 2 ; 11 K—K 3,
R—Kt 7 ; 12 R × P, R × P ; 13 K—B 3, R—Kt 8 ;
14 R—K Kt 2, R × R ; 15 K × R, and White must win
this pawn ending.　One must feel inclined to believe
that Black failed to foresee White's 14 R—K Kt 2,
which transformed a Rook ending, with its attendant
chance of a draw, into an ending without Rooks which is
manifestly lost ; Black's 10th move supports this
assumption.　But fundamentally, this inattention was
undoubtedly due to a wrong diagnosis of the ending :
he relied on his distant passed pawn on the K R file,
which he expected to counterbalance White's united
passed pawns in the centre.　In overestimating the value
of his K R P, he failed to take into account the weakness
of his K Kt P.　In end games all details are of an
importance often as great as major considerations.

　Another example of the same kind is shown in Diag.
143.　Black has a very bad game, he is subjected to
an attack which should win through.　In these circumstances, he is justified in seeking to bring about an end
game, and to this end the Queens must be exchanged.
Now if White could be made himself to effect this
exchange all would be well and Black's game could be
held.　But if Black has to do it, then, after the recapture
by the Kt P, Black's Q Kt P would remain backward,
lamentably weak and practically helpless.　Its defence by
... B—B 1 ; is hardly adequate, as White's Knight obtains
admirable strong points at Q 6, Q Kt 6 and Q B 5.
Probably Black reasoned thus : the position is almost
lost, cannot be held against the attack in the middle
game, and so any sort of ending will be preferable.

No. 143. Black to play.

Dr. Euwe *v.* Capablanca
Carlsbad, 1929

We must state here that, although the game actually
ended in a draw owing to some tactical opportunities
which arose suddenly, the ending is lost for Black after
1 ... Q × Q ; 2 Kt P × Q, K—K 2 ; 3 K R—Kt 1,
R × R ; 4 R × R, B—B 1 ; 5 K—B 1, P—K 4 ;
(possibly Black had great expectations from this counter-
attack, which isolated one of White's pawns, but fate
decreed otherwise, and incidentally proved that general
considerations, the fundamentals of a position, are of
greater consequence than such fortuitous happenings) ;
6 Kt × P, R × P ; 7 K—K 2, P—B 3 ; 8 Kt—B 4,
R—Q 1 ; 9 R—R 7, K—Q 2 ; 10 Kt—Kt 6 *ch*, K—
B 2 ; 11 B—R 6. Thus, in spite of Black's valiant
efforts, White has succeeded in concentrating all his
forces against the hapless Kt P, which now must fall.
Only ten moves were needed to obtain this position.

In this example Black was unable to transfer the *onus*
of exchanging Queens to his adversary, and, by doing
it himself, he drifted into an unfavourable ending.
When a player has the choice of several types of ending,
his positional judgment undergoes a searching test.

Here is Diag. 144.   The game is drifting towards

No. 144.   White to play.

Euwe *v.* Alekhine
Match, 1935

the end game.   The exchange of all the pieces is practically compulsory and White thereby will recover his
lost piece.   But he can choose between several exchanges
which lead to widely different positions, with different
chances in the ending.   Here is one method : 1 R × B,
Q × Q ; 2 R × R *ch*, K × R ; 3 P × Q, and here is
another : 1 R × R *ch*, K × R ; 2 Q—B 4 *ch*, Q—B 2 ;
3 Q × B, Q × Q; 4 P × Q.   There appears to be little
difference, and yet the first ending is a draw, and the
second is a loss for White in not more than three or four
moves.   The characteristics of each position had to be
grasped and weighed up beforehand : in the one case
White obtained doubled pawns at K Kt 3 and K Kt 5,
in the other at K B 2 and K B 3.   In the second case
White is unable, in the time at his disposal, to obtain
a defended passed pawn which would counterbalance
Black's united passed pawns on the Q side; in the first
case he can easily obtain passed pawns.

A last example (Diag. 145) in which Black again

has a choice of two different endings by means of a
series of exchanges.   Here is the first alternative : 1 ...

No. 145. Black to play.

Dr. Alekhine *v.* Bogoljubow
Match, 1934

Kt × Kt P ; 2 B × Kt, B × Kt ; 3 P × P, and here is the
second : 1 ... P × P ; 2 P × P, Kt × P ; 3 B × Kt,
B × Kt. In the first instance Black does not win a pawn
but he inflicts on White the drawback of isolated pawns
on the K file which hinder their own Q B to a serious
degree.   In the second case, although Black wins a
pawn, White's Q B gains full freedom of movement.
Thus two principles are involved, and Black must give
preference to one or the other.

Black chose the first and only drew the game.   The
fight would have been much more severe had he chosen
the second.   A pawn is a pawn, as the saying is, and
moreover, whilst White would still have an isolated
pawn, Black's distant passed pawn on the Q R file and
his chance of obtaining a passed pawn on the K side
would have improved his prospects.   What the actual
result would have been it is difficult to say, the game
would have to be played afresh.

It is only by practical play, taking all these things into account, that proper judgment and a correct appreciation of the coming end game can be developed.

CONCLUSION

Journey's end. We may now rest and look back upon our labours, and review what we have learnt, what we have discovered. We shall have achieved a good deal if we but realize that the end game is not merely a matter of automatic calculation, of pure technique, but that it is based on the same principle of simple logic as is the rest of the game, and that it is equally rich in imagination. Here again the *dictum* holds good : "Chess is a game of the understanding and not of memory." The essence of this book is found in the general explanations ; variations count for little. The earnest student can find all he wants of this nature in the prodigious work on the subject by I. Rabinovich, to whom I gladly pay my humble tribute—463 pages in double columns, 412 diagrams and 312 questions—an admirable and exhaustive treatise, which, however, is not for him who has yet to grasp the nature of end game play.

The student will find many points of importance and interest in the valuable if short works on the end game by Sosin and by Rödl. The works of Berger and Chéron are also invaluable, and I am indebted to all those named for some interesting examples and ideas.

I hope that this first attempt to write a reasoned treatise on the end game will raise the standard of play of the vast army of amateurs, on whom the future of our game, after all, depends.

ANSWERS TO QUESTIONNAIRE

Diag. 15, page 30.

After 1 ... Q × R ; 2 P × Q, P × P ; White draws as follows :
3 K—Kt 2, K—B 5 ; 4 K—R 3, P—Kt 7 ; 5 K—R 2,
(5 K × P, would lose as Black obtains the opposition by 5 ...
K × P ;) 5 ... K × P ; 6 K × P, and White has the opposition
and draws the game, thanks to the manœuvre 5 K—R 2, and
then only 6 K × P, "losing" a *tempo.*

Diag. 16, page 31.

The white King threatens two points, and the "poles" are
Q 6 and K Kt 5. White needs three moves to reach K B 4
from Q B 5 ; Black's King also takes three moves from his
K 2 to his K R 4. According to our system of related
squares the win is as follows : 1 K—R 2, K—Kt 1 ; 2 K—
R 3, K—B 1 ; 3 K—Kt 2, K—Kt 2 ; 4 K—Kt 3, K—B 2 ;
5 K—B 2, K—B 1 ; 6 K—Q 2, K—B 2 ; 7 K—K 2,
K—Kt 2 ; 8 K—Q 3, K—B 2 ; 9 K—Q 4, and wins.

No. 146.
Answer to Exercise No. 16

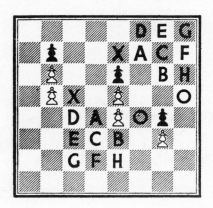

Diag. 28, page 60.

White wins with the move, but he only draws if the move is Black's : 1 K—B 2, K—K 2 ; 2 K—K 3, K—K 3 ; 3 K—K 4, K—B 3 ; 4 K—Q 5, (note this important manœuvre, the only means of forcing back the adverse King and clearing the way for the pawn) K—K 2 ; 5 K—K 5, K—B 2 ; 6 K—Q 6, K—B 1 ; 7 K—K 6, K—K 1 ; 8 P—K 4, K—B 1 ; 9 K—Q 7, and wins.   Or 1 ... K—K 2 ; 2 K—B 2, K—K 3 ; 3 K—K 3, K—K 4 ; 4 K—B 3, K—B 4 ; (always maintaining the opposition) 5 P—K 4 *ch*, K—K 4 ; 6 K—K 3, K—K 3 ; 7 K—Q 4, K—Q 3 ; 8 P—K 5 *ch*, K—K 3 ; 9 K—K 4, K—K 2 ; 10 K—B 5, K—B 2 ; 11 P—K 6 *ch*, K—K 2 ; 12 K—K 5, K—K 1 ; 13 K—Q 6, K—Q 1 ; 14 P—K 7 *ch*, draw. White's King never succeeded in getting in front of his pawn. Note that the black King's manœuvres at all times had the object of allowing him to assume the opposition after every advance by the white King.

Diag. 29, page 60.

White draws with or without the move.   1 K—B 2, P—Kt 5 ; (if 1 ... P—R 5 ; 2 K—Kt 2 ;) 2 K—Kt 2, P—B 6 *ch* ; 3 K—Kt 3, P—R 5 *ch* ; 4 K—B 2, P—R 6 ; 5 K—Kt 3, P—R 7 ; 6 K×R P, P—B 7 ; 7 K—Kt 2, P—Kt 6 ; 8 K—B 1, and the King prevails against the three pawns and captures them all.   If 1 ... P—R 5 ; 2 K—Kt 4, winning the pawns.   The game is drawn because the black King is in a stalemate position.

Diag. 34, page 68.

The white King has a double task in preventing the black King from stopping the white pawn, whilst himself keeping the adverse pawn from queening.   To this end he employs the well-known zig-zag manœuvre, keeping the geometrical idea to the fore.   1 K—B 5, P—Kt 4 ; (1 ... K—Kt 3 ; 2 P—Kt 4, K—B 2 ; 3 P—Kt 5, K—K 2 ; 4 K—B 6, K—Q 1 ; 5 K—Kt 7, P—Kt 4 ; 6 P—Kt 6, P—Kt 5 ; 7 K—R 8, P—Kt 6 ; 8 P—Kt 7, P—Kt 7 ; 9 P—Kt 8 (Q) *ch*,) 2 P—Kt 4, P—Kt 5 ; 3 K—Q 4, (entering the "square") 3 ... K—Kt 4 ; 4 P—Kt 5, P—Kt 6 ; (4 ...

K—B 5 ; 5 P—Kt 6, P—Kt 6 ; 6 P—Kt 7, P—Kt 7 ;
7 P—Kt 8 (Q) *ch*,) 5 K—K 3, K—Kt 5 ; 6 P—Kt 6,
K—R 6 ; 7 P—Kt 7, P—Kt 7 ; 8 K—B 2, K—R 7 ;
9 P—Kt 8 (Q) *ch*, and wins. In nearly all variations White
queens with check with decisive results.

Diag. 35, page 69.
1 K—Q 5, P—R 4 ; 2 P—Kt 6 *ch*, K × P ; 3 K × P, P—
R 5 ; 4 P—B 7, P—R 6 ; 5 P—B 8 (Q), and wins. The
authors give a more lengthy solution which tends to keep the
white King within the "square" of the adverse R P, but
leading to the same result : 1 K—B 4, K—Kt 3 ; (1 ...
P—R 4 ; 2 K—Kt 5, P—Q 4 ; 3 K × P, remaining within
the "square") 2 K—B 5, K—B 2 ; 3 K—B 6, K—Kt 3 ;
4 K—K 6, K—B 2 ; 5 K—Q 5, reverting to the variation
given above.

Diag. 44, page 87.
1 P—B 5, P × P ; 2 P—Kt 6, P—B 5 *ch* ; 3 K—Kt 2,
(the geometrical idea, forcing the win) 3 ... K—K 7 ; 4
P—Kt 7, P—B 6 *ch* ; 5 K—Kt 3, P—B 7 ; 6 P—Kt 8 (Q),
P—B 8 (Q) ; 7 Q—B 4 *ch*, K—K 8 ; 8 Q × Q *ch*, K × Q ;
9 K—B 4, wins. White's third move forced Black to play
his King to K 7 (or else 3 ... P—B 6 *ch* ; 4 K—B 1,)
allowing the exchange of Queens.

Diag. 45, page 87.
At first sight it seems that Black is in an uncomfortable
situation. He has an isolated and a backward pawn against
White's two united passed pawns. But the black King can
hold up these pawns and, in addition, Black can obtain a
dangerous passed pawn on the K Kt file by giving up the
K B P. Black will then possess two passed pawns, isolated
but at a distance of three ranks, and, as we already know,
such pawns do not require the assistance of their King.
All Black is required to do is to keep his King within the
square of the white Q side pawns. The win is as follows :
1 ... P—B 5 ; 2 P × P *ch*, K—Q 3 ; (the solution !) 3 P—
Kt 6, (3 P—R 5, P—Kt 6 ; 4 P—R 6, K—B 2 ; or 3
K—K 2, P—Kt 6 ; 4 K—B 3, P—Q 6 ;) 3 ... P—Kt 6 ;
4 P—Kt 7, K—B 2 ; 5 K—K 2, P—Q 6 *ch* ; and wins.

Diag. 53, page 104.

White has a great advantage in his two united passed pawns, well advanced and well supported. Of Black's advanced pawns, one is lost, and, should the other one manage to queen, his King is in such a position that mate is threatened. Alternatively, White, exploiting the geometrical idea, can force the exchange of Queens and remain with an extra pawn : 1 Q—Kt 5, (a very strong move, which has several objects : it guards the King against a perpetual check, threatens the future Queen at Q B 1 and co-operates in the mating threat by the potential new Queen.) 1 ... P—B 7 ; 2 P—B 7 *dis. ch,* K—B 2 ; 3 P—B 8 (Q), Q—B 6 *ch* ; (the pawn must not queen because of mate in four) 4 K—R 2, P—B 8 (Q) ; (his Q 7 is guarded by the white Queen at her K Kt 5) 5 Q (Kt 5)—Q 8 *ch,* K—B 3 ; 6 Q (B 8)—K 8 *ch,* and mate in two cannot be prevented.

Diag. 54, page 104.

White has an extra pawn : by sacrificing his K side pawns, he could have obtained a passed pawn on the Q side, which would have won easily. Having missed this chance, he could still have won, but he overlooked the perpetual check. 1 P—B 3, Q—R 8 *ch* ; 2 K—B 2, Q—Q 8 ; 3 Q—B 8 *ch,* K—Kt 2 ; 4 Q × P, (the decisive mistake ! with 4 Q—B 3 *ch,* followed by 5 Q—Q 4, he would have maintained winning chances) 4 ... Q—Q 7 *ch* ; 5 K—Kt 3, P—Q 5 ; (and here is the trap : this advanced pawn, if not captured, might yet win the game) 6 P × P, Q—Kt 4 *ch* ; and draws by perpetual check.

Diag. 61, page 116.

Prevented by his adversary from approaching his pawn, the black King achieves his aim from the opposite direction : 1 ... R—K 8 *ch* ; 2 K—Q 4, (keeping the black King away from K 3) 2 ... K—K 7 ; 3 P—B 5, K—B 6 ; 4 K—Q 5, K—B 5 ; 5 P—B 6, K—Kt 4 ; 6 P—B 7, R—K B 8 ; 7 K—K 6, K—Kt 3 ; and wins the pawn as in example 57.

Diag. 62, page 116.

1 P—R 6, R—Q 8 *ch* ; (1 ... R—Q R 8 ; 2 P—B 7,) 2 K—B 8, R—Q R 8 ; 3 K—Kt 7, R—Kt 8 *ch* ; 4 K—R 8,

R—Q B 8 ; 5 P—R 7, K—B 5 ; (5 … R × P ; 6 K—Kt 7,)
6 K—Kt 7, R—Kt 8 *ch* ; 7 K—B 7, R—Q R 8 ; 8 K—
Kt 6, R—Kt 8 *ch* ; 9 K—B 5, R—Q R 8 ; 10 P—B 7,
R—B 8 *ch* ; 11 K—Kt 4, R—Kt 8 *ch* ; 12 K—R 3, R—
R 8 *ch* ; 13 K—Kt 2, and wins.

Diag. 78, page 142.

It is to be noted that, if White forces the exchange of Rooks
now, his King will be at a distance of two ranks from his
rival. Therefore White will try to get his King nearer, as
he cannot shut off Black's King by : 1 R—Kt 2, K—B 6 ;
etc. Hence : 1 K—Kt 5, R—K 5 ; 2 K—B 5,
R—K 4 *ch* ; 3 K—B 4, R—K 1 ; 4 K—B 3, K—Q 6 ;
5 R—Kt 2, R—B 1 *ch* ; 6 K—Kt 2, K—B 6 ; 7 R—K 2,
draw. Actually, the game was continued with less precision
as follows : 6 K—Kt 3, K—B 6 ; 7 R—Kt 7, R—B 8 ;
(this should have been prevented on White's sixth move)
8 R—Kt 8, R—Q R 8 ; 9 K—B 3, R × P ; 10 K—K 3,
(or 10 R—Q R 8, P—R 6 ; 11 R—B 8 *ch*, K—Kt 7 ;
12 R—Kt 8 *ch*, K—B 8 ; 13 R—Q R 8, K—Kt 8 ; 14
R—R 7, R—R 8 ; and wins) 10 … R—R 7 ; (this again
leads to a draw, whereas 10 … P—R 6 ; would win) 11
R—B 8 *ch*, (11 R—Q R 8, draws) 11 … K—Kt 7 ; 12
R—Kt 8 *ch*, K—B 8 ; 13 R—B 8 *ch*, K—Kt 8 ; 14 R—
Kt 8 *ch*, R—Kt 7 ; 15 R—Q R 8, R—Kt 6 *ch* ; 16 K—
Q 4, P—R 6 ; 17 K—B 4, K—Kt 7 ; 18 R—R 8, R—
B 6 *ch* ; and wins (see Diag. 61).

Diag. 79, page 143.

Black could save the game only if his King were more
favourably placed, so that he could give up his Rook for
the advanced white pawn. As it is he must lose : 1 …
R—B 3 ; (1 … R—B 8 ; 2 P—K 7, R—K 8 ; 3 P—
K 8 (Q),) 2 K—Q 7, K—Kt 3 ; 3 P—K 7, R—B 2 ;
4 K—Q 6, R × P ; 5 K × R, K—B 4 ; 6 K—Q 6, (White
must not allow his King to remain backward and to be cut
off by the adverse King) 6 … P—Kt 4 ; 7 K—Q 5, K—B 5 ;
8 K—Q 4, P—Kt 5 ; 9 R—B 8 *ch*, K—Kt 6 ; 10 K—K 3,
P—R 7 ; (10 … K—R 7 ; 11 K—B 4,) 11 R—Q R 8,
K—R 6 ; 12 R × P, P—Kt 6 ; 13 K—B 3, and wins.

Admire the calm with which White delays the capture of the pawn until the last moment.

Diag. 88, page 158.

Thanks to the distant passed pawn the game ended in a draw as follows : 1 R—K R 6, R—R 7 ; 2 K—B 3, R—R 6 *ch* ; 3 K—B 2, R—Q 6 ; 4 R × P, P—R 5 ; 5 P—Q 5, P—R 6 ; 6 R—R 7 *ch*, K—B 3 ; 7 R—R 7, K—K 4 ; 8 R—R 5, R—Q 7 *ch* ; 9 K—B 3, R—Q 6 *ch* ; 10 K—K 2, R—Q Kt 6 ; 11 K—B 2, R—Kt 7 *ch* ; 12 K—Kt 3, R—Kt 6 *ch* ; 13 K—R 4, R—Kt 7 ; 14 K—R 3, P—R 7 ; 15 P—Q 6 *dis. ch*, (15 P—Kt 4, K—B 5 ; 16 P—Q 6, R—Q 7 ; 17 R—R 4 *ch*, K—Kt 4 ;) 15 ... K × P ; 16 P—Kt 4, K—B 3 ; 17 K—Kt 3, K—Kt 3 ; 18 R—R 8, K—Kt 4 ; 19 P—R 3, (19 P—R 4, R—Kt 6 *ch* ; 20 K—B 4, R—Kt 5 *ch* ; followed by ... R—R 5 ;) 19 ... K—Kt 5 ; 20 K—B 4, (a little better is 20 K—R 4, K—Kt 6 ; 21 K—Kt 5, R—Kt 8 ; 22 P—R 4, P—R 8 (Q) ; 23 R × Q, R × R ; 24 P—R 5, K—B 5 ; 25 P—R 6, K—Q 4 ; draw) 20 ... R—B 7 ; 21 R—Kt 8 *ch*, K—B 6 ; 22 R—Q R 8, K—Kt 5 ; draw.   Where did White go wrong ?   He certainly brought all his units into awkward positions on moves 2–5.   It may be noted that 2 R × P, R × P ; 3 R × P, R × P ; 4 R—K 5, R—K 7 *ch* ; also leads to a draw, but he could have played : 2 R × P, R × P ; 3 P—R 4, P—R 5 ; (3 ... R—Kt 5 *ch* ; 4 K—Q 5,) 4 R—B 5 *ch*, K—K 3 ; 5 R—K 5 *ch*, and 6 P—R 5, preserving two passed pawns. But he played for safety and found safety in a draw.

Diag. 89, page 159.

Even with improvements suggested after analysis, this game ends in a draw, but not without several subtle turns on both sides : 1 ... R—B 6 ; 2 K—Q 2, R—B 7 *ch* ; 3 K—K 3, P—Kt 7 ; 4 P—B 4, K—B 2 ; 5 R—Kt 6, K—K 2 ; 6 K—K 4, K—Q 2 ; 7 K—B 5, K—K 2 ; 8 R—Kt 3, R—Q 7 ; 9 K—Kt 6, K—K 3 ; 10 K—Kt 7, draw.

Diag. 93, page 165.

In order to win the black pawn, the white King must get behind the pawn. He must therefore evade the Rook's barrage : 1 Q—R 7 *ch*, K—K 3 ; 2 Q—B 7, R—B 4 ;

(the Rook will at all times try to remain on its fourth rank, supported by the pawn) 3 Q—Q 8, R—K 4 ; 4 Q—K 8 ch, K—Q 4 ; 5 Q—Q B 8, R—K 5 ch ; 6 K—B 5, (the first stage ; now the King must get close to the pawn) 6 ... R—K 4 ch ; 7 K—B 6, R—K 5 ; 8 Q—B 3, R—K 3 ch ; 9 K—B 7, R—K 4 ; 10 K—B 8, R—K 5 ; 11 Q— Q 3 ch, R—Q 5 ; 12 Q—B 5 ch, K—B 5 ; 13 Q—B 2 ch, K—Q 4 ; 14 K—K 7, K—K 4 ; 15 K—Q 7, R—Q 4 ; 16 Q—K 2 ch, K—B 5 ; 17 K—B 6, R—Q 5 ; 18 K— Kt 5, K—B 4 ; 19 Q—K 3, R—K 5 ; 20 Q—Q 3, K— K 4 ; 21 K—B 6, R—Q 5 ; 22 Q—K 3 ch, and wins.

Diag. 94, page 166.

Thanks to a perpetual check, Black succeeds in drawing the game. For this result he has to thank the lack of co-operation between the two Rooks and the vulnerable position of the adverse King : 1 R—B 7 ch, K—Q 1 ; 2 R—B 8 ch, K—K 2 ; 3 P—K 6, P—Kt 3 ; 4 R—B 7 ch, K—Q 1 ; 5 R—Q 7 ch, K—B 1 ; (5 ... B×R ; 6 P—K 7 ch,) 6 P—K 7, P×B ; 7 R—Q 8 ch, K—B 2 ; 8 R×B, Q×P ch ; 9 K—R 1, Q—B 6 ch ; 10 K—Kt 1, Q—Kt 5 ch ; draw.

Diag. 98, page 182.

White wins as follows : 1 B—R 4, K—Kt 4 ; 2 B—B 2, K—R 3 ; 3 B—B 5, B—K 4 ; 4 B—K 7, K—Kt 3 ; 5 B—Q 8 ch, K—B 3 ; 6 B—B 6, B—R 7 ; 7 B—Q 4, B—Kt 6 ; 8 B—R 7, B—B 5 ; 9 B—Kt 8, B—K 6 ; 10 B—R 2, B—R 2 ; 11 B—Kt 1. The object of the white Bishop's manœuvres is to drive the hostile Bishop from the diagonal K R 2—Q Kt 8 and to force it to occupy the short diagonal Q R 7—Q Kt 8. In order to achieve this object, the Bishop must reach its Q Kt 8, and in order to prevent it, the black King must occupy his Q R 3.

Diag. 99, page 183.

White wins as follows : 1 ... Kt—B 3 ; (1 ... Kt—R 3 ; 2 K—B 8, K—Kt 3 ; 3 Kt—B 3, K—R 7 ; 4 Kt—K 4, K—Kt 6 ; 5 Kt—Q 6,) 2 K—B 7, K—B 4 ; 3 Kt—Q 2, Kt—Kt 5 ; (3 ... K—Kt 4 ; 4 Kt—K 5 ch, or 3 ... K—K 4 ; 4 Kt—B 4 ch, K—B 4 ; 5 Kt—Q 6 ch, K—Kt 4 ; 6 Kt—

K 4 *ch*,) 4 K—B 8, (4 P—Kt 8 (Q), Kt—R 3 *ch* ;) 4 ...
Kt—R 3 ; 5 Kt—B 4, K—K 3 ; 6 Kt—Kt 6, K—B 3 ;
7 Kt—B 8, K—Kt 3 ; (7 ... K—K 3 ; 8 Kt—K 7, K—
B 3 ; 9 Kt—Kt 8 *ch*,) 8 Kt—Q 6, K—R 2 ; 9 Kt—B 7,
Kt—Kt 1 ; 10 Kt—Kt 5 *ch*.   White's Knight must attack
the black Knight and sacrifice itself so that the pawn can
queen.   Care must be taken that the capture is not effected
with a check.

Diags. 110 and 111, page 207.
   In both positions White has a manifest advantage, as in both
cases the Knight, strongly posted at Q 4, is superior to the
Bishop, which has to guard weaknesses created by the
advance of the Q side pawns ; and yet the position in Diag.
110 resulted in a draw as follows : 1 K—K 2, K—Kt 3 ;
2 K—Q 2, K—B 3 ; 3 K—B 3, K—K 2 ; 4 P—R 3,
K—Q 1 ; 5 P—Kt 4, P×P *ch* ; 6 P×P, K—K 2 ; 7
K—Kt 3, K—Q 1 ; 8 Kt—K 2, K—K 2 ; 9 K—B 3,
B—B 1 ; 10 K—Q 4, B—R 3 ; 11 Kt—B 3, K—Q 1 ;
12 Kt—Kt 1, K—K 2 ; 13 Kt—Q 2, K—Q 1 ; 14 Kt—
Kt 3, K—K 2 ; 15 P—B 5, K—B 3 ; 16 P—B 6, (here is
the mistake : with 16 K—B 3, White would have won :
16 ... B—Kt 2 ; 17 P—B 6, B—B 1 ; 18 Kt—Q 4,
K—K 2 ; 19 K—Kt 3, K—Q 1 ; 20 K—R 4, K—K 2 ;
21 K—Kt 5, followed by the sacrifice of the Knight for the
Q Kt P.) 16 ... B—Q 6 ; (the saving clause.   The Bishop
is freed and can guard its pawns from in front.) 17 K—B 3,
P—Kt 4 ; draw.
   In Diag. 111, where Black's weaknesses were less pronounced, White succeeded in winning the game : 1 ... B—
K 1 ; (a bad move, although it lays a little trap : 2 Kt—K 6,
K—Q 2 ; 3 Kt—B 8 *ch*, K—K 2 ; 4 Kt×P, K—B 2 ;
and the Knight is caught.   He should, however, have played
1 ... P—Q R 4 ;) 2 Kt—B 6 *ch*, B×Kt ; (or else, after 2
... K—Q 2 ; there follows 3 Kt—Kt 8 *ch*, winning a pawn)
3 P×B, K—B 2 ; 4 K—Q 5, K—K 2 ; 5 P—Q R 4,
P—Q R 4 ; 6 K—Q 4, K—B 2 ; 7 K—B 3, K—K 2 ;
8 P—Kt 4, K—B 2 ; 9 P×P, P×P ; 10 K—Q 4, K—
K 1 ; 11 K—Q 5, K—B 2 ; and Black resigned in view of
the threat P—B 5.

Diag. 127, page 233.

Black has good winning chances on account of his distant passed pawn : 1 Q—K B 2, P—Q R 4 ; 2 B—Q 4, P—R 5 ; 3 K—Kt 2, Q—Kt 6 ; 4 Q—K 2, B—Kt 3 ; 5 B×B, Q×B ; 6 Q—Q 3, Q—R 4 ; 7 Q—R 3, Q—Q 7 *ch* ; 8 K—R 3, Q—Q 8 ; 9 Q—B 5, Q—Q 6 ; 10 Q—R 5, Q—B 5 ; (10 ... P—R 6 ; 11 P—K 4,) 11 Q—R 7, Q—Kt 5 ; 12 Q—K B 7, Q—R 4 ; 13 P—K 4, P×P ; 14 Q—K 8, (14 P—B 5, Q—R 3 ;) 14 ... Q—B 4 *ch* ; 15 K—Kt 2, P—R 6 ; (in the actual game 15 ... Q—Q 4 ; was played with a drawn conclusion : 16 Q×P, P—K 6 *dis. ch* ; 17 K—Kt 1, Q—Q 6 ; 18 Q—K 8, Q—Kt 8 *ch* ; 19 K—Kt 2, Q—B 7 *ch* ; 20 K—R 3, Q—B 4 *ch* ; 21 K—Kt 2, Q—Q 4 *ch* ; 22 K—R 3, Q—B 6 ; 23 Q—K 6, Q—B 8 *ch* ; 24 K—R 4,) 16 Q—R 4, P—K 6 ; 17 Q×P, Q—K 5 *ch* ; 18 K—any, P—K 7. Compare the black King's secure abode with the white King's uneasy wanderings.

Diag. 128, page 233.

Black's position is superior because of White's isolated Q P and his doubled pawns on the K Kt file. But the win is not an easy one if White restricts himself to a stubborn defence by B—Q 3, P—B 3, K—B 2, and K—K 3. Instead of this he undertakes an expedition for the capture of Black's K R P. He thus loses much time and in the end, as in example 122, his Knight is out of play, which leads to the loss of the game : 1 Kt—B 4, P—K Kt 4 ; 2 Kt×R P, Kt—B 4 ; 3 P—K Kt 4, Kt×P ; (no doubt White thought that this exchange, getting rid of his isolated pawn, would prove favourable, but, for a long time, he loses the services of his Knight.) 4 B—Q 1, B—Q 4 ; 5 P—R 3, (5 P— Q Kt 3, Kt—Kt 4 ;) 5 ... B—Kt 6 ; 6 B×B, (6 B—B 3, Kt×B *ch* ; 7 P×Kt, B—Q 8 ; 8 K—Kt 2, P—B 4 ; 9 Kt— Kt 3, K—B 3 ;) 6 ... Kt×B ; 7 Kt—Kt 3, Kt—Q 7 ; 8 P—Kt 4, P—Kt 4 ; (or 8 ... Kt—Kt 8 ; 9 P—R 4, Kt—B 6 ; 10 P—R 5, Kt—Q 4 ;) 9 Kt—K 2, Kt—Kt 8 ; 10 Kt—Q 4, Kt×P ; 11 Kt—B 6, K—K 1 ; 12 P—Kt 3, (12 Kt×P, K—Q 2 ; winning the Knight which, after losing its way on the K side, is in trouble on the Q side. How like a Knight !) 12 ... K—Q 2 ; 13 Kt—Kt 8 *ch*, K—Q 3 ; 14 P—B 4, Kt—B 7 ; and White resigns.

Diag. 135, page 240.

As White has the move, he deprives his adversary of his spare move by playing his own, P—Q R 4, and thus wins the game : 1 P—Q R 4, K—B 5 ; 2 K—K 3, K—Kt 5 ; 3 K—Q 4, K×P ; 4 K—B 4, P—R 4 ; (compulsory) 5 P×P, P—Kt 5 ; 6 P—R 6, (6 P×P *stalemate.*) 6 ... P—Kt 6 ; 7 P—R 7, P—Kt 7 ; 8 P—R 8 (Q), P—Kt 8 (Q) ; 9 Q—K 8 *mate.*   Note the clever use of the *Zugzwang* where the adverse King is in a stalemate position.

Diag. 136, page 241.

1 ... K—Kt 6 ; 2 Kt×Kt, P—R 5 ; 3 P—R 6, P—R 6 ; 4 P—R 7, P—B 3 *ch* ; (the *finesse* which blocks the long black diagonal and allows Black also to make a Queen) 5 Kt×P, P—R 7 ; 6 P—R 8 (Q), P—R 8 (Q) ; draw.

A CATALOGUE OF SELECTED DOVER BOOKS
IN ALL FIELDS OF INTEREST

A CATALOGUE OF SELECTED DOVER BOOKS IN ALL FIELDS OF INTEREST

CELESTIAL OBJECTS FOR COMMON TELESCOPES, T. W. Webb. The most used book in amateur astronomy: inestimable aid for locating and identifying nearly 4,000 celestial objects. Edited, updated by Margaret W. Mayall. 77 illustrations. Total of 645pp. 5⅜ x 8½.
20917-2, 20918-0 Pa., Two-vol. set $9.00

HISTORICAL STUDIES IN THE LANGUAGE OF CHEMISTRY, M. P. Crosland. The important part language has played in the development of chemistry from the symbolism of alchemy to the adoption of systematic nomenclature in 1892. ". . . wholeheartedly recommended,"—Science. 15 illustrations. 416pp. of text. 5⅝ x 8¼. 63702-6 Pa. $6.00

BURNHAM'S CELESTIAL HANDBOOK, Robert Burnham, Jr. Thorough, readable guide to the stars beyond our solar system. Exhaustive treatment, fully illustrated. Breakdown is alphabetical by constellation: Andromeda to Cetus in Vol. 1; Chamaeleon to Orion in Vol. 2; and Pavo to Vulpecula in Vol. 3. Hundreds of illustrations. Total of about 2000pp. 6⅛ x 9¼.
23567-X, 23568-8, 23673-0 Pa., Three-vol. set $26.85

THEORY OF WING SECTIONS: INCLUDING A SUMMARY OF AIRFOIL DATA, Ira H. Abbott and A. E. von Doenhoff. Concise compilation of subatomic aerodynamic characteristics of modern NASA wing sections, plus description of theory. 350pp. of tables. 693pp. 5⅜ x 8½.
60586-8 Pa. $7.00

DE RE METALLICA, Georgius Agricola. Translated by Herbert C. Hoover and Lou H. Hoover. The famous Hoover translation of greatest treatise on technological chemistry, engineering, geology, mining of early modern times (1556). All 289 original woodcuts. 638pp. 6¾ x 11.
60006-8 Clothbd. $17.95

THE ORIGIN OF CONTINENTS AND OCEANS, Alfred Wegener. One of the most influential, most controversial books in science, the classic statement for continental drift. Full 1966 translation of Wegener's final (1929) version. 64 illustrations. 246pp. 5⅜ x 8½. 61708-4 Pa. $4.50

THE PRINCIPLES OF PSYCHOLOGY, William James. Famous long course complete, unabridged. Stream of thought, time perception, memory, experimental methods; great work decades ahead of its time. Still valid, useful; read in many classes. 94 figures. Total of 1391pp. 5⅜ x 8½.
20381-6, 20382-4 Pa., Two-vol. set $13.00

THE PHILOSOPHY OF HISTORY, Georg W. Hegel. Great classic of Western thought develops concept that history is not chance but a rational process, the evolution of freedom. 457pp. 5⅜ x 8½.   20112-0 Pa. $4.50

LANGUAGE, TRUTH AND LOGIC, Alfred J. Ayer. Famous, clear introduction to Vienna, Cambridge schools of Logical Positivism. Role of philosophy, elimination of metaphysics, nature of analysis, etc. 160pp. 5⅜ x 8½. (Available in U.S. only)   20010-8 Pa. $2.00

A PREFACE TO LOGIC, Morris R. Cohen. Great City College teacher in renowned, easily followed exposition of formal logic, probability, values, logic and world order and similar topics; no previous background needed. 209pp. 5⅜ x 8½.   23517-3 Pa. $3.50

REASON AND NATURE, Morris R. Cohen. Brilliant analysis of reason and its multitudinous ramifications by charismatic teacher. Interdisciplinary, synthesizing work widely praised when it first appeared in 1931. Second (1953) edition. Indexes. 496pp. 5⅜ x 8½.   23633-1 Pa. $6.50

AN ESSAY CONCERNING HUMAN UNDERSTANDING, John Locke. The only complete edition of enormously important classic, with authoritative editorial material by A. C. Fraser. Total of 1176pp. 5⅜ x 8½.
20530-4, 20531-2 Pa., Two-vol. set $14.00

HANDBOOK OF MATHEMATICAL FUNCTIONS WITH FORMULAS, GRAPHS, AND MATHEMATICAL TABLES, edited by Milton Abramowitz and Irene A. Stegun. Vast compendium: 29 sets of tables, some to as high as 20 places. 1,046pp. 8 x 10½.   61272-4 Pa. $14.95

MATHEMATICS FOR THE PHYSICAL SCIENCES, Herbert S. Wilf. Highly acclaimed work offers clear presentations of vector spaces and matrices, orthogonal functions, roots of polynomial equations, conformal mapping, calculus of variations, etc. Knowledge of theory of functions of real and complex variables is assumed. Exercises and solutions. Index. 284pp. 5⅝ x 8¼.   63635-6 Pa. $5.00

THE PRINCIPLE OF RELATIVITY, Albert Einstein et al. Eleven most important original papers on special and general theories. Seven by Einstein, two by Lorentz, one each by Minkowski and Weyl. All translated, unabridged. 216pp. 5⅜ x 8½.   60081-5 Pa. $3.00

THERMODYNAMICS, Enrico Fermi. A classic of modern science. Clear, organized treatment of systems, first and second laws, entropy, thermodynamic potentials, gaseous reactions, dilute solutions, entropy constant. No math beyond calculus required. Problems. 160pp. 5⅜ x 8½.
60361-X Pa. $3.00

ELEMENTARY MECHANICS OF FLUIDS, Hunter Rouse. Classic undergraduate text widely considered to be far better than many later books. Ranges from fluid velocity and acceleration to role of compressibility in fluid motion. Numerous examples, questions, problems. 224 illustrations. 376pp. 5⅝ x 8¼.   63699-2 Pa. $5.00

THE SENSE OF BEAUTY, George Santayana. Masterfully written discussion of nature of beauty, materials of beauty, form, expression; art, literature, social sciences all involved. 168pp. 5⅜ x 8½. 20238-0 Pa. $2.50

ON THE IMPROVEMENT OF THE UNDERSTANDING, Benedict Spinoza. Also contains *Ethics, Correspondence,* all in excellent R. Elwes translation. Basic works on entry to philosophy, pantheism, exchange of ideas with great contemporaries. 402pp. 5⅜ x 8½. 20250-X Pa. $4.50

THE TRAGIC SENSE OF LIFE, Miguel de Unamuno. Acknowledged masterpiece of existential literature, one of most important books of 20th century. Introduction by Madariaga. 367pp. 5⅜ x 8½.
20257-7 Pa. $4.50

THE GUIDE FOR THE PERPLEXED, Moses Maimonides. Great classic of medieval Judaism attempts to reconcile revealed religion (Pentateuch, commentaries) with Aristotelian philosophy. Important historically, still relevant in problems. Unabridged Friedlander translation. Total of 473pp. 5⅜ x 8½. 20351-4 Pa. $6.00

THE I CHING (THE BOOK OF CHANGES), translated by James Legge. Complete translation of basic text plus appendices by Confucius, and Chinese commentary of most penetrating divination manual ever prepared. Indispensable to study of early Oriental civilizations, to modern inquiring reader. 448pp. 5⅜ x 8½. 21062-6 Pa. $4.00

THE EGYPTIAN BOOK OF THE DEAD, E. A. Wallis Budge. Complete reproduction of Ani's papyrus, finest ever found. Full hieroglyphic text, interlinear transliteration, word for word translation, smooth translation. Basic work, for Egyptology, for modern study of psychic matters. Total of 533pp. 6½ x 9¼. (Available in U.S. only) 21866-X Pa. $5.95

THE GODS OF THE EGYPTIANS, E. A. Wallis Budge. Never excelled for richness, fullness: all gods, goddesses, demons, mythical figures of Ancient Egypt; their legends, rites, incarnations, variations, powers, etc. Many hieroglyphic texts cited. Over 225 illustrations, plus 6 color plates. Total of 988pp. 6⅛ x 9¼. (Available in U.S. only)
22055-9, 22056-7 Pa., Two-vol. set $12.00

THE ENGLISH AND SCOTTISH POPULAR BALLADS, Francis J. Child. Monumental, still unsuperseded; all known variants of Child ballads, commentary on origins, literary references, Continental parallels, other features. Added: papers by G. L. Kittredge, W. M. Hart. Total of 2761pp. 6½ x 9¼.
21409-5, 21410-9, 21411-7, 21412-5, 21413-3 Pa., Five-vol. set $37.50

CORAL GARDENS AND THEIR MAGIC, Bronsilaw Malinowski. Classic study of the methods of tilling the soil and of agricultural rites in the Trobriand Islands of Melanesia. Author is one of the most important figures in the field of modern social anthropology. 143 illustrations. Indexes. Total of 911pp. of text. 5⅝ x 8¼. (Available in U.S. only)
23597-1 Pa. $12.95

TONE POEMS, SERIES II: TILL EULENSPIEGELS LUSTIGE STREICHE, ALSO SPRACH ZARATHUSTRA, AND EIN HELDEN-LEBEN, Richard Strauss. Three important orchestral works, including very popular *Till Eulenspiegel's Marry Pranks*, reproduced in full score from original editions. Study score. 315pp. 9⅜ x 12¼. (Available in U.S. only)
23755-9 Pa. $7.50

TONE POEMS, SERIES I: DON JUAN, TOD UND VERKLARUNG AND DON QUIXOTE, Richard Strauss. Three of the most often performed and recorded works in entire orchestral repertoire, reproduced in full score from original editions. Study score. 286pp. 9⅜ x 12¼. (Available in U.S. only)
23754-0 Pa. $7.50

11 LATE STRING QUARTETS, Franz Joseph Haydn. The form which Haydn defined and "brought to perfection." *(Grove's)*. 11 string quartets in complete score, his last and his best. The first in a projected series of the complete Haydn string quartets. Reliable modern Eulenberg edition, otherwise difficult to obtain. 320pp. 8⅜ x 11¼. (Available in U.S. only)
23753-2 Pa. $6.95

FOURTH, FIFTH AND SIXTH SYMPHONIES IN FULL SCORE, Peter Ilyitch Tchaikovsky. Complete orchestral scores of Symphony No. 4 in F Minor, Op. 36; Symphony No. 5 in E Minor, Op. 64; Symphony No. 6 in B Minor, "Pathetique," Op. 74. Bretikopf & Hartel eds. Study score. 480pp. 9⅜ x 12¼.
23861-X Pa. $10.95

THE MARRIAGE OF FIGARO: COMPLETE SCORE, Wolfgang A. Mozart. Finest comic opera ever written. Full score, not to be confused with piano renderings. Peters edition. Study score. 448pp. 9⅜ x 12¼. (Available in U.S. only)
23751-6 Pa. $11.95

"IMAGE" ON THE ART AND EVOLUTION OF THE FILM, edited by Marshall Deutelbaum. Pioneering book brings together for first time 38 groundbreaking articles on early silent films from *Image* and 263 illustrations newly shot from rare prints in the collection of the International Museum of Photography. A landmark work. Index. 256pp. 8¼ x 11.
23777-X Pa. $8.95

AROUND-THE-WORLD COOKY BOOK, Lois Lintner Sumption and Marguerite Lintner Ashbrook. 373 cooky and frosting recipes from 28 countries (America, Austria, China, Russia, Italy, etc.) include Viennese kisses, rice wafers, London strips, lady fingers, hony, sugar spice, maple cookies, etc. Clear instructions. All tested. 38 drawings. 182pp. 5⅜ x 8.
23802-4 Pa. $2.50

THE ART NOUVEAU STYLE, edited by Roberta Waddell. 579 rare photographs, not available elsewhere, of works in jewelry, metalwork, glass, ceramics, textiles, architecture and furniture by 175 artists—Mucha, Seguy, Lalique, Tiffany, Gaudin, Hohlwein, Saarinen, and many others. 288pp. 8⅜ x 11¼.
23515-7 Pa. $6.95

THE COMPLETE BOOK OF DOLL MAKING AND COLLECTING, Catherine Christopher. Instructions, patterns for dozens of dolls, from rag doll on up to elaborate, historically accurate figures. Mould faces, sew clothing, make doll houses, etc. Also collecting information. Many illustrations. 288pp. 6 x 9. 22066-4 Pa. $4.50

THE DAGUERREOTYPE IN AMERICA, Beaumont Newhall. Wonderful portraits, 1850's townscapes, landscapes; full text plus 104 photographs. The basic book. Enlarged 1976 edition. 272pp. 8¼ x 11¼.
23322-7 Pa. $7.95

CRAFTSMAN HOMES, Gustav Stickley. 296 architectural drawings, floor plans, and photographs illustrate 40 different kinds of "Mission-style" homes from *The Craftsman* (1901-16), voice of American style of simplicity and organic harmony. Thorough coverage of Craftsman idea in text and picture, now collector's item. 224pp. 8⅛ x 11. 23791-5 Pa. $6.00

PEWTER-WORKING: INSTRUCTIONS AND PROJECTS, Burl N. Osborn. & Gordon O. Wilber. Introduction to pewter-working for amateur craftsman. History and characteristics of pewter; tools, materials, step-by-step instructions. Photos, line drawings, diagrams. Total of 160pp. 7⅞ x 10¾. 23786-9 Pa. $3.50

THE GREAT CHICAGO FIRE, edited by David Lowe. 10 dramatic, eye-witness accounts of the 1871 disaster, including one of the aftermath and rebuilding, plus 70 contemporary photographs and illustrations of the ruins—courthouse, Palmer House, Great Central Depot, etc. Introduction by David Lowe. 87pp. 8¼ x 11. 23771-0 Pa. $4.00

SILHOUETTES: A PICTORIAL ARCHIVE OF VARIED ILLUSTRATIONS, edited by Carol Belanger Grafton. Over 600 silhouettes from the 18th to 20th centuries include profiles and full figures of men and women, children, birds and animals, groups and scenes, nature, ships, an alphabet. Dozens of uses for commercial artists and craftspeople. 144pp. 8⅜ x 11¼.
23781-8 Pa. $4.00

ANIMALS: 1,419 COPYRIGHT-FREE ILLUSTRATIONS OF MAMMALS, BIRDS, FISH, INSECTS, ETC., edited by Jim Harter. Clear wood engravings present, in extremely lifelike poses, over 1,000 species of animals. One of the most extensive copyright-free pictorial sourcebooks of its kind. Captions. Index. 284pp. 9 x 12. 23766-4 Pa. $7.95

INDIAN DESIGNS FROM ANCIENT ECUADOR, Frederick W. Shaffer. 282 original designs by pre-Columbian Indians of Ecuador (500-1500 A.D.). Designs include people, mammals, birds, reptiles, fish, plants, heads, geometric designs. Use as is or alter for advertising, textiles, leathercraft, etc. Introduction. 95pp. 8¾ x 11¼. 23764-8 Pa. $3.50

SZIGETI ON THE VIOLIN, Joseph Szigeti. Genial, loosely structured tour by premier violinist, featuring a pleasant mixture of reminiscenes, insights into great music and musicians, innumerable tips for practicing violinists. 385 musical passages. 256pp. 5⅝ x 8¼. 23763-X Pa. $3.50

GEOMETRY, RELATIVITY AND THE FOURTH DIMENSION, Rudolf Rucker. Exposition of fourth dimension, means of visualization, concepts of relativity as Flatland characters continue adventures. Popular, easily followed yet accurate, profound. 141 illustrations. 133pp. 5⅜ x 8½.
23400-2 Pa. $2.75

THE ORIGIN OF LIFE, A. I. Oparin. Modern classic in biochemistry, the first rigorous examination of possible evolution of life from nitrocarbon compounds. Non-technical, easily followed. Total of 295pp. 5⅜ x 8½.
60213-3 Pa. $4.00

PLANETS, STARS AND GALAXIES, A. E. Fanning. Comprehensive introductory survey: the sun, solar system, stars, galaxies, universe, cosmology; quasars, radio stars, etc. 24pp. of photographs. 189pp. 5⅜ x 8½. (Available in U.S. only)
21680-2 Pa. $3.00

THE THIRTEEN BOOKS OF EUCLID'S ELEMENTS, translated with introduction and commentary by Sir Thomas L. Heath. Definitive edition. Textual and linguistic notes, mathematical analysis, 2500 years of critical commentary. Do not confuse with abridged school editions. Total of 1414pp. 5⅜ x 8½.
60088-2, 60089-0, 60090-4 Pa., Three-vol. set $18.50

DIALOGUES CONCERNING TWO NEW SCIENCES, Galileo Galilei. Encompassing 30 years of experiment and thought, these dialogues deal with geometric demonstrations of fracture of solid bodies, cohesion, leverage, speed of light and sound, pendulums, falling bodies, accelerated motion, etc. 300pp. 5⅜ x 8½.
60099-8 Pa. $4.00

Prices subject to change without notice.

Available at your book dealer or write for free catalogue to Dept. GI, Dover Publications, Inc., 180 Varick St., N.Y., N.Y. 10014. Dover publishes more than 175 books each year on science, elementary and advanced mathematics, biology, music, art, literary history, social sciences and other areas.